Global Trends in Human Resource Management

Global Trends in Human Resource Management
A Twenty-Year Analysis

Edward E. Lawler III and John W. Boudreau

Stanford Business Books
An Imprint of Stanford University Press
Stanford, California

Stanford University Press
Stanford, California
©2015 by the Board of Trustees of the
Leland Stanford Junior University.
All rights reserved.

Special discounts for bulk quantities of Stanford Business Books
are available to corporations, professional associations, and other
organizations. For details and discount information, contact the
special sales department of Stanford University Press.
Tel: (650) 736-1782, Fax: (650) 736-1784

Printed in the United States of America on acid-free,
archival-quality paper

Library of Congress Cataloging-in-Publication Data
Lawler, Edward E., III, author.
 Global trends in human resource management : a twenty-year
analysis / Edward E. Lawler III and John W. Boudreau.
    pages cm
 Includes bibliographical references.
 ISBN 978-0-8047-9129-8 (pbk. : alk. paper)
 1. Personnel management. I. Boudreau, John W., author. II. Title.
 HF5549.L2885 2015
 658.3—dc23
                                                2015004814

ISBN 978-0-8047-9455-8 (electronic)

Typeset by Classic Typography in 10½/14 Palatino

CONTENTS

TABLES, FIGURES, AND EXHIBITS

TABLES

Tables, Figures, and Exhibits

FIGURES

EXHIBITS

PREFACE AND ACKNOWLEDGMENTS

This book reports the results from the seventh study done by the Center for Effective Organizations of the human resource (HR) function in large corporations. Like the previous studies, it measures whether the HR function is changing and whether it is an effective strategic partner. The study also analyzes how organizations can more effectively manage their human capital. It gathered data on many of the same topics and the same companies that we studied in 1995, 1998, 2001, 2004, 2007, and 2010, and we have compared data from our earlier studies with data we collected in 2013 in order to measure changes. For the second time, we collected data from multiple countries so that we can determine how corporations in the United States differ from those of other countries. Information on how the data for this study were collected are in appendix B, which presents information on the characteristics of the sample. A copy of the questionnaire used in the study, along with the responses for the US sample, are in appendix C.

We are deeply indebted to Walt Cleaver and Human Resource People and Strategy for their support of all seven of our studies. Thanks also go to Jay Jamrog, Kevin Oakes, and the Institute for Corporate Productivity (i4cp) for its support of our 2007, 2010, and 2013 surveys. A number of individuals and organizations helped us with international data collection. We offer special thanks to our research partners who helped us with data collection; we list them in appendix A.

We also thank Lorelei Oriel Palacpac for her help in preparing the manuscript. Alice Yee Mark, Aaron Griffith, and Nora Osganian helped with the data collection and did a terrific job analyzing the data.

The Marshall School of Business of the University of Southern California deserves special thanks and recognition for its continuing support of the activities of the Center for Effective Organizations. In addition, we thank the corporate sponsors of the center for their support of CEO and its mission; their support is vital to the overall success of the center and is responsible for enabling us to do the kind of research reported here.

The Center for Effective Organizations has been and continues to be focused on doing research that improves organizational effectiveness. During 2014, it celebrated its thirty-fifth-year anniversary.

Special thanks go to Susan Mohrman, who has made many contributions to this research effort. She and Ed did the first three surveys, and she worked with us on the fourth.

THE AUTHORS

Edward E. Lawler III is Distinguished Professor of Business and Director of the Center for Effective Organizations in the Marshall School of Business at the University of Southern California (USC). He joined USC in 1978 and during 1979 founded and became director of the university's Center for Effective Organizations. He has consulted with over one hundred organizations on employee involvement, organizational change, and HR management and has been honored as a top contributor to the fields of organizational development, organizational behavior, corporate governance, and human resource management.

The author of over 400 articles and 50 books, his articles have appeared in leading academic journals as well as *Fortune, Harvard Business Review,* and leading newspapers including *USA Today* and the *Financial Times.* His books include *Rewarding Excellence* (2000), *Corporate Boards: New Strategies for Adding Value at the Top* (2001), *Organizing for High Performance* (2001), *Treat People Right* (2003), *Human Resources Business Process Outsourcing* (2004), *Built to Change* (2006), *America at Work* (2006), *The New American Workplace* (2006), *Talent: Making People Your Competitive Advantage* (2008), *Useful Research: Advancing Theory and Practice* (2011), *Management Reset: Organizing for Sustainable Effectiveness* (2011), *Effective Human Resource Management: A Global Analysis* (2012), and *The Agility Factor* (2014). For more information, visit http://www.edwardlawler.com and http://ceo.usc.edu.

John W. Boudreau, professor and research director at the University of Southern California's Marshall School of Business and Center for Effective Organizations, is recognized worldwide for his breakthrough research on superior human capital, talent, and sustainable competitive advantage. He consults and conducts executive development with companies worldwide that seek to maximize their employees' effectiveness by discovering the specific strategic bottom-line impact of superior people and human capital strategies.

Boudreau has more than two hundred publications, including books such as *Retooling HR: Using Proven Business Tools to Make Better Decisions about Talent* (2010) and *Beyond HR: The New Science of Human Capital,* with Peter M. Ramstad (2007), *Short Introduction to Strategic Human Resources,* with Wayne Cascio (2012), *Transformative HR,* with Ravin Jesuthasan (2011), *Effective Human Resource Management: A Global Analysis,* with Edward Lawler (2012), and *Investing in People,* with Wayne F. Cascio, now in its second edition (2011).

Boudreau's large-scale research studies and focused field research address the future of the global HR profession, HR measurement and analytics, decision-based HR, executive mobility, HR information systems, and organizational staffing and development. His scholarly research has been published in *Management Science*, *Academy of Management Executive*, *Journal of Applied Psychology*, *Personnel Psychology*, *Asia-Pacific Human Resource Management*, *Human Resource Management*, *Journal of Vocational Behavior*, *Human Relations*, *Industrial Relations*, and *Journal of Human Resources Costing and Accounting*. Features on his work have appeared in *Harvard Business Review*, the *Wall Street Journal*, *Fortune*, *Fast Company*, and *Businessweek*, among others.

He is the recipient of the 2013 Michael Losey award from the Society for Human Resource Management for excellence in research that has contributed to the HR profession. His research received the Academy of Management's Organizational Behavior New Concept and Human Resource Scholarly Contribution awards. He received the 2009 Chairman's Award from the International Association for Human Resources Information Management for lifetime achievement in HR information management. He is a fellow of the National Academy of Human Resources, the Society for Industrial and Organizational Psychology, and the American Psychological Association.

Global Trends in Human Resource Management

CHAPTER 1

What HR Needs to Do

A changing workforce, global competition, advances in information technology, new knowledge, an uneven recovery from the 2008 global recession, demands for sustainable organizational performance, and a host of other changes are forcing organizations to constantly examine and reevaluate how they operate. They are using new technologies, changing their structures, redesigning work, relocating their workforces, and improving work processes to respond to an increasingly demanding, unpredictable, and global competitive environment (Lawler and Worley 2011). These important changes have significant implications for how their human capital should be managed and how their human resource functions should be designed and operated. But are organizations changing their human capital management policies, practices and processes? Are they redesigning their HR functions?

Over the past decade, it has been difficult to find a management book or business magazine that does not point out how many of the changes in the business world have made human capital—people—an organization's most important asset. Human capital management has been the focus of a great deal of writing focused on finding, motivating, developing, and monitoring the right talent. The annual reports of many corporations in North America, Europe, and Australia argue that their human capital and intellectual property are their most important assets. In many organizations, compensation is one of the largest costs, if not the largest one. In service organizations, it often represents 70 to 80 percent of the total cost of doing business. Adding the costs of training and other HR management activities to compensation costs means that the HR function often has the responsibility for a very large and growing portion of an organization's total expenditures.

In most organizations, the compensation cost of human capital is not the only, or even the most, important determinant of an organization's effectiveness. Even when compensation accounts for very little of the cost of doing business, human capital has a significant impact on the performance of most organizations (Cascio 2000; Cascio and Boudreau 2011). In essence, without effective human capital, organizations are likely to have little or no revenue. Even the most automated production facilities require skilled, motivated employees to operate them. Knowledge work organizations depend on employees to develop, use, and manage their most important asset, knowledge. Thus, although human capital does not appear on the balance sheet of corporations, it represents an increasingly large percentage of many organizations' market valuation (Lev 2001; Huselid, Becker, and Beatty 2005).

In an increasing number of organizations, having the best talent and talent management processes can be a continuous, difference-making source of competitive advantage. It can make companies more innovative and agile, better able to develop superior products and customer knowledge, and offer superior services (Worley, Williams, and Lawler, 2014).

Role of the HR Organization

Because of the way the business environment has changed, there are more and more ways the HR function can add value to an organization. For decades, it has added value primarily by performing administrative tasks. But two other roles that it can play allow it to add greater value. Lawler (1995) has developed this line of thought by describing three roles HR can take on. The first is the familiar HR management role (exhibit 1.1).

The second is the role of business partner (exhibit 1.2). It emphasizes developing systems and practices to ensure that a company's human resources have the needed competencies and motivation to perform effectively. In this approach, HR has a seat at the table when business issues are discussed and brings an HR perspective to these discussions. When it comes to designing HR systems and practices, this approach focuses on creating systems and practices that support the business strategy. HR focuses on the effectiveness of the human capital management practices and process improvements in them. HR is expected to help implement changes and help managers effectively deal with people issues.

The business partner approach positions the HR function as a value-added part of an organization so that it can contribute to business performance by effectively managing what is the most important capital of most organizations, their human capital (Ulrich and Brockbank 2005; Lawler 2008). But this approach may not be one that enables the HR function to add the greatest value given the increasingly important role that talent plays in determining organizational performance. By becoming a strategic contributor (see exhibit 1.3), HR has the potential to add more value in situations where human capital performance can be a major difference maker.

Acting as a strategic contributor means that HR plays a role that includes helping the organization develop its strategy. Not only does HR have a seat at the strategy table, it helps to set the table with information about organizational capabilities, talent analytics, and the labor

AIMS	Support business.
	Provide HR services.
PROCESS	Build performance management capabilities.
	Develop managers: link competencies to job requirements and career development.
	Plan succession.
	Enhance organizational change capabilities.
	Build an organization-wide HR network.
PLANNING	HR (and all other functions) inspect business plans; inputs from HR may be inserted in the planning process.

Exhibit 1.1. HR management

AIMS	Line management owns human resources as a part of its role.
	HR is an integral member of management teams.
	Culture of the firm evolves to fit with strategy and vision.
PROCESS	Organize HR flexibly around the work to be done (programs and projects, outsourcing).
	Focus on the development of people and organizations (road maps, teams, organizational design).
	Leverage competencies, manage learning linkages; build organizational work redesign capabilities.
PLANNING	An integral component of strategic and business planning by the management team.

Exhibit 1.2. Business partner

AIMS	HR is a major influence on business strategy.
	HR systems drive business performance.
PROCESS	Self-service for transactional work.
	Transactional work outsourced.
	Knowledge management.
	Focus on organizational development.
	Change management.
	HR processes tied to business strategies.
PLANNING	HR is a key contributor to strategic planning and change management.

Exhibit 1.3. Strategic contributor

market. It helps shape and enhance strategies by bringing human capital decision science to strategy discussions. It helps organizations operate in ways that help it perform well financially, socially, and environmentally.

In a knowledge business, a firm's strategy must be closely linked to its talent. Thus, the HR function needs to be positioned to play a major role in both strategy formulation and implementation. Expertise in attracting, retaining, developing, deploying, motivating, and organizing human capital is critical to both. Ideally the HR function should be knowledgeable not just about the business and about talent; it should also be the expert in organizational and work design issues so that it can help develop needed organizational capabilities and facilitate organizational change.

To be a strategic contributor, HR executives need, in addition to knowing HR, an expert understanding of business strategy, organizational design, and change management, and they need to know how integrated HR practices and strategies can support organizational designs and strategies. This role requires extending their focus beyond delivery of the HR services and practices that are associated with being a business partner to a focus on making decisions about talent, organizational design, and business strategy.

To be an effective strategic contributor, HR needs to offer a perspective that is often missing in discussions of business strategy and change: knowledge of the human capital factors and the organizational changes that are critical in determining whether a strategy can be implemented. Many more strategies fail in execution than in their conception (Lawler and Worley 2006). What sounds good often cannot be implemented for a variety of reasons having to do with talent management and organizational culture.

Despite compelling arguments supporting HR management as a key strategic issue in most organizations, our research and that of others finds that HR executives usually are not strategic contributors and do not use data to guide their decision making (Lawler 1995; Brockbank 1999; Lawler, Boudreau, and Mohrman 2006; Lawler and Boudreau 2009, 2012). All too often, HR is largely an administrative function headed by individuals whose roles are focused on cost control and administrative activities (Ulrich 1997; Lawler and Mohrman 2003; Boudreau and Ramstad 2005a; Lawler and Boudreau 2009, 2012). Missing almost entirely from the list of HR focuses in our 2010 global survey of HR in large corporations were such key organizational challenges as improving productivity, increasing quality, facilitating mergers and acquisitions, managing knowledge, implementing change, developing business strategies, and improving the ability of the organization to execute strategies (Lawler and Boudreau 2012). Since these areas are critical determinants of organizational performance, the HR function was missing a great opportunity to add value.

There is some evidence that the HR function is beginning to redefine its role in order to increase the value it adds. The first six phases of the study collected data in 1995, 1998, 2001, 2004, 2007, and 2010. The results showed evidence of some change in large US corporations, but there was more discussion of change than actual change (Lawler and Mohrman 2003; Lawler et al., 2006; Lawler and Boudreau 2009, 2012). In addition, there is evidence of change in the profession. The leading professional association for HR, SHRM, has grown to over 270,000 members. Until 1984, SHRM was known as the American Society for Personnel Administration, a name that reflected HR's administrative role in organizations. Nevertheless, although it has changed its name, it still is more focused on personnel administration than on talent management and business strategy.

Creating Change

Describing the new role of HR is only the first step in transitioning the HR function to be a business partner that contributes to organizational effectiveness. For decades, the HR function has been organized and staffed to carry out administrative activities. Changing that role will require a different mix of activities and people. It will necessitate reconfiguring the HR function to support changing business strategies and organizational designs. It also will require the employees in the HR function to have very different competencies from those they traditionally have had (Ulrich, Younger, Brockbank, and Ulrich 2012).

It is clear that information technology is playing an increasingly important role in the future of the HR function (Lawler, Ulrich, Fitz-enz, and Madden 2004; Boudreau 2010). Administrative tasks that have been traditionally performed by the HR function can be done by employees and managers on a self-service basis. Today's HR information systems (HRIS) simplify and speed up virtually every administrative HR task: salary administration, job posting and placement, address changes, family changes, and benefits administration, for example. . What is more, HR systems are available around the clock, and with mobile technology, they can be accessed from virtually anywhere by anyone, thus making self-service possible, convenient, and efficient.

Perhaps the greatest value of HRIS results from enabling the integration and analysis of HR activities, thus guiding strategy development and implementation. Metrics can be easily tracked and analyses performed that make it possible for organizations to develop and allocate their human capital more effectively (Boudreau and Ramstad 2007; Lawler, Levenson, and Boudreau 2004).

It is increasingly possible to measure and analyze the effectiveness of many HR policies and practices. With big data and a strategic mind-set, HR can be a data-driven function that practices evidence-based management. Business leaders can now be held accountable for HR measures such as turnover, employee attitudes, bench strength, and performance distributions.

A strong case can be made that HR needs to develop much better metrics and analytics capabilities. Our previous six studies identified metrics as one of four characteristics of HR systems that lead to HR's being a strategic partner. Managers want measurement systems that inform their decisions about human capital. All too often, however, HR focuses on the traditional paradigm of delivering HR services quickly, cheaply, and in ways that satisfy their clients but fail to use HR measures to make a true strategic difference in an organization's performance (Boudreau and Ramstad 1997, 2003). The issue is how to use HR measures to make a true strategic difference in an organization's performance.

Boudreau and Ramstad (2007) have identified four critical components of a measurement system that drive strategic change and organizational effectiveness: logic, analysis, measures, and process. Measures certainly are essential, but without the other three components, they are destined to remain isolated from the true purpose of the HR measurement systems.

Boudreau and Ramstad (1997) have also proposed that HR can make great strides by learning how more mature and powerful decision sciences have evolved their measurement systems in order to improve decision making. They identify three anchor points—efficiency, effectiveness, and impact—that connect decisions about resources such as money and customers to organizational effectiveness and that can be used to understand HR measurement:

1. *Efficiency* asks, "What resources are used to produce our HR policies and practices?" Typical indicators are cost-per-hire and time-to-fill vacancies.

2. *Effectiveness* asks, "How do our HR policies and practices affect the talent pools and organizational structures to which they are directed?" It thus refers to the effects of HR policies and practices on human capacity (a combination of capability, opportunity and

motivation) and the resulting aligned actions of the target talent pools. Effectiveness includes trainees' increased knowledge, better-selected applicants, stronger qualifications, and performance ratings of those receiving incentives.

3. *Impact* poses the hardest question of the three: "How do differences in the quality or availability of different talent pools affect strategic success?" This question is a component of talent segmentation, just like market segmentation is for marketers: "How do differences in the buying behavior of different customer groups affect strategic success?"

Most HR measurement systems largely reflect the question of efficiency, though there is some attention to effectiveness as well through focusing on such things as turnover, attitudes and bench strength (Gates 2004). Rarely do organizations consider impact (such as the relative effect of different talent pools on organizational effectiveness). More important, it is rare that HR measurement is specifically directed toward where it is most likely to have the greatest effect: on key talent. Attention to non-financial outcomes and sustainability also needs to be increased, as strategic HR can affect these as well (Boudreau and Ramstad 2005a).

The Emerging HR Decision Science

The majority of HR practices, benchmarks, and measures still reflect the traditional HR paradigm of excellence, defined as delivering high-quality HR services in response to client needs. Even as the field advocates more strategic HR, it is often defined as delivering the HR services that are important to executive clients: leadership development, competency systems, board governance, and so on. But this traditional service delivery paradigm is fundamentally limited because it assumes that clients know what they need. Market-based HR and accountability for business results should also be recognized as important (Gubman 2004). However, all too often, they amount to merely using marketing techniques or business results to assess the popularity of traditional HR services and their association with financial outcomes.

Fields such as finance have a different approach. They have augmented their service delivery paradigm with a decision science paradigm that teaches clients the frameworks to make good choices. Significant improvements in HR decisions will be attained not by applying finance and accounting formulas to HR programs and processes, but by learning how these fields evolved into the powerful, decision-supporting functions they are today. Their evolution provides a blueprint for what should be next for HR. The answer lies not just in benchmarking HR in other organizations, but in evolving to be similar to more strategic functions such as finance and marketing.

In marketing, decision science informs decisions about customers. In finance, decision science informs decisions about money. In human capital, a decision science should inform decisions about organizational talent and decisions made both within and outside the HR function. Boudreau and Ramstad (2005a, 2007) have labeled this emerging decision science "talentship" because it focuses on decisions that improve the stewardship of the hidden and apparent talents of current and potential employees.

Strategic Focuses

Human resource organizations exist in organizational environments that are as turbulent as the competitive environments in which companies find themselves. As companies take measures to survive and prosper, they make changes and introduce strategic initiatives that change the organization, the competencies it has, the way it manages its human resources, and its expectations of and relationships to its employees (Boudreau and Jesuthasan 2011; Lawler and Worley 2011).

A key driver of an organization's approach to organizing and performing is its business strategy. Thus, in order to understand how the HR function operates and what makes it effective, it is important to examine how its characteristics are related to the strategic focuses of the organization in which it operates. We have done this in our past studies and do it in this study as well.

Table 1.1 shows the prevalence of five strategic focuses that are often part of a company's business strategy. It also shows that in our US sample, the items measuring strategic focus statistically factor into five types: growth, information, knowledge, sustainability, and innovation. The focus concerned with information was rated the highest strategy in 1998, and the item on customer focus was the most highly rated single item. There are a few significant differences in the data from the different surveys. However, there is no overall trend that shows some focuses consistently increasing and others decreasing. Instead the results suggest that the focuses vary in importance based on what is happening during a particular time period.

Table 1.2 presents the strategic focus data for each country in our study. Building a global presence is the focus that shows the largest differences. The European and India companies have the greatest focus on it and China the least. China is the country that is the most different, with the lowest ratings across the board. This is not surprising given that it is less developed than the other countries and does not have a history of capitalism with its focus on competitive strategies.

Table 1.1. Strategic focuses, United States							
	Means						
Strategic Focus	**1995**[1]	**1998**[2]	**2001**[3]	**2004**[4]	**2007**[5]	**2010**[6]	**2013**[7]
Growth	**3.1**	**3.4**[4]	**3.0**	**2.9**[2]	**3.1**	**3.0**	**3.2**
Building a global presence	3.4	3.2	3.0	2.9	3.1	3.1	3.2
Acquisitions	2.8[2]	3.5[1,4,6]	3.1	2.9[2]	3.2	3.0[2]	3.3
Information-based strategies	—	**4.0**	**4.0**[7]	**3.9**	**3.8**	**3.8**	**3.7**[3]
Customer focus	—	4.4	4.4[7]	4.4	4.4	4.3	4.1[3]
Technology leadership	—	3.6	3.5	3.4	3.2	3.3	3.3
Knowledge-based strategies	—	—	**3.3**	**3.4**	**3.3**	**3.3**	**3.2**
Talent management	—	—	3.7[7]	3.7	3.6	3.4	3.4[3]
Knowledge / intellectual capital management	—	2.9	2.9	3.1	3.1	3.2	3.0
Sustainability	—	—	—	—	**3.6**[7]	**3.6**[7]	**3.2**[5,6]
Innovation	—	—	—	—	**3.6**	**3.4**	**3.3**

Response scale: 1 = little or no extent; 2 = some extent; 3 = moderate extent; 4 = great extent; 5 = very great extent. Empty cells indicate that the item was not asked in that year.
[1,2,3,4,5,6,7] Significant differences between years ($p \leq .05$).

Table 1.2. Strategic focuses, by country							
	Means						
Strategic Focus	**United States**[1]	**Canada**[2]	**Australia**[3]	**Europe**[4]	**United Kingdom**[5]	**India**[6]	**China**[7]
Growth	**3.2**[2,7]	**2.6**[1,4,6]	**3.0**[7]	**3.4**[2,7]	**3.2**[7]	**3.4**[2,7]	**2.2**[1,3,4,5,6]
Building a global presence	3.2[7]	2.6[4,5,6]	2.7[4]	3.9[2,3,7]	3.7[2,7]	3.7[2,7]	2.3[1,4,5,6]
Acquisitions	3.3[2,7]	2.6[1]	3.3[7]	2.9[7]	2.8	3.2[7]	2.1[1,3,4,6]
Information-based strategies	**3.7**[7]	**3.7**	**3.6**	**3.7**	**3.7**	**3.8**[7]	**3.2**[1,6]
Customer focus	4.1[7]	4.3[7]	4.0	3.9	4.1[7]	4.0[7]	3.4[1,2,5,6]
Technology leadership	3.3	3.1	3.1	3.5	3.4	3.6[7]	3.0[6]
Knowledge-based strategies	**3.2**[7]	**2.9**	**3.1**	**3.2**	**3.3**	**3.3**[7]	**2.7**[1,6]
Talent management	3.4[7]	3.0	3.1	3.5[7]	3.4	3.3[7]	2.8[1,4,6]
Knowledge /intellectual capital management	3.0	2.8	3.0	2.9	3.2	3.2[7]	2.6[6]
Sustainability	**3.2**	**3.2**	**3.0**	**3.7**[7]	**3.5**[7]	**3.5**[7]	**2.9**[4,5,6]
Innovation	**3.3**	**3.0**	**3.2**	**3.5**	**3.3**	**3.3**	**2.9**

Response scale: 1 = little or no extent; 2 = some extent; 3 = moderate extent; 4 = great extent; 5 = very great extent.
[1,2,3,4,5,6,7] Significant differences between countries ($p \leq .05$).

The highest-rated focus in every country is customer focus. Also highly rated is talent management. The high ratings for these two strategic focuses are an important point with respect to the role HR plays in strategy formulation and implementation. Given the close tie between them and HR policies and practices, it is logical that HR should play a major role in strategy development and implementation.

On balance, the strategic focus data support the point that organizations exist in complex, dynamic environments and need a variety of strategic and organizational initiatives to position themselves to perform successfully. In order to add value and act as a strategic contributor, the HR function needs to help ensure that the organizational capabilities and competencies exist to cope with a dynamic environment and changing organizational focuses. It is important to look at how the HR function is performing and changing, as well as how it is being driven by companies' strategies.

Management Approaches

The management approach that organizations take varies widely and should influence what the HR function can and should do. In the 2007, 2010, and 2012 surveys, we asked the respondents how much their company used these five management approaches:

- *Bureaucratic*: hierarchical structure, tight job description, top-down decision making

- *Low-cost operator*: low wages, minimum benefits, focus on cost reduction and controls

- *High involvement*: flat structure, participative decisions, commitment to employee development and careers

- *Global competitor*: complex, interesting work, best talent, low commitment to employee development and careers

- *Sustainable*: agile design, focus on financial performance and sustainability

The first four of these approaches are described in more detail in O'Toole and Lawler (2006). The fifth, sustainable management, is fully described by Lawler and Worley (2011). As can be seen in table 1.3, sustainable management is the most frequently used in the US companies studied. The second most frequently used is global competitor, which is also the only one that is used more often in 2013 than in 2007. These results most likely are due to changes in the business environment as more and more organizations are competing globally and experiencing demands for sustainable performance.

The results from our international sample, shown in table 1.4, are similar to the US results: the sustainable approach is used the most by the companies in our international sample, and the low-cost-operator approach is used the least.

The noticeable outlier is China. As it did in 2010, it uses the low-cost-operator and bureaucratic approaches the most and the high-involvement

Table 1.3. Management approaches, United States

To what extent do the following approaches describe how your organization is managed?	2013 Percentages					Means		
	Little or No Extent	Some Extent	Moderate Extent	Great Extent	Very Great Extent	2007[1]	2010[2]	2013[3]
Bureaucratic (hierarchical structure, tight job descriptions, top-down decision making)	10.5	34.3	27.3	23.8	4.2	2.66	2.82	2.77
Low-cost operator (low wages, minimum benefits, focus on cost reduction and controls)	32.6	27.7	27.7	9.2	2.8	2.07	2.02	2.22
High involvement (flat structure, participative decisions, commitment to employee development and careers)	7.0	30.3	31.0	26.8	4.9	3.04	3.05	2.92
Global competitor (complex, interesting work; best talent; low commitment to employee development and careers)	11.3	23.2	33.8	23.9	7.7	2.55[3]	2.66	2.94[1]
Sustainable (agile design, focus on financial performance and sustainability)	7.1	12.8	39.7	29.8	10.6	—	3.33	3.24

Note: The empty cell signifies that the item was not asked in that year.

[1,2,3] Significant differences between years ($p \leq .05$).

Table 1.4. Management approaches, by country

To what extent do the following approaches describe how your organization is managed?	Means						
	United States[1]	Canada[2]	Australia[3]	Europe[4]	United Kingdom[5]	India[6]	China[7]
Bureaucratic (hierarchical structure, tight job descriptions, top-down decision making)	2.8	2.8	2.9	3.1	2.9	2.8	3.2
Low-cost operator (low wages, minimum benefits, focus on cost reduction and controls)	2.2[6,7]	2.0[6,7]	2.6	2.2[6,7]	1.8[6,7]	2.9[1,2,4,5]	3.0[1,2,4,5]
High involvement (flat structure, participative decisions, commitment to employee development and careers)	2.9	2.8	2.9	2.7	2.6	2.9	2.5
Global competitor (complex interesting work; hire best talent; low commitment to employee development and careers)	2.9[7]	2.5[4]	2.3[4]	3.4[2,3,7]	3.1[7]	3.0[7]	2.4[1,4,5,6]
Sustainable (agile design, focus on financial performance and sustainability)	3.2	3.3	3.1	3.4	3.3	3.6[7]	2.9[6]

Response scale: 1 = little or no extent; 2 = some extent; 3 = moderate extent; 4 = great extent; 5 = very great extent.

[1,2,3,4,5,6,7] Significant differences between countries ($p \leq .05$).

---

approach the least in comparison to the other countries. It also is a relatively low user of the global competitor approach. The most obvious explanation for the tendency of China to use different management approaches is its level of economic and management development.

Throughout this book, we look at how US corporations that use these five approaches operate. They do not include all possible management approaches, and we do not expect that any company will be managed in one way. We use them because they provide a way to identify the overall management approach that a large corporation is taking and how HR practices are related to the way a company is managed.

Organizational Design

Organizational design is a key factor in enabling organizations to develop capabilities and perform in ways that produce a competitive advantage (Galbraith 2014). Organizational design is more than structure; it includes elements such as management processes, rewards, people systems, information systems, and work processes. These elements must fit with the strategy and with each other for an organization to perform effectively.

Organizational designs involve complex trade-offs and contingencies. Clearly no single design approach fits all organizations. As new business models emerge—complex partnerships, globally integrated firms, customer-focused designs, and network organizations—new approaches and organizational forms need to be created to deal with the complex performance requirements that organizations must address. Furthermore, multibusiness corporations are recognizing that different businesses exist in different markets and face varying requirements. Consequently, variation in organizational design is increasing both within multibusiness corporations and between businesses (Galbraith 2014). Thus, for the company and the HR function, one size does not fit all situations. Different organizational forms require different HR contributions, and thus different HR functional designs and systems.

Contributing to effective organizational design is a major domain in which the HR function has the opportunity to add strategic value (Lawler 2008). Increasingly, the only sustainable competitive advantage is the ability to organize effectively, respond to change, and manage well (Mohrman, Galbraith, Lawler, and Associates 1998; Lawler and Worley 2006; Worley et al. 2014). Confirmation of this statement is provided by Lawler, Mohrman, and Benson's (2001) longitudinal study of the Fortune 1000, which shows a significant relationship between firm financial performance and the adoption of new management practices designed to increase a firm's capabilities. Further confirmation of this is provided by data showing that agile firms outperform all others over the long term. (Worley et al. 2014).

Lawler (2008) has identified four approaches to talent management that need to be supported by different organizational designs and HR practices. For example, the low-cost-operator approach calls for an organizational design that has highly structured jobs and excellent control systems. The high-involvement and the global competitor approaches require interesting, challenging jobs as well as flat structures that put people in contact with the external environment. The fourth approach, sustainable management, calls for a focus on how an organization affects the environment, society, and its employees. Both picking the right approach to management and then implementing it effectively are opportunities for the HR function to add significant value.

Design of the HR Function

All parts of organizations—operating units and staff functions alike—need to be designed to deliver high value. For staff groups, doing so requires the development of a business model—a value proposition defining what kind of value they will deliver that the company is willing to pay for because their work strengthens company performance. It also requires them to determine how best to deliver their services.

The HR function must think about whether the elements of its design indeed create a high-performance organization—one capable of delivering maximum value while consuming the fewest possible resources. Doing so means concentrating on the way HR organizes to deliver routine transactions services, traditional HR systems development and administration, and strategic business support.

HR must develop structures, competencies, customer linkages, metrics, management processes, rewards, and information technology to ensure that scarce resources are optimally deployed to deliver value. In addition to making sure the HR function is optimally designed, HR can add value by helping design the key features of the rest of the organization.

In many respects, it is useful to think of HR functions as multiple product businesses. They have customers, products and services, revenue, and competitors (self-service, vendors, and consulting firms). In order to exist, they need to perform in a way that makes them the "best buy."

Organizational design decisions for HR, as well as for companies as a whole, are made in response to four key questions:

1. *Which activities should be centralized and leveraged, and which should be decentralized in order to provide focus on the unique needs of different parts of the organization?* Organizations are combining centralization and decentralization, trying to be big (coordinated) in functions such as purchasing when there is an advantage to being big and small (decentralized and flexible) in functions such as new product development when there are advantages to being small and agile.

2. *Which functions should be performed in-house and which should be outsourced?* Companies should outsource when they can purchase high-quality services and products more inexpensively or reliably than they can generate internally.

3. *Which functions should be hierarchically controlled, and which should be integrated and controlled laterally?* In some areas, organizations function in a lateral manner, integrating and creating synergies across various parts of the organization, creating cross-functional units to carry out entire processes, and collaborating with suppliers and customers. Organizations are searching for ways to leverage across business units while setting up organizational and management approaches that give the optimal levels of flexibility and control to various business units.

4. *Which processes should be IT based?* Today most organizations have electronic systems that can do a great deal of the administrative work of HR, but what is it advantageous to have them do?

Traditionally HR (and many other staff groups such as IT) has been organized in a hierarchical manner, and it has seen its mission as designing, administering, and enforcing adherence to HR policies and systems. As a result, all too often HR has been seen as an expensive and necessary evil that consumes resources disproportionate to the value that it adds to the organization. A number of changes in structure and process are being advocated for HR:

- Decentralizing business support to operating units in order to increase responsiveness

- Contracting with business units for the services that are to be delivered, and perhaps even requiring services to be self-funding as a way of ensuring that businesses get only the services that they are willing to pay for and that they see as contributing to business performance

- Creating efficient central services units or outsourcing transactional services, or both

- Creating centers of excellence that provide expert services, often in a consulting capacity

- Increasing the rotation of people within various staff functions and between staff and line, and having fewer lifelong careers within a narrow staff function, in order to broaden the perspectives of HR staff professionals and increase their awareness of business issues, as well as increasing the depth of understanding of HR issues among line management

- Expanding the scope of the HR function to include communications and sustainability, to mention just two areas

Conclusion

The future of the HR function in organizations is uncertain. On the one hand, if it does not change, it could end up being largely an administrative function that manages an information technology–based HR system and vendors who do most of the HR administrative work. On the other hand, it could become a driver of organizational effectiveness and business strategy. In many organizations, one of the key determinants of competitive advantage is effective human capital management. More than ever before, the effectiveness of an organization depends on its ability to address issues such as knowledge management, change management, and capability building, all of which could fall into the domain of the HR function. The unanswered question at this point is whether HR will rise to the occasion and address these issues.

In order to increase its contribution to organizational effectiveness, HR must rethink its basic value proposition, structure, services, and programs in order to address how it can add value in today's economy with new organizational forms, business strategies, and performance demands. HR faces a formidable challenge in helping organizations deal with the human issues that are raised by large-scale strategic change. To deal with these challenges effectively, HR has to focus on how it is organized and its competencies and role in business strategy.

There is some evidence that the situation of HR is changing and that the function is beginning to redefine its role in order to increase the value it adds. Data collected in 1995, 1998, 2001, 2004, 2007, and 2010 found evidence of some change in large US corporations, but there has been more talk of change than actual change (Lawler and Mohrman 2003; Lawler et al. 2006; Lawler and Boudreau 2009, 2012). If this is true in the 2013 results examined in this book, it will be additional evidence that HR is not doing what it needs to do in order to be a key contributor to organizational effectiveness.

CHAPTER 2

The Role of HR

- HR spends the majority of its time on services, controlling, and record keeping.

- How HR spends its time has not changed since 1995.

- HR executives report that in the past, they spent more time on services, controlling, and record keeping than they do currently, but data from earlier surveys do not support this claim.

- What HR does is related to the organization's management approach. For example, bureaucratic organizations have HR functions that spend time on services, controlling, and record keeping.

- The HR function in Chinese organizations spends the least amount of time being a strategic contributor.

A key issue for HR functions is how they divide their time between providing services and doing higher value-added business partner and strategic work. A major criticism of HR functions for decades has been that they are too bogged down in administration and policing. The results of our previous surveys support this conclusion. They have consistently shown that HR functions spend over 50 percent of their time on service provision, auditing, and maintaining records.

Time Allocation

As with our previous surveys, respondents were asked to estimate the percentage of time that their HR function currently spends in carrying out five roles and how much time was spent on them five to seven years ago. Figure 2.1 shows that the US respondents report the function currently spends the most time on service provision and as a strategic business partner. When the time spent on service provision is combined with the time spent on records and auditing/controlling, respondents report that 53.9 percent of their time is currently spent on administration and services.

The responses from India, Canada, Australia, Europe, and the United Kingdom are very similar to the US responses. The data from them (table 2.1) show only small differences among these countries and in comparison to the United States. The results for China show a much smaller amount of time spent being a strategic business contributor. What most likely accounts for this is the different levels of economic development in China. However, it is worth noting that India is also a developing country but does not have results like those for China. This most likely is due to their different business histories.

When asked about what their HR's time allocation was five to seven years ago, US HR executives report significant change in how their function's time is spent when they look back. They report that they now spend less time (54 percent versus 73 percent) on record keeping,

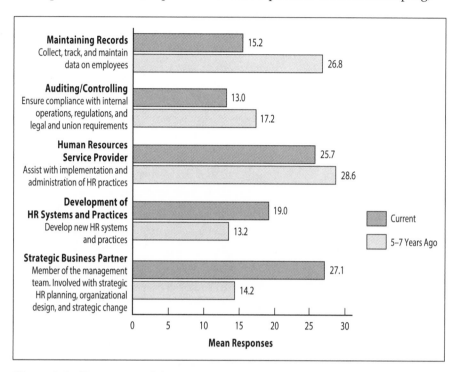

Figure 2.1. Percentage of time spent on HR roles

Table 2.1. Percentage of current time spent on various HR roles, by country							
	Means						
HR Roles	**United States[1]**	**Canada[2]**	**Australia[3]**	**Europe[4]**	**United Kingdom[5]**	**India[6]**	**China[7]**
Maintaining records Collect, track, and maintain data on employees	15.2[7]	17.9	12.7[7]	22.3	15.9	19.1	23.7[1,3]
Auditing/controlling Ensure compliance with internal operations, regulations, and legal and union requirements	13.0[7]	9.9[7]	14.0	13.5	11.0[7]	14.4	16.6[1,2,5]
HR service provider Assist with implementation and administration of HR practices	25.7[2]	36.4[1,4,6,7]	28.2	24.6[2]	28.1	26.0[2]	28.1[2]
Development of HR systems and practices Develop new HR systems and practices	19.0	15.8	17.3	16.5	16.3	20.2	18.0
Strategic business partner Member of the management team; involved with strategic HR planning, organizational design, and strategic change	27.1[7]	19.9	27.9[7]	23.1[7]	28.7[7]	20.2	13.7[1,3,4,5]
[1,2,3,4,5,6,7] Significant differences between countries ($p \leq .05$).							

auditing, and service provision and more time (27 percent versus 46 percent) on developing new HR systems and practices and being a strategic business contributor.

Our results from the other countries are very similar to those from the United States with respect to how they say HR spent its time five to seven years ago. A comparison between tables 2.1 and 2.2 shows that the estimates of how time is spent suggests that in all countries, the time spent on strategy has increased over the previous five to seven years. This movement toward spending more time on strategic business issues appears to be the right way for HR to change because it means that HR can add more value.

Overall, our respondents are reporting a significant and encouraging movement toward HR becoming a strategic contributor and doing higher value-added activities. However, before we conclude that this has actually occurred, it is important to compare the results for the United States from 1995, 1998, 2001, 2004, 2007, 2010, and 2013. The US data from 1995, 1998, 2001, 2004, 2007, and 2014 are very similar to those collected in 2013 when the same questions were asked (see tables 2.3 and 2.4). There is no significant change in the current responses or in the responses concerning five to seven years ago from 1995 to 2013. In other words, there has been no major change in any of the responses about how time is spent from 1995 to 2013. This raises serious questions about the validity of the reports by our respondents about how things were in the past.

It might be expected that the 2013 estimates of how things were five to seven years earlier would be somewhat in line with how things were

Table 2.2. Percentage of time spent five to seven years ago on various HR roles, by country

HR Roles	Means						
	United States[1]	Canada[2]	Australia[3]	Europe[4]	United Kingdom[5]	India[6]	China[7]
Maintaining records Collect, track, and maintain data on employees	26.8	26.1	22.3	31.0	24.1	28.7	32.7
Auditing/controlling Ensure compliance with internal operations, regulations, and legal and union requirements	17.2[2,7]	9.8[1,7]	16.9	14.3[7]	15.5	16.0[7]	22.7[1,2,4,6]
HR service provider Assist with implementation and administration of HR practices	28.6[2]	41.5[1,4,6,7]	33.6	28.7[2]	34.6	26.2[2]	26.4[2]
Development of HR systems and practices Develop new HR systems and practices	13.2[7]	12.3	16.1[7]	14.2	11.8	15.9[7]	9.5[1,3,6]
Strategic business partner Member of the management team; involved with strategic HR planning, organizational design, and strategic change	14.2[7]	10.3	11.0	11.8	13.9	13.2	8.6[1]

[1,2,3,4,5,6,7] Significant differences between countries ($p \leq .05$).

Table 2.3. Percentage of current time spent on various HR roles, United States

HR Roles	Means						
	1995[1]	1998[2]	2001[3]	2004[4]	2007[5]	2010[6]	2013[7]
Maintaining records Collect, track, and maintain data on employees	15.4	16.1	14.9	13.2	15.8	13.6	15.2
Auditing/controlling Ensure compliance with internal operations, regulations, and legal and union requirements	12.2	11.2	11.4	13.3	11.6	12.5	13.0
HR service provider Assist with implementation and administration of HR practices	31.3[7]	35.0[5,7]	31.3[7]	32.0[7]	27.8[2]	30.4	25.7[1,2,3,4]
Development of HR systems and practices Develop new HR systems and practices	18.6	19.2	19.3	18.1	19.2	16.7	19.0
Strategic business partner Member of the management team; involved with strategic HR planning, organizational design, and strategic change	22.0	20.3[6,7]	23.2	23.5	25.6	26.8[2]	27.1[2]

[1,2,3,4,5,6,7] Significant differences between years ($p \leq .05$).

Table 2.4. Percentage of time spent five to seven years ago on various HR roles, United States

HR Roles	Means						
	1995[1]	1998[2]	2001[3]	2004[4]	2007[5]	2010[6]	2013[7]
Maintaining records Collect, track, and maintain data on employees	23.0	25.6	26.7	25.9	26.3	23.2	26.8
Auditing/controlling Ensure compliance with internal operations, regulations, and legal and union requirements	19.5[4,5,6]	16.4	17.1	14.8[1]	15.2[1]	15.7[1]	17.2
HR service provider Assist with implementation and administration of HR practices	34.3	36.4[7]	33.1	36.4[7]	33.0	32.8	28.6[2,4]
Development of HR systems and practices Develop new HR systems and practices	14.3	14.2	13.9	12.6	13.5	14.4	13.2
Strategic business partner Member of the management team; involved with strategic HR planning, organizational design, and strategic change	10.3	9.4[6,7]	9.1[6,7]	9.6[6,7]	12.1	13.9[2,3,4]	14.2[2,3,4]

[1,2,3,4,5,6,7] Significant differences between years ($p \leq .05$).

said to be in our 2010 study, and especially in our 2007 study (six years ago), but they are not. Instead, rather than showing a change in time spent, the 1995, 1998, 2001, 2004, 2007, and 2010 results for how time is spent are the same as the results for 2013. This finding suggests that the HR executives who responded in 2013, as well as those who responded in 1995, 1998, 2001, 2004, 2007, and 2010, may have perceived more change in their role than has actually taken place. In short, they may be guilty of wishful thinking and a selective memory.

What should we believe: Retrospective reports of the way things were or data from the past about the way things were at the time the data were collected? The answer is obvious: most individuals are much better at reporting how things are now than about what they were like years ago. Reports concerning the past often include changes that reflect favorably on the individual. In this case, it is possible that HR executives want to see themselves as more of a strategic contributor now than they were in the past. This is quite likely, given the many books and articles that have called for this to happen and the advantages it offers those in the HR profession.

The complete lack of change in the report of how time is spent is surprising and concerning: the results from 1995 are almost identical to those from 2013. It is an understatement to say that the worlds of business and HR have changed dramatically since 1995. Thus, it is surprising, even shocking, that how HR spends its time has not changed. Each time we have done our survey, we have expected to see some change in how HR spends its time, but no sign of change has appeared. The likelihood that HR has not changed makes us wonder what, if anything, can cause HR to spend more time on being a strategic business partner.

It is worth noting that there is one explanation for the lack of change in the reports of how HR spends its time that suggests some progress. HR executives might have gained a much better understanding of what is involved in being a strategic contributor. As a result of their development, they are setting a higher standard for what constitutes strategic work. If this is true, it could be that HR is doing more strategic partner work even though it does not report any change in time allocation.

It is not too surprising that HR continues to report it has changed, even though it most likely has not. We have seen this pattern in each of our previous surveys, and it raises the question of whether this is a problem. It may be a major problem if it leads to HR executives' believing they have made progress toward an objective they feel is important when in fact they have not.

Strategic Focuses

The relationships between the strategic focuses of an organization and how HR spends its time are shown in table 2.5. The correlations in the table show a clear pattern: maintaining records and auditing/controlling are negatively related to all the strategic focuses and the negative relationships for auditing/controlling are statistically significant. We found a similar result in our 2004, 2007, and 2010 studies. Apparently the weaker an organization's strategic focus is in these areas, the more the HR function spends its time maintaining records

Table 2.5. Relationship of HR roles to strategic focuses					
HR Roles	**Strategic Focuses**				
	Growth	**Information-Based Strategies**	**Knowledge-Based Strategies**	**Sustainability**	**Innovation**
Maintaining records	–.01	–.15^t	–.13	–.10	–.10
Auditing/controlling	–.01	–.23**	–.20*	–.12	–.24**
HR service provider	.07	.13	.01	.10	–.03
Development of HR systems and practices	.07	.17*	.10	.09	.10
Strategic business partner	–.08	.05	.14^t	.02	.16^t
Significance level: $^t p \leq .10$, $^* p \leq .05$, $^{**} p \leq .01$, $^{***} p \leq .001$.					

and auditing/controlling. Given the lack of a strategic focus, this may be the best thing HR can do.

The time that the HR function spends on strategic business activities is positively related to four of the strategic focuses. Time spent on developing HR systems is positively related to all of the five strategic focuses. Although the relationships are not strong, this finding suggests that HR becomes much more involved in strategic business activities when the organization has a clear strategic focus, regardless of what that focus is. One implication of this finding is that in order for HR to become more strategic, organizations themselves may need to become more strategic. One way for this to happen is for HR to provide leadership to the rest of the organization in this area. If it can accomplish this, we believe there is a good chance that HR will spend more time on strategy and the development of HR systems that support their organization strategy and less time on recording and auditing.

Management Approaches

The management approach that organizations take has a low, but in some cases a significant, relationship to how HR spends its time. As shown in table 2.6, taking the bureaucratic approach is associated with spending significantly more time maintaining records and auditing and significant less time being a strategic contributor. The results for the low-cost-operator approach are similar. As might be expected, strategic business partnering and developing HR systems are slightly higher in high-involvement organizations and maintaining records is slightly lower. This result reinforces the point that what HR does is at least partially determined by the way an organization is managed. Simply stated, bureaucratic organizations have bureaucratic HR functions.

Table 2.6. Relationship of HR roles to management approaches					
	Management Approaches				
HR Roles	Bureaucratic	Low-Cost Operator	High Involvement	Global Competitor	Sustainable
Maintaining records	.23**	.18*	–.15ᵗ	–.08	–.07
Auditing/controlling	.29***	.17*	–.11	–.08	–.11
HR service provider	–.07	.08	–.02	.10	.12
Development of HR systems and practices	–.07	–.15ᵗ	.13	.13	–.02
Strategic business partner	–.24**	–.22**	.13	–.05	.01
Significance level: ᵗ$p \leq .10$, *$p \leq .05$, **$p \leq .01$, ***$p \leq .001$.					

Conclusion

The obvious conclusion is that HR has not significantly changed how it allocates its time since we began this research in 1995. In all of the countries we studied, it remains a function that spends the majority of its time on services, controlling, and record keeping. HR executives report that they are spending more time providing strategic services than they did 5-7 years ago, but our longitudinal data do not support that conclusion. Our data on management approaches and strategy provide one likely reason why there has not been much change. The management approaches and strategies that call for a change in how HR operates are only now gaining market share.

Our findings that HR has not changed how it spends its time and spends relatively little time on strategy make it particularly important that throughout this book, we focus on HR's strategic role. We need to establish what it can and should be. We also need to determine what changes are needed in order to make change happen and, finally, what the advantages are of HR performing a more strategic role.

CHAPTER 3

HR's Engagement with Boards

- HR is most likely to help boards in the United States with executive compensation and succession planning.

- HR provides little help to boards with sustainability and board effectiveness.

- Providing support to boards is clearly an area where HR could do more.

- China stands out as the country where HR provides the least help to boards.

- Help to boards is higher when an organization's management approach is either high involvement or sustainable management.

HR expertise and information is critical to many of the issues that corporate boards deal with. They range from executive compensation to talent management. This raises the important question of whether boards, when they face these issues, call on HR. If they do, it is a clear indication that HR at least has a part-time seat at the most important decision-making table in most organizations. If it does not, it is hard to see how HR can play a significant role with respect to most key strategic decisions.

Board Help

Table 3.1 shows the responses to a question about the type of help HR gives to boards in US firms. The question was first asked in 2004, so there are data from 2004, 2007, 2010, and 2013.

Executive compensation and succession have been and continue to be the two issues on which HR is most likely to be asked for help in US corporations. This finding is not surprising, given that these are areas where most HR functions should be able to provide help and where board members are likely to see HR as a knowledgeable source of help. It is disappointing that such organizational issues as change consulting and strategic readiness receive such low ratings. These two functions and three others have average ratings below "asking for help to a moderate extent" (3.0). Particularly low are help with board effectiveness and sustainability.

The fact that workforce condition is the fourth most requested area is a positive. This is an area where HR should have good information; it is a critical organizational performance determinant and an area where a

Table 3.1. HR extent of help to boards, United States

HR Extent of Help	2013 Percentages					Means			
	Little or No Help	Some Help	Moderate Help	Great Help	Very Great Help	2004[1]	2007[2]	2010[3]	2013[4]
Executive compensation	4.0	5.6	5.6	31.0	54.0	4.2	4.1	3.9[4]	4.3[3]
Addressing strategic readiness	12.9	25.8	32.3	24.2	4.8	2.8	2.8	2.8	2.8
Executive succession	4.8	9.5	8.7	37.3	39.7	3.8	3.8	3.7	4.0
Change consulting	18.5	26.6	29.0	20.2	5.6	2.6	2.7	2.6	2.7
Developing board effectiveness/corporate governance	30.9	22.8	26.0	18.7	1.6	2.5	2.5	2.2	2.4
Risk assessment	19.2	24.8	34.4	18.4	3.2	2.4	2.6	2.6	2.6
Information about the condition or capability of the workforce	10.7	20.5	33.6	26.2	9.0	3.3	3.3	3.2	3.0
Board compensation	17.6	13.4	18.5	27.7	22.7	3.4[3]	3.0	2.8[1,4]	3.2[3]
Sustainability[a]	26.2	25.4	30.3	15.6	2.5	—	—	—	2.4

[a]This topic was new for 2013.

[1,2,3,4]Significant differences between years ($p \leq .05$).

high rating is warranted. If HR performs well in areas like it and executive succession, it may well be asked for help in executing change and strategic readiness. So far, however, this does not seem to be happening. A comparison of the 2004, 2007, 2010, and 2013 results reveals few significant changes in these areas. In comparison to 2010, the 2013 data shows more use of HR only with respect to board and executive compensation. Overall, it is clear that in most companies, HR has its foot in the boardroom door, but that is all, and there is no evidence of this changing.

International Results

The data from the other developed countries in the study (see table 3.2) are similar to the US data, but with some interesting differences. This is not surprising since all of the countries have different board structures and are subject to different regulations and board rules. If anything is a surprise, it is that the differences among the developed countries are not greater. As it is, boards in the United States and Canada seem to ask for the least organizational development help. Across all of the areas, Canadian boards stand out among the developed countries by asking for the least help.

Not surprisingly, the results from China are different given the ownership structures that include government-owned firms. It is somewhat surprising that the differences are not larger. As it is, three differences stand out: corporate boards in China ask for less help with executive compensation, succession, and board compensation. These are the three

Table 3.2. HR extent of help to boards, by country							
	Means						
HR Extent of Help	**United States[1]**	**Canada[2]**	**Australia[3]**	**Europe[4]**	**United Kingdom[5]**	**India[6]**	**China[7]**
Executive compensation	4.3[2,6,7]	3.5[1]	3.8[7]	3.7[7]	4.3[7]	3.6[17]	2.8[1,3,4,5,6]
Addressing strategic readiness	2.8	2.3[3,5,6]	3.2[2]	3.0	3.2[2]	3.3[2,7]	2.5[6]
Executive succession	4.0[2,7]	2.9[1,5]	3.7[7]	3.5[7]	4.0[2,7]	3.5[7]	2.6[1,3,4,5,6]
Change consulting	2.7[6]	2.3[6]	3.3	3.0	3.2	3.3[1,2,7]	2.6[6]
Developing board effectiveness/corporate governance	2.4[6]	2.2[6]	2.6	2.4[6]	2.9	3.2[1,2,4,7]	2.1[6]
Risk assessment	2.6	2.4[6]	2.9	2.4[6]	2.8	3.1[2,4,7]	2.3[6]
Information about the condition/capability of the workforce	3.0	2.7[6]	3.5	3.2	3.5	3.5[2]	3.1
Board compensation	3.2[2,7]	2.3[1,5]	2.8	2.8	3.4[2,7]	3.1[7]	2.2[1,5,6]
Sustainability[a]	2.4	2.1	2.8	2.8	2.8	—	2.6

[a]India was not asked to respond to this question.

Response scale: 1 = little or no extent; 2 = some extent; 3 = moderate extent; 4 = great extent; 5 = very great extent.

[1,2,3,4,5,6,7] Significant differences between countries ($p \leq .05$).

areas where US boards ask for the most help. It almost goes without saying that the different labor markets that US and Chinese firms face, as well as the history of board governance in the two countries, most likely accounts for this difference.

Strategic Focuses

The relationship between the help provided to the board and the strategic focuses of organizations is shown in table 3.3. As might be expected because of the direct relationship to human capital, boards ask for more help in these areas when organizations have knowledge-based strategies. Organizations with a focus on innovation have boards that are high users of HR in change consulting and workforce capability. Somewhat surprising, the lowest relationships are with growth.

The strongest relationship in table 3.3 is with sustainability. When sustainability is a strategic focus, boards do ask for HR help. This is an interesting point that we discuss more in chapter 10 when we look at the data on HR and sustainability.

The use of HR help for board compensation and board effectiveness shows the weakest relationships to most of the strategic focuses. This is not surprising since support with compensation and board effectiveness is needed regardless of the strategy. Workforce information is related to three of the focuses, a result that likely reflects the close connection

Table 3.3. Relationship of strategic focuses to board help

HR Extent of Help	Strategic Focuses				
	Growth	Information-Based Strategies	Knowledge-Based Strategies	Sustainability	Innovation
Executive compensation	–.02	.05	.19*	–.01	.21*
Addressing strategic readiness	–.09	.09	.24**	.14	.16^t
Executive succession	–.13	.02	.20*	.01	.14
Change consulting	–.10	.12	.20*	.05	.29***
Developing board effectiveness/corporate governance	.05	–.06	.05	.11	.08
Risk assessment	–.15^t	.01	.15^t	.01	.08
Information about the condition/capability of the workforce	–.11	.24**	.28**	.06	.28**
Board compensation	.03	–.09	.02	–.03	–.01
Sustainability	.06	.08	.17^t	.40***	.10

Significance level: $^t p \leq .10$, $^* p \leq .05$, $^{**} p \leq .01$, $^{***} p \leq .001$.

between most strategies and workforce issues. The relationships are not strong, but it does seem that the more an organization has a strategic focus other than growth, the more likely it is to use HR.

Management Approaches

Table 3.4 shows the relationship between the management approaches and board help. The strongest relationships are with the high-involvement approach and the low-cost-operator approach. The more that the high-involvement approach to management is used, the more active HR is with the board. This finding makes good sense and reinforces the point that when organizations take talent seriously as a source of competitive advantage, HR organizations can and do play a more important role (Lawler 2008). Also supporting this conclusion are the negative relationship between the bureaucratic and the low-cost-operator approaches and how active HR is with the board. This finding is not surprising given the reality that neither of these approaches places great importance on human capital.

The sustainable approach shows a strong positive relationship to boards getting help from HR with respect to sustainability. This is not surprising given the emphasis this approach puts on human capital.

Conclusion

HR has a limited role when it comes to supporting boards. Its major support areas are executive compensation and succession. In most areas, its level of support has not changed, but it has increased with respect

Table 3.4. Relationship of management approaches to board help

HR Extent of Help	Management Approaches				
	Bureaucratic	Low-Cost Operator	High Involvement	Global Competitor	Sustainable
Executive compensation	–.16ᵗ	–.08	.24**	.18*	.08
Addressing strategic readiness	–.08	–.07	.28**	.00	.12
Executive succession	–.10	–.08	.22*	.10	.15ᵗ
Change consulting	–.12	–.25**	.33***	–.04	.06
Developing board effectiveness/corporate governance	–.09	–.04	.14	.02	.08
Risk assessment	.06	.02	.03	–.11	.01
Information about the condition/capability of the workforce	–.08	–.22*	.25**	–.04	.02
Board compensation	–.12	–.08	.17ᵗ	.18ᵗ	.16ᵗ
Sustainability	–.09	–.05	.25**	.09	.23*

Significance level: ᵗ$p \le .10$, *$p \le .05$, **$p \le .01$, ***$p \le .001$.

to executive and board compensation. The management approach of an organization has a strong relation to its overall level of support. It is high in high-involvement and sustainable management organizations and low in bureaucratic and low-cost-operator organizations. Providing support to boards is clearly an area where HR could do more. There is little doubt that if it did more with boards, it could play a larger role in formulating and implementing business strategies. The key question at this point is what it needs to do in order to do more.

- In most US organizations, HR is not a full partner in business strategy, but it does have an input role.

- The country in our survey where HR has the smallest role in business strategy is China.

- HR's role in strategy shows little change from 1998 to 2012.

- HR plays a major role in strategy when organizations have a strong strategic focus and practice high-involvement management and sustainable management.

- HR is involved in organizational diagnosis and change rather than strategic direction (mergers, new business, options, and choices).

- HR strategy activity is related to HR's strategic role but not to organizational performance.

The involvement that an organization's HR function has in the development and implementation of strategy—how much and what kind—is a critical determinant of its influence and the value it adds. There is a growing consensus among executives and researchers that human capital needs to be given more and better-informed consideration because it should be an important determinant of what strategies an organization can and should pursue (Boudreau 2010; Lawler 2008; Lawler and Worley 2011). It also should be a key determinant of how a strategy is pursued.

Type of Involvement

HR's involvement in business strategy can take a variety of forms. Figure 4.1 shows that in 2013, virtually all HR functions reported that they are involved in business strategy. However, in over 70 percent of the companies studied, HR is less than a full partner in the eyes of their HR executives and managers. When the 2013 data are compared to those of 1998, 2001, 2004, 2007, and 2010, there is no statistically significant change in the extent to which HR reports being involved in business strategy (see Lawler and Boudreau 2012 for data from 1998 to 2010). If there is any tendency, it is for HR to be slightly less involved in 2013 than it used to be. Thus, the data do not suggest that the HR function is becoming more of a strategic partner in most organizations; instead, at best, it has a stagnant position.

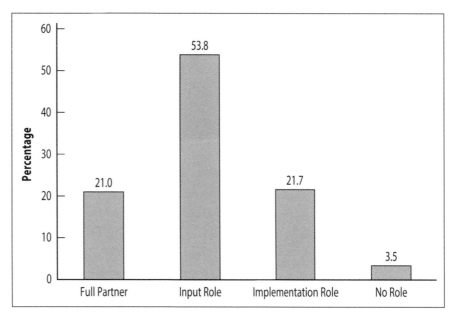

Figure 4.1. HR's role in business strategy: Results from current global HR study

International Results

The international data in table 4.1 are similar to the US data with the exception of China. In all the countries except China, HR may not be a full partner, but at least it has an input role with respect to business strategy. In China, HR rarely has a full partner or input role.

Table 4.1. HR's role in business strategy, by country							
Role in Strategy	**Percentages**						
	United States[1]	**Canada[2]**	**Australia[3]**	**Europe[4]**	**United Kingdom[5]**	**India[6]**	**China[7]**
No role	3.5	4.4	4.3	14.0	0.0	11.3	23.4
Implementation role	21.7	24.4	26.1	20.9	25.8	34.0	37.7
Input role	53.8	42.2	39.1	44.2	38.7	30.2	27.3
Full partner	21.0	28.9	30.4	20.9	35.5	24.5	11.7
Mean	2.92[7]	2.96[7]	2.96[7]	2.72	3.10[7]	2.68	2.27[1,2,3,5]

[1,2,3,4,5,6,7] Significant differences between countries ($p \leq .05$).

Strategic Focuses

The role that HR plays in the strategy process is related to an organization's strategic focus. As can be seen in table 4.2, when HR has a full partner role, all of the strategic focuses except growth are higher. The strongest relationships are with knowledge and sustainability. Overall,

Table 4.2. Strategic focuses and HR's role in business strategy

Role in Strategy	Strategic Focuses				
	Growth	Information-Based Strategies	Knowledge-Based Strategies	Sustainability	Innovation
No role[1]	4.1	3.3	2.7	2.4	3.0
Implementation role[2]	3.0	3.5	2.9[4]	3.3	3.1
Input role[3]	3.4	3.7	3.2[4]	3.2	3.2
Full partner[4]	2.9	3.9	3.6[2,3]	3.3	3.7

Response scale: 1 = little or no extent; 2 = some extent; 3 = moderate extent; 4 = great extent; 5 = very great extent.

[1,2,3,4] Significant difference ($p \leq .05$) from one other role in strategy.

Table 4.3. Management approaches and HR's role in business strategy

Role in Strategy	Management Approaches				
	Bureaucratic	Low-Cost Operator	High-Involvement	Global Competitor	Sustainable
No role[1]	3.4	3.0	2.0[4]	2.8	3.4
Implementation role[2]	3.0	2.5	2.5[4]	2.8	2.9
Input role[3]	2.8	2.1	3.0	3.1	3.3
Full partner[4]	2.3	2.0	3.4[1,2]	2.8	3.5

Response scale: 1 = little or no role; 2 = some role; 3 = moderate role; 4 = great role; 5 = very great role.

[1,2,3,4] Significant difference ($p \leq .05$) from one other role in strategy.

HR is most likely to play a major role in strategy when a clear strategy exists. The exception here is when growth is the focus: the more it is a focus, the less likely it is that HR plays a full partner role in business strategy.

Management Approaches

Table 4.3 shows the relationship between HR's role in strategy and an organization's management approach. It shows that when HR has a full partner role in strategy, high-involvement management and sustainable management are the most common management approaches. But in low-cost-operator and bureaucratic companies, it is unlikely that HR plays a full partner role in strategy. These findings are not surprising; they fit well with how these approaches think about the role of people. With high-involvement and sustainable management, people are front and center, whereas in the others, they are "something to be dealt with." These results do raise an interesting question about causation: Does this relationship exist because the HR strategy role leads to high involvement and sustainable management or the reverse? It is a question that the data cannot answer, but our view is that the major direction of causation is from the management style to role of HR. That said, the reverse no doubt is true in some companies.

Strategy Activities

HR can make a number of contributions to the strategy process in a business; some involve implementation, while others involve strategy development. Table 4.4 presents the data from a question that identifies some key specific activities that HR may engage in with respect to business strategy (it was asked for the first time in 2004).

When it comes to strategy, HR executives report that they are particularly likely to be involved in designing an organization's structure and planning for the implementation of strategy. Implementation is a logical area for HR, so it is not surprising that this is rated as a major involvement area for it. A comparison of the 2004, 2007, 2010, and 2013 data shows no significant changes in HR's involvement in strategy activities, which is consistent with the finding reported in chapter 2 that HR has not changed its time allocation over this period.

Perhaps the best summary of the results concerning business strategy is that HR is more likely to play a role in the implementation of it than in the development of it or making key decisions concerning what it will be. Finally, it is worth noting that, as we pointed out in chapter 3, HR is not likely to be involved with the corporate board in discussions of business strategy or in identifying new business opportunities.

Table 4.4. Business strategy activities, United States					
	Means				Correlation with HR Role in Strategy
Activities	2004[1]	2007[2]	2010[3]	2013[4]	
Help identify or design strategy options	2.9	3.0	2.8	2.7	.54***
Help decide among the best strategy options	3.0	3.1	2.9	2.8	.58***
Help plan the implementation of strategy	3.6	3.8	3.6	3.5	.58***
Help identify new business opportunities	2.0	2.2	2.0	1.9	.44***
Assess the organization's readiness to implement strategies	3.5	3.5	3.2	3.3	.59***
Help design the organizational structure to implement strategy	3.8	3.9	3.6	3.7	.60***
Assess possible merger, acquisition, or divestiture strategies	2.9	3.0	2.7	2.9	.31***
Work with the corporate board on business strategy	2.6	2.9[4]	2.6	2.4[2]	.53***

Response scale: 1 = little or no extent; 2 = some extent; 3 = moderate extent; 4 = great extent; 5 = very great extent.

[1,2,3,4] Significant difference ($p \leq .05$) between years.

Significance level: [1]$p \leq .10$, *$p \leq .05$, **$p \leq .01$, ***$p \leq .001$.

Table 4.4 also shows the relationship between business strategy activities and HR's role in strategy. Not surprisingly, HR executives see this relationship as strong, which indicates that these activities are associated with the degree of involvement HR has in the strategy process. The weakest relationship is with assessing mergers and divestitures, although even here, the relationship is quite strong.

International Results

The international data in table 4.5 show some differences among countries. India stands out as the country where HR is most active in business strategy activities, particularly identifying and deciding among strategy options. No country reports a high level of HR involvement in strategy, and China stands out as the country where HR is the least active. This finding is consistent with the finding that in China, HR is rarely a full partner in strategy development and implementation.

Strategic Focuses

As can be seen in table 4.6, there are numerous, significant relationships between the company's strategic focus areas and the role that HR plays in the strategy process. Three of the strategic focuses—information, knowledge, and innovation—are associated with HR's active involvement in almost all of the business strategy activities listed in table 4.6. Knowledge-based strategies are related to all activities, whereas growth is related only to assessing merger and divestiture actions.

Table 4.5. Business strategy activities, by country							
	Means						
Activities	United States[1]	Canada[2]	Australia[3]	Europe[4]	United Kingdom[5]	India[6]	China[7]
Help identify or design strategy options	2.7[7]	2.8[7]	2.8	2.7[7]	2.5	3.0[7]	2.0[1,2,4,6]
Help decide among the best strategy options	2.8[7]	2.8[7]	2.8[7]	2.9[7]	2.7[7]	3.0[7]	2.0[1,2,3,4,5,6]
Help plan the implementation of strategy	3.5[7]	3.3[7]	3.5[7]	3.6[7]	3.5[7]	3.6[7]	2.5[1,2,3,4,5,6]
Help identify new business opportunities	1.9[6]	1.8[6]	2.2	2.1	1.9	2.5[1,2]	2.0
Assess the organization's readiness to implement strategies	3.3[7]	2.9	3.3[7]	3.1[7]	3.3[7]	3.3[7]	2.4[1,3,4,5,6]
Help design the organizational structure to implement strategy	3.7[7]	3.3	3.8[7]	3.8[7]	3.8[7]	3.7[7]	2.9[1,3,4,5,6]
Assess possible merger, acquisition, or divestiture strategies	2.9[7]	2.3	2.5	2.4	2.6	3.0[7]	2.0[1,6]
Work with the corporate board on business strategy	2.4[6]	2.4	2.8[7]	2.8[7]	2.7[7]	3.0[1,7]	1.9[3,4,5,6]

Response scale: 1 = little or no extent; 2 = some extent; 3 = moderate extent; 4 = great extent; 5 = very great extent.

[1,2,3,4,5,6,7] Significant differences between countries ($p \le .05$).

Table 4.6. Relationship of business strategy activities to strategic focuses					
	Strategic Focuses				
Activities	**Growth**	**Information-Based Strategies**	**Knowledge-Based Strategies**	**Sustainability**	**Innovation**
Help identify or design strategy options	−.09	.30***	.46***	.15^t	.29***
Help decide among the best strategy options	−.07	.26**	.39***	.08	.25**
Help plan the implementation of strategy	.04	.28***	.37***	−.01	.31***
Help identify new business opportunities	−.04	.13	.28***	.14	.23**
Assess the organization's readiness to implement strategies	.02	.13	.45***	.02	.34***
Help design the organization structure to implement strategy	.11	.13	.33***	.09	.27***
Assess possible merger, acquisition, or divestiture strategies	.24**	.12	.25**	.06	.21*
Work with the corporate board on business strategy	−.10	−.03	.22*	−.09	.18*

Response scale: 1 = little or no extent; 2 = some extent; 3 = moderate extent; 4 = great extent; 5 = very great extent.

Significance level: $^t p \leq .10$, *$p \leq .05$, **$p \leq .01$, ***$p \leq .001$.

It is a bit surprising that a strategic focus on growth has weak relationships to all but one of the strategy activities of the HR function while three others—innovation, information, and knowledge—have strong, positive relationships. The strength of the relationships with them does indicate that the more that corporations have a strategic focus, the more the HR function engages in these strategy activities. This is not surprising, since in order to effectively perform most of the strategy activities studied, HR needs the guidance of a well-articulated strategy it can help develop and implement. In total, the results on strategic focuses suggest that almost regardless of the strategic focus in an organization, there are HR strategy activities that are relevant and important.

Management Approaches

The relationships between business strategy activities and management approaches are shown in table 4.7. Many of the relationships are statistically significant and paint a clear picture. Bureaucratic and low-cost-operator companies tend to have HR functions that are relatively inactive with respect to strategy. The opposite is true of high-involvement organizations: their HR functions are very active in both strategy creation and implementation. Sustainable management organizations also tend to have active HR organizations, but the relationship is not as strong as it is for high involvement. In the case of global competitor organizations, there is no relationship with HR strategy activities. Overall, how an organization is managed clearly makes a difference in

Table 4.7. Relationship of business strategy activities to management approaches

Activities	Management Approaches				
	Bureaucratic	Low-Cost Operator	High Involvement	Global Competitor	Sustainable
Help identify or design strategy options	−.09	−.10	.34***	.07	.25**
Help decide among the best strategy options	−.12	−.07	.26**	.11	.16^t
Help plan the implementation of strategy	−.21*	−.17*	.43***	.08	.12
Help identify new business opportunities	−.06	−.06	.16^t	−.03	.12
Assess the organization's readiness to implement strategies	−.23**	−.10	.35***	.11	.17*
Help design the organizational structure to implement strategy	−.29***	−.09	.31***	.09	.15^t
Assess possible merger, acquisition, or divestiture strategies	−.19*	−.09	.13	.05	.16^t
Work with the corporate board on business strategy	−.18*	−.01	.18*	.02	.18*

Response scale: 1 = little or no extent; 2 = some extent; 3 = moderate extent; 4 = great extent; 5 = very great extent.

Significance level: $^t p \leq .10$, $^* p \leq .05$, $^{**} p \leq .01$, $^{***} p \leq .001$.

Table 4.8. HR strategy, United States

HR Strategy	Means				Correlation with HR Role in Strategy (2013)
	2004[1]	2007[2]	2010[3]	2013[4]	
Data-based talent strategy	2.7	2.6	2.7	2.5	.37***
A human capital strategy integrated with business strategy	3.2	3.3[4]	3.0	2.9[2]	.54***
Provides analytical support for business decision making	2.9	2.8	2.8	2.6	.35***
Provides HR data to support change management	3.2	3.0	3.0	2.8	.42***
HR drives change management.	3.4	3.2	3.1	3.1	.53***
Makes rigorous data-based decisions about human capital management	2.7	2.6	2.7	2.4	.42***

Response scale: 1 = little or no extent, 2 = some extent, 3 = moderate extent, 4 = great extent, 5 = very great extent.

[1,2,3,4] Significant differences between years ($p \leq .05$).

Significance level: $^t p \leq .10$, $^* p \leq .05$, $^{**} p \leq .01$, $^{***} p \leq .001$.

---

the strategy activities of HR, but it is not certain why. Is it because the management approach influences the HR function, or vice versa? Our view is that in most cases, it is the former.

HR Strategy

Data on the HR strategy of organizations are presented in table 4.8. The results from 2004, 2007, 2010, and 2013 are essentially identical. With respect to the level of activity, none of the mean scores are particularly high. The highest in 2010 and in 2013 is 3.1 on a five-point scale. It appears that to a moderate extent, HR drives change management, develops a human capital strategy that is integrated with business strategy, and provides HR data to support change management.

HR is not particularly active in the use of data and analytics. Data-based decision making about human capital and data-based talent strategies are the lowest-rated HR strategy activities. A comparison of 2013 data with the 2004, 2007, and 2010 data shows no major changes in what HR does, but it does show slightly lower overall ratings in 2013 (questions were asked only in 2004, 2007, 2010, and 2013). This finding, consistent with the point that HR is not changing, is nevertheless a bit surprising given the growing interest in HR analytics, big data, and the importance of human capital.

It is interesting to look back at the results of our 2007 survey. HR executives responding to it said that all of the items in table 4.8 were activities they would increase (the question was not asked in 2010 or 2013), but they apparently have not. In 2007, all of the strategy items were rated near the top of the scale (2.6 or greater on a three-point scale) in terms of the future focus of the HR organization. Apparently these items represent the way that HR planned to be involved in the strategy process, but there are no data to suggest this is has happened. Thus, there is a major question concerning when and if these activities will be put in place. HR executives said in both our 2004 and 2007 surveys that they planned to do these things, but as we have noted, the 2007 and the 2010 data shows no change, and the comparison between 2010 and 2013 shows a slight drop.

The correlations between the current activity levels and HR's overall role in strategy are also presented in table 4.8. All are high. The data-based talent strategies item has a low correlation, as it did in 2010, but it is still highly significant. Why this relationship is relatively weak is not entirely clear given that it is potentially an important part of the strategy process. One possibility is that effective measurement systems require not just data but sound analytics, good logic, and attention to change management processes (Boudreau and Ramstad 2006). It may be that today's HR data focus primarily on the quality of measures and do not sufficiently reflect the other elements of a complete data-based decision strategy.

What the results in table 4.8 do show is a clear pattern of the types of underused HR activities that are related to having a role in strategy. They provide a useful set of practices that HR organizations should consider adopting in order to play an important role in strategy formulation. However, the fact that there has been no change in their adoption from 2004 to 2013 raises the question of whether they are practices that most HR functions will ever put in place.

International Results

The international data on HR strategy are similar to the 2013 US data: they show significant differences only with respect to India and China. China clearly shows the lowest ratings among the countries in the study, whereas India tends to have the highest ratings, particularly with respect to making rigorous data-based decisions.

Strategic Focuses

Table 4.9 shows the relationship between an organization's strategic focuses and its HR strategy activities. There are a number of strong significant relationships, with the exception of the growth strategic focus, which is not significantly related to any of the HR strategy activities. Overall, this result reinforces the point that if an organization has a clear strategic focus, HR is likely to be actively engaged in the strategic HR activities. Most of the HR strategy items show significant correlations with all of the strategic focuses. This finding suggests that all of the activities are potentially useful activities in most organizations.

Perhaps the most interesting data in the table are about the pattern of strong correlations between knowledge-based strategies and the HR strategy items. It is clear that when an organization has a knowledge-based strategy, it is particularly likely to emphasize the role of HR processes and measures—as it should, since talent is a particularly critical asset in organizations with knowledge-based strategies. This finding is further confirmation of the future importance of HR strategic activities since more and more organizations are developing knowledge-based strategies.

Table 4.9. Relationship of current HR strategy to strategic focuses					
	Strategic Focuses				
HR Strategy	**Growth**	**Information-Based Strategies**	**Knowledge-Based Strategies**	**Sustainability**	**Innovation**
Data-based talent strategy	.03	.14	.38***	.16†	.24**
A human capital strategy integrated with business strategy	.03	.22**	.52***	.13	.32***
Provides analytical support for business decision making	−.03	.26**	.33***	.22**	.19*
Provides HR data to support change management	−.07	.25**	.34***	.17*	.25**
HR drives change management	−.05	.19*	.39***	.17*	.31***
Makes rigorous data-based decisions about human capital management	.03	.28***	.47***	.30***	.30***

Response scale: 1 = little or no extent; 2 = some extent; 3 = moderate extent; 4 = great extent; 5 = very great extent.
Significance level: $^†p \leq .10$, $^*p \leq .05$, $^{**}p \leq .01$, $^{***}p \leq .001$.

Table 4.10. Relationship of current HR strategy to management approaches

HR Strategy	Management Approaches				
	Bureaucratic	**Low-Cost Operator**	**High Involvement**	**Global Competitor**	**Sustainable**
Data-based talent strategy	−.07	−.05	.23**	.12	.25**
A human capital strategy integrated with business strategy	−.21**	−.19*	.34***	.07	.24**
Provides analytical support for business decision making	−.08	−.11	.24**	.04	.24**
Provides HR data to support change management	−.10	−.19*	.27***	−.04	.16ᵗ
HR drives change management	−.24**	−.14	.35***	.01	.12
Makes rigorous data-based decisions about human capital management	−.12	−.12	.30***	.03	.26**

Response scale: 1 = little or no extent; 2 = some extent; 3 = moderate extent; 4 = great extent; 5 = very great extent.
Significance level: $^t p \le .10$, $^* p \le .05$, $^{**} p \le .01$, $^{***} p \le .001$.

Management Approaches

The human capital strategy activities in table 4.10 show a number of significant correlations with four of the five management approaches. It is interesting that all of the activities are negatively correlated with the low-cost-operator and bureaucratic approaches and positively correlated with the high-involvement and the sustainable management approaches. This once again highlights the large difference in how these approaches treat talent and the HR function. It clearly is much more important and strategic in high-involvement organizations.

Conclusion

Overall, the data suggest that HR still has a considerable way to go when it comes to adding value as a strategic contributor. In most organizations, it is still not a major contributor to the business strategy process. This is particularly true in the case of organizations in China. The low level of strategy involvement in China is not surprising given its level of economic development. It is surprising and disappointing in the case of the other countries.

The data suggest that HR is making little progress in the United States. Overall the 2013 results are very similar to the 1998 results. Although a lot has changed in the world of business since 1998, our data suggest that HR has not. It has not become a major strategic business contributor or made a major commitment to developing HR strategy. This is true even though a number of business changes have occurred that would seem to be ones that would lead to HR being more of a strategic partner.

On the encouraging side, HR executives do report being active in a number of areas that are directly tied to the strategic direction of the business. These range from human capital recruitment and development through organizational design and strategy development. The challenge for HR is to increase the degree to which it is involved in strategy-related activities so that it can become a full partner in the high-value-added area of business strategy. One finding that suggests this might happen is the higher level of strategy activities in knowledge-based organizations. As more and more organizations in developed countries focus on knowledge, HR may start engaging in more strategy activities. Another finding that is encouraging is the high level of strategy activities in high-involvement firms. These too are likely to increase in the developed world. This finding once again makes the point that the role of HR is tied to and most likely determined by the organization's overall strategy and management approach.

CHAPTER 5

HR Decision Science

- Decision science sophistication relates significantly to HR's strategic role.

- All decision science activities are rated at moderate levels, with "educating business leaders" particularly low rated, similar to results in 2007 and 2010.

- HR's value added through services and decision support has a stronger correlation with HR's strategic role than value added through compliance.

- Levels of decision science sophistication were generally rated lower in China than in other countries.

- Bureaucratic and low-cost operation approaches are negatively related to decision science sophistication, while high-involvement and sustainable approaches are positively related.

Decision science provides a framework of principles and decision rules, based on valid evidence, to guide leaders' strategic choices (Boudreau and Ramstad 2007). A classic example of decision science in management is portfolio theory in finance, which informs decision frameworks such as return on investment, return on equity, and diversification of investments. A striking feature of decision science frameworks is that their objective is not simply to improve the quality of decisions about financial resources, but to improve the validity and consistency of the mental models that leaders use when they consider such decisions. The key issues are not only the overall sophistication and quality of decisions, but also the quality of the principles underlying those decisions.

Similar to the finance discipline, higher-quality human capital decisions occur if HR professionals and other managers have valid and logical frameworks that help them understand how human capital affects sustainable organizational effectiveness, and if they are educated and held accountable for using that understanding to identify and make vital choices that involve strategic human capital. For HR to be a truly transformative function, leaders must use valid principles to guide their decisions (Boudreau and Jesuthasan 2011). The state of HR's decision science, however, is far less mature than those of finance, marketing, and some management disciplines. Despite the importance of HR decision science, there has been little research describing the decision frameworks that HR and other business leaders use or the quality and prevalence of the systems that are used to educate business leaders. This chapter presents findings on the quality of human capital decisions and the relationship between decision quality and the strategic role of HR.

Quality of Decisions about Talent and Human Capital

Table 5.1 shows the results of questions that ask about the quality of decision making by non-HR and HR leaders when it comes to human capital and, by comparison, other important resources. The first item poses the fundamental question of whether their organization excels in the competition for critical talent. HR leaders rate their organization as moderately effective in competing for key talent, and this has remained virtually the same since 2007, when we first posed the question.

For the question that taps the definition of talentship ("decisions that depend on or impact affect capital are as rigorous, logical, and strategically relevant as decisions [about more tangible] resources," the average

Table 5.1. HR decision making, United States				
Decision Making	**Means**			**2013 Correlation with HR Role in Strategy**
	2007[1]	**2010[2]**	**2013[3]**	
We excel at competing for and with talent where it matters most to our strategic success.	3.2	3.1	3.2	**.35*****
Business leaders' decisions that depend on or affect human capital (e.g., layoffs, rewards) are as rigorous, logical, and strategically relevant as their decisions about resources such as money, technology, and customers.	2.9	3.0	2.8	**.34*****
Business leaders understand and use sound principles when making decisions about:				
1. Motivation	2.7	2.8	2.8	**.24****
2. Development and learning	2.8	2.9	2.8	**.39*****
3. Culture	2.9	3.1	3.0	**.32*****
4. Organization design	2.8	2.8	2.7	**.39*****
5. Business strategy	3.6	3.8	3.7	**.35*****
6. Finance	4.0	4.0	3.9	**.27****
7. Marketing	3.5	3.5	3.3	**.10**
HR leaders have a good understanding about where and why human capital makes the biggest difference in their business.	3.2	3.3	3.2	**.48*****
Business leaders have a good understanding about where and why human capital makes the biggest difference in their business.	3.2	3.1	3.1	**.39*****
HR systems educate business leaders about their talent decisions.	2.5[3]	2.4	2.2[1]	**.35*****
HR adds value by ensuring compliance with rules, laws, and guidelines.	3.5	3.4	3.2	**.04**
HR adds value by delivering high-quality professional practices and services.	3.6	3.6	3.4	**.41*****
HR adds value by improving talent decisions inside and outside the HR function.	3.6	3.5	3.5	**.54*****

Response scale: 1 = little or no extent; 2 = some extent; 3 = moderate extent; 4 = great extent; 5 = very great extent.

[1,2,3]Significant difference ($p \leq .05$) between years.

rating is just below the midpoint and has not changed since 2007 (Boudreau and Ramstad 2007). This is also true for business leaders' use of sound principles when making decisions in the four talent principle items in table 5.1 (numbered 1 through 4). For HR executives, all the ratings are at the midpoint or slightly below, suggesting only moderate decision quality where human capital is involved. The fact that we see virtually no improvement in these items over the past six years is interesting considering the rapidly growing awareness that human and intellectual capital is increasingly vital.

Are the elements of HR decision quality important? The correlation results for these items are notable. There are significant correlations between HR's role in strategy and perceptions of the quality of business leader decisions and principles. This is especially true when it comes to the four talent principle items in table 5.1 (1 to 4). All of these items have statistically significant correlations with the item measuring HR's role in strategy, and at about equal levels. In the 2010 survey, the "culture" item had a much higher correlation than the other items, which may reflect the popularity of culture as an explanation for the demise or survival of many iconic organizations during the 2008 economic downturn. It appears that in 2013, leaders' decision quality about culture was about equally related to HR's role in strategy as the other talent principle areas.

Items 5, 6, and 7 provide a useful comparison to talent decisions because they describe decision areas that are more traditionally the domain of business leaders. Here, the average decision quality ratings by business leaders are considerably higher than they are for the talent-related areas, just as they were in the 2007 and 2010 surveys, suggesting that HR executives regard business leaders as more adept at the traditional management decision sciences than they are for talent.

The correlations with HR's role in strategy show a somewhat low (though still statistically significant) correlation between item 6 (finance) and a nonsignificant relationship with item 7 (marketing). These results suggest that HR's strategic role is more strongly related to managers' prowess in talent-related areas than in non-talent-related areas, but the distinction is far less significant in 2013 than in prior years. It appears that when non-HR managers use sound principles in all areas of management, they increasingly have HR executives play a stronger strategic role and one that is not confined to decision areas that are talent related. This is good news in that it implies that leaders with stronger decision science capability in all areas do not try to substitute their HR strategic capability for that of HR leaders, but rather appear to welcome a stronger HR role. The stronger are leaders' talent and organization decision abilities, the stronger the strategic role of HR is.

Two items in table 5.1 refer to talent segmentation. They ask whether HR leaders and business leaders understand where and why human capital makes the biggest difference in their business. These items receive moderate ratings, virtually the same as in the past two surveys going back six years. Again, the ratings displayed strong positive correlations between these items and HR's strategic role. Talent segmentation, particularly a deep understanding of where there is pivotal return on improved performance, may be both a result of and perhaps a precursor to a stronger strategic role for HR.

If business leaders are to learn to make sound talent decisions, then the HR systems they use should educate them about the quality of those decisions in the same way that management systems in finance, marketing, and operations management provide clear feedback regarding managers' decision quality (Boudreau and Ramstad 2007; Boudreau 2010). Yet the question regarding HR systems for educating business leaders suggests that such education remains stubbornly low. The 2013 results mirror the results in 2007 and 2010; this question has the lowest ratings of any of the decision science questions. Yet the correlation between this question and HR's strategic role has been positive and significant in every wave of the survey, just as it is in 2013. There is a significant and apparently untapped opportunity to improve how well HR systems educate leaders about talent decisions. One potential gain resulting from this education is a stronger strategic role for HR.

Finally, the last three items in table 5.1 ask about how HR adds value. Boudreau and Ramstad (2007) suggested that mature professions evolve to a balance of adding value through compliance, services, and decision support. Table 5.1 shows that HR executives believe that HR adds value to a moderate or great extent in all three areas (ratings between 3 and 4). However, the overall level of value added by HR leaves room for improvement in all three areas. The correlation pattern with HR's role in strategy is notable. HR executives show a strong association between their perceptions of HR's strategic role and the value added by HR through services and decision support. When it comes to value added through compliance, however, the correlation with HR's strategic role is much smaller and nonsignificant. This may be because compliance is an expected basic outcome, and that improving it greatly makes little difference to the quality of HR's strategic contributions or that it is not seen as a distinguishing element compared to high-quality services and decision support.

Overall, on the one hand, managers most likely have increased their awareness of the importance of human capital and their role in nurturing and deploying it. HR data and scorecards are more available, providing a basis for improved decisions. On the other hand, there is a great deal that managers still do not know about talent segmentation, motivation, culture, and learning. HR executives likely can see this gap, and it is reflected in their ratings. These executives often say, "Our business leaders don't know what they don't know," when it comes to sound principles of human capital decisions.

HR executives, who see room for improvement, may need to provide tangible examples of more sophisticated human capital decision principles. As with the development of the decision sciences of marketing and finance, one would hope to see an HR decision science develop so that it will become clear that competing effectively with and through human capital requires that leaders both inside and outside HR are not satisfied with the traditional HR service delivery paradigm. They will realize that it must be extended to include making better decisions about human capital where it matters most to strategic success (Boudreau and Ramstad 1997, 2005a, 2005b, 2005c, 2007). Unfortunately, progress in this arena appears to be quite slow, maybe even nonexistent.

International Results

Table 5.2 presents the international results. Overall, most of the differences arise when comparing the Chinese data with those from other countries. The ratings in the Chinese sample are generally lower than the ratings in the other countries, and many of the differences re statistically significant.

The pattern of ratings for each country is very similar to the results for the US sample reported in table 5.1. Most ratings fall near the midpoint of the scale, with the exception of the degree to which HR systems educate business leaders about their talent decisions, which is rated lower. In all of the countries, business leaders' use of sound principles is rated higher in traditional management arenas (items 5, 6, and 7) than in talent management and human capital (items 1 through 4). Thus, the conclusions reached for the United States seem to hold for all the national samples in the survey. There appears to be a solid but not exemplary level of talent decision science in all these countries, with multiple opportunities for improvement in how well HR systems educate business leaders about their decisions.

As with other elements of HR, China appears to be at an earlier stage of HR development when it comes to advancing a decision science. This is similar to what we found in the 2010 survey.

The sample of HR managers from India presents some interesting patterns. The ratings are quite similar to those of the Western countries and higher than China's ratings. However, the Indian HR managers rate the

Table 5.2. HR decision making, by country

Decision Making	Means						
	United States[1]	Canada[2]	Australia[3]	Europe[4]	United Kingdom[5]	India[6]	China[7]
We excel at competing for and with talent where it matters most to our strategic success.	3.2[7]	2.7	3.0	3.0	3.3[7]	3.1[7]	2.5[1,5,6]
Business leaders' decisions that depend on or affect human capital (e.g., layoffs, rewards) are as rigorous, logical, and strategically relevant as their decisions about resources such as money, technology, and customers.	2.8	2.9	3.0	2.9	3.0	3.0	2.5
Business leaders understand and use sound principles when making decisions about:							
1. Motivation	2.8	2.4[6]	2.6	3.1	2.8	3.2[2]	2.9
2. Development and learning	2.8[4]	2.7[4]	2.8	3.4[1,2,7]	2.9	3.3[7]	2.7[4,6]
3. Culture	3.0	2.7	2.6	3.0	2.9	3.3	2.9
4. Organizational design	2.7[6]	2.5[6]	2.7	2.7[6]	2.8	3.4[1,2,4,7]	2.6[6]
5. Business strategy	3.7[7]	3.4[7]	3.4	3.5[7]	3.8[7]	3.6[7]	2.8[1,2,4,5,6]
6. Finance	3.9[7]	3.7[7]	3.8[7]	3.8[7]	4.0[7]	3.7[7]	2.9[1,2,4,5,6]
7. Marketing	3.3	3.2	3.2	3.1	3.5	3.5	3.1
HR leaders have a good understanding about where and why human capital makes the biggest difference in their business.	3.3[7]	3.3[7]	3.5[7]	3.3[7]	3.3	3.3[7]	2.6[1,2,4,5,6]
Business leaders have a good understanding about where and why human capital makes the biggest difference in their business.	3.1[7]	3.0	3.4[7]	2.9	3.1	3.5[7]	2.5[1,3,6]
HR systems educate business leaders about their talent decisions.	2.2[6]	2.2[6]	2.3	2.3[6]	2.2[6]	3.1[1,2,4,5,7]	2.2[6]
HR adds value by ensuring compliance with rules, laws, and guidelines.	3.2	3.5[7]	3.4	3.5[7]	2.8[6]	3.6[57]	2.8[2,4,6]
HR adds value by delivering high-quality professional practices and services.	3.4[7]	3.7[7]	3.6[7]	3.6[7]	3.6[7]	3.5[7]	2.7[1,2,3,4,5,6]
HR adds value by improving talent decisions inside and outside the HR function.	3.5[7]	3.5[7]	3.3	3.5[7]	3.4[7]	3.4[7]	2.7[1,2,4,5,6]

Response scale: 1 = little or no extent; 2 = some extent; 3 = moderate extent; 4 = great extent; 5 = very great extent.

[1,2,3,4,5,6,7] Significant differences between countries ($p \leq .05$).

items higher than the Western HR managers do. For example, Indian HR managers gave their managers higher marks for using sound principles of organizational design (item 4) and motivation (item 1) than most Western countries. Indian HR managers also rated their systems higher on the question of educating non-HR leaders about the quality of their talent decisions.

HR Decision Science Sophistication and HR's Role in Strategy

The correlations between the HR decision science questions and the perception of HR's role in strategy in table 5.1 show a similar pattern to earlier surveys, as noted above. The results show many significant and positive correlations between the ratings of the decision science items and HR's role in strategy. Two correlations were not significant: those between ratings of business leader decision capability in marketing and between HR's value added through compliance. Generally, where decision science principles are rated highly, so is HR's role in strategy.

We do not know the causal direction of the relationships with strategy involvement. These results suggest that when organizations achieve high HR strategy involvement, HR managers perceive themselves and their business leaders as better on all elements of the HR decision science. The causal direction may go from strategic role to decision science sophistication. This interpretation is consistent with the typical situation that we see in organizations, where a handful of HR executives are highly skilled at talent segmentation and strategic insights. Often they developed this ability through fortuitous career opportunities to observe and participate in business strategy development and implementation. This interpretation supports efforts to get HR executives more involved in strategy as a way to build and convey the HR decision science.

The causal direction may also be that enhancing the decision science capability of managers outside HR leads to HR strategic involvement. Our results suggest that some HR executives already have opportunities for full partnership in strategy development and implementation, but in general HR executives do not rate highly the decision science capability of non-HR managers (average ratings in table 5.1 are at the moderate point on the scale). Improving the decision science capability of managers outside of HR may make them more effective at working with strategically involved HR executives.

Strategic Focuses

The relationship between the extent to which organizations are pursuing different strategic focuses and the extent to which they perceive the different elements of a sophisticated HR decision science is shown in table 5.3 Clearly, the pattern of significant associations varies greatly among the different strategic focuses.

Excellence in competing for talent and the extent to which HR decisions by business executives are made with the same rigor as decisions about other key resources are significantly related to the strategic focuses. The exception is a focus on growth, which shows very few significant correlations and contains many negative correlations. This suggests that how strongly an organization emphasizes growth has little to do with the level of these HR decision science items. A focus on sustainability also shows few correlations with these decision science items.

Table 5.3. Relationship of HR decision making to strategic focuses

Decision Making	Strategic Focuses				
	Growth	Information-Based Strategies	Knowledge-Based Strategies	Sustainability	Innovation
We excel at competing for and with talent where it matters most to our strategic success.	−.08	.26**	.27**	.09	.29***
Business leaders' decisions that depend on or affect human capital (e.g., layoffs, rewards) are as rigorous, logical, and strategically relevant as their decisions about resources such as money, technology, and customers.	−.05	.28***	.35***	.09	.35***
Business leaders understand and use sound principles when making decisions about:					
1. Motivation	−.14	.32***	.35***	.05	.28**
2. Development and learning	−.08	.25**	.41***	.19*	.27**
3. Culture	−.18*	.24**	.42***	.24**	.23**
4. Organizational design	−.16ᵗ	.16ᵗ	.31***	.15ᵗ	.27**
5. Business strategy	−.01	.25**	.23**	.18*	.33***
6. Finance	.06	.16ᵗ	.11	−.01	.10
7. Marketing	−.07	.26**	.11	.07	.34***
HR leaders have a good understanding about where and why human capital makes the biggest difference in their business.	−.04	.22*	.33***	.12	.29***
Business leaders have a good understanding about where and why human capital makes the biggest difference in their business.	−.10	.30***	.44***	.10	.27**
HR systems educate business leaders about their talent decisions.	−.04	.14	.21*	.08	.19*
HR adds value by ensuring compliance with rules, laws, and guidelines.	−.09	.16ᵗ	.11	.17ᵗ	.13
HR adds value by delivering high-quality professional practices and services.	−.06	.14	.27**	.19*	.18*
HR adds value by improving talent decisions inside and outside the HR function.	.08	.17*	.31***	.16ᵗ	.26**

Response scale: 1 = little or no extent; 2 = some extent; 3 = moderate extent; 4 = great extent; 5 = very great extent.

Significance level: Significance level: ᵗ$p \leq .10$, *$p \leq .05$, **$p \leq .01$, ***$p \leq .001$.

The results for the growth focus are similar to what we observed in the 2010 and 2007 samples. Also, the correlations for the innovation strategy have generally increased compared to 2007 and are mostly statistically significant (see Lawler and Boudreau 2012 for 2007 and 2010 results). In 2007, pursuing innovation was not strongly associated with excellence in the human capital decision science, but in 2010, this changed and once again is associated in 2013. It may be that the significance of high-quality human capital decisions for innovation has become more apparent; it certainly is consistent with the reality that talent quality is fundamental for innovation to occur. Possibly, at earlier stages of innovation, organizations focused on more traditional resources such as technology, alliances, and intellectual property protection, but as innovation has matured and become more competitive, the significance of human capital and high-quality talent decisions has become more apparent to leaders.

This idea seems to apply more generally as well. The results for items reflecting HR leaders' and business leaders' understanding of talent segmentation (where and why human capital makes the biggest difference), as well as the three items reflecting how HR adds value, showed a significant pattern change from 2007 to 2013. In 2007, these items were generally uncorrelated with the different strategic focuses, though a few correlations with the knowledge-based strategic emphasis were significant. The 2010 data show strong correlations with these items across all strategies except growth, and this pattern seems to be sustained in the 2013 results. Such a generalized shift suggests that HR decision science quality may be becoming a more generalized factor in a broad array of strategic focuses.

It is interesting that the pursuit of a growth strategy and a sustainability strategy is not highly correlated with the talent items. This suggests that organizations pursuing growth and sustainability strategies may not have internalized the connection between high-quality talent decisions and their strategies' success. In separate research on organizational sustainability, we find that leaders who are driving the sustainability strategy are often found in functions other than HR (Lawler and Worley 2011). They are more likely to be in logistics and manufacturing; indeed HR is often not even represented on key sustainability committees and decision bodies within organizations. This may explain why pursuit of a sustainability strategy shows less of a relationship with the talent decision science items.

It is also notable that across all strategies, HR's ability to add value through compliance is not significantly correlated with the strategic focuses, while delivering high-quality services and improving talent decisions more often correlates significantly. Again, compliance is seen as "table stakes" rather than as a differentiating factor when it comes to HR being an important contributor.

Management Approaches

Table 5.4 shows the relationship between the HR decision-making items and the five management approaches. In general, the results suggest that the level of HR decision science is much more strongly associated with the high-involvement and sustainable management approaches than with the other three approaches. This is consistent with the idea that in the high-involvement approach, there is a major reliance on talent alignment, commitment and trust at all levels of the organization and that it demands business leaders attend to talent and human capital issues. It is also consistent with the idea that in sustainability-focused approaches, there is a higher level of attention to outcomes that go beyond the traditional financial or competitive growth outcomes. The three other approaches (bureaucratic, low cost, global) rely on a more traditional approach in which leaders outside HR may be held less accountable for making high-quality HR decisions because they focus on more traditional resources and perceive that their results depend less on effective talent management.

Table 5.4. Relationship of HR decision making to management approaches

Decision Making	Management Approaches				
	Bureaucratic	Low-Cost Operator	High Involvement	Global Competitor	Sustainable
We excel at competing for and with talent where it matters most to our strategic success.	–.23**	–.25**	.36***	.08	.26**
Business leaders' decisions that depend on or affect human capital (e.g., layoffs, rewards) are as rigorous, logical, and strategically relevant as their decisions about resources such as money, technology, and customers.	–.13	–.12	.31***	–.03	.27**
Business leaders understand and use sound principles when making decisions about:					
1. Motivation	–.06	–.04	.44***	.06	.29***
2. Development and learning	–.13	–.16^t	.49***	–.02	.16^t
3. Culture	–.17^t	–.09	.51***	–.08	.25**
4. Organizational design	–.16^t	–.19*	.44***	.07	.25**
5. Business strategy	–.11	–.24**	.34***	.04	.22*
6. Finance	.02	–.07	.21*	–.05	.26**
7. Marketing	.01	–.09	.18*	–.11	.11
HR leaders have a good understanding about where and why human capital makes the biggest difference in their business.	–.24**	–.27**	.30***	–.05	.09
Business leaders have a good understanding about where and why human capital makes the biggest difference in their business.	–.13	–.19*	.34***	–.04	.21*
HR systems educate business leaders about their talent decisions.	–.07	–.06	.16^t	.04	.14
HR adds value by ensuring compliance with rules, laws, and guidelines.	.01	–.24**	.14	–.17^t	.03
HR adds value by delivering high-quality professional practices and services.	–.19*	–.16^t	.28***	–.11	.13
HR adds value by improving talent decisions inside and outside the HR function.	–.32***	–.19*	.41***	.04	.24**

Response scale: 1 = little or no extent; 2 = some extent; 3 = moderate extent; 4 = great extent; 5 = very great extent.

Significance level: $^t p \le .10$, $^* p \le .05$, $^{**} p \le .01$, $^{***} p \le .001$.

It is notable that the strategic focus of sustainability in table 5.3 produced far fewer significant correlations than the sustainable management approach in table 5.4. The question posed in table 5.4 was, "To what extent do these describe how your organization operates?" In table 5.3, the item was, "To what extent is each of the following strategic initiatives present in your organization?" It may be that in responding to the item in table 5.4 that emphasizes description, the respondents were considering a broad and less formal emphasis on sustainability, while when responding to the item in table 5.3 that emphasizes operational activity, they were considering specific sustainability initiatives. The HR decision science items may emerge more when considering a broader operating approach, while HR decision quality is still relatively tangential to specific sustainability initiatives.

Regarding the other three management approaches in table 5.4, "bureaucratic," "low-cost operator," and "global competitor," the results are quite different from those for the sustainable and high-involvement approaches. Generally the correlations are nonsignificant for global competitor, meaning that there is little relationship with the extent or quality of the HR decision science. For the bureaucratic and low-cost-operator management approaches, table 5.4 clearly shows that an emphasis on the bureaucratic approach or the low-cost-operator approach is negatively associated with all the HR decision science elements, the same elements that are generally significantly and positively associated with the high-involvement and sustainable approaches. This pattern was present in our 2007 survey, became stronger in the 2010 survey, and is quite pronounced in the 2013 survey.

Low-cost-operator strategies place a premium on efficiency and low overhead, which often means very lean budgets for HR investments, often seen as overhead. It also may imply a focus on talent except as labor costs, not investments. Thus, for HR executives in such organizations, the consequences of a least-cost-possible approach to talent may mean accepting that the organization will not excel in the talent competition and that resources to build, use, and disseminate an HR decision science are limited.

For organizations that approach management with a bureaucratic model, we surmise that issues of human capital and workforce management are delegated to a formal HR function and are managed largely through formal systems. This is not to say that such systems are unsophisticated or inattentive to human capital issues, but they are generally not as much designed to enhance talent decisions as they are to ensure that proper processes are followed. This is somewhat supported by the fact that the item assessing whether HR adds value through compliance is less negatively correlated than the other items with the bureaucratic management approach.

The correlations with HR adding value through decision support (the bottom row of table 5.4) generally follow the patterns of the other items with strong positive correlations for the high-involvement and sustainable approaches, moderate for the global competitor approach, and significantly negative for the bureaucratic and low-cost-operator approaches. The pattern suggests that the bureaucratic and low-cost-operator approaches actually engender a decreasing emphasis on HR value through services and decisions, while high-involvement and sustainable approaches increase the emphasis on this sort of value.

Finally, it is notable that the global competitor approach seems to consistently fall between the strong human capital decision emphasis of the high-involvement and sustainable approaches and the negative human capital decision emphasis of the bureaucratic and low-cost-operator approaches. This is consistent with the results of the 2007 and 2010 surveys. We surmise that organizations with the global competitor approach may use a combination of HR decision-making approaches given the diversity of their operations and workforces. It also may mean that human capital decision management is not a major focus for them.

Conclusion

HR executives rate the human capital decision making both inside and outside HR as moderately effective. Thus, there is significant room for improvement. An important finding is the striking correlation between HR leaders' perceptions of business leader talent decision sophistication and HR's role in strategy. It would appear that there is synergy between HR's strategic role and non-HR executives' ability to make strong decisions about talent and HR.

The HR decision science facility of organizations appears to vary with the strategy they pursue. It is more sophisticated when they pursue information-based, knowledge-based, and innovation business strategies than when they pursue growth or sustainability strategies. It is also more sophisticated in high-involvement and sustainable management approaches. This suggests that business leader sophistication and HR contribution is higher in strategies where there is a strong line of sight between human capital and business outcomes and where managers' talent decisions are clearly tied to business and strategic results. High-involvement and sustainable organizations may create a culture and values that emphasize not just the capability of HR to manage the workforce well, but that it is the responsibility of all leaders to do so.

Generally our findings argue strongly for the strategic value of organizations having a strong human capital decision support capacity both within and outside their HR functions. There is much room for improvement, as the average ratings of decision quality in 2013 are still close to the midpoint of the rating scale, as they were in earlier surveys. The 2013 results provide strong evidence of the positive association between an organization's decision science capacity and HR's role in strategy, particularly in organizations pursuing management approaches and strategies that are workforce intensive and high involvement.

CHAPTER 6

HR Organization

- The design of HR functions has changed since 1995. Centers of excellence have become more common, as has self-service.

- The degree to which HR practices vary within an organization has decreased.

- HR does little to develop HR talent by rotating people within, into, and out of the function.

- Most HR functions have not yet adopted HR talent development to a great extent.

- Results suggest that what HR needs to do to become more of strategic contributor is to use information technology, establish centers of excellence, and develop HR talent.

The organizational and operational approaches that an HR function employs have a major impact on what it is able to do and how well it performs. This study examined practices and structures that have been suggested as potential ways for HR to become more of a business partner and, in some cases, a strategic contributor. The approaches were grouped into three scales based on a statistical analysis. The items and the US mean responses to the items are shown in table 6.1.

Organizational Design

The organizational design practices that HR uses the most are those concerned with decentralization and HR service units. A comparison of the 1995 and 2013 results shows a significant increase in the use of HR centers of excellence. Most of this change appears to have occurred between 1995 and 2004; there is little evidence of recent change. This is the time period when the business partner model of HR became popular and organizations felt the need for greater HR expertise.

A particularly popular practice from 1995 to 2013 is decentralized generalists who support the business units of a company. This configuration is a possible way to position HR as a business partner by getting it close to the customers. It too has not increased in popularity since 1995.

The use of corporate centers of excellence complements the use of decentralized HR generalists by giving them a source of expert help. Growth in the use of centers of excellence is consistent with the idea of HR being a business partner since it can provide a higher level of business-relevant HR expertise. Having HR processing centers can help

Table 6.1. HR organization, United States

HR Organization	Means							Correlation with HR Role in Strategy
	1995[1]	1998[2]	2001[3]	2004[4]	2007[5]	2010[6]	2013[7]	
HR service units	**3.0[4,5,6,7]**	**3.2**	**3.3**	**3.5[1]**	**3.5[1]**	**3.4[1]**	**3.4[1]**	**.28***
Centers of excellence provide specialized expertise.	2.5[2,3,4,5,6,7]	3.1[1]	3.1[1]	3.3[1]	3.4[1]	3.3[1]	3.5[1]	.30***
Administrative processing is centralized in shared services units.	3.5	3.4	3.4	3.7	3.5	3.5	3.4	.18*
Decentralization	**3.3[6]**	**3.3[6]**	**3.3[6]**	**3.1**	**3.1**	**2.9[1,2,3]**	**3.0**	**−.09**
Decentralized HR generalists support business units.	3.6	3.9	4.0	3.9	3.7	3.6	3.6	.11
HR practices vary across business units.	2.9[4,5,6,7]	2.6	2.6	2.3[1]	2.5[1]	2.3[1]	2.4[1]	−.25**
HR talent development	**2.1**	**2.2**	**2.1**	**2.2**	**2.1**	**2.0**	**2.0**	**.40***
People rotate within HR.	2.6	2.8	2.8	2.8	2.7	2.5	2.7	.39***
People rotate into HR.	1.8	1.8	1.8	1.8	1.7	1.8	1.7	.24**
People rotate out of HR to other functions.	1.8	1.9[7]	1.9[7]	1.9[7]	1.8	1.8	1.6[2,3,4]	.28***

Response scale: 1 = little or no extent, 2 = some extent, 3 = moderate extent, 4 = great extent, 5 = very great extent.

[1,2,3,4,5,6,7] Significant differences ($p \leq .05$) between years.

Significance level: [1]$p \leq .10$, *$p \leq .05$, **$p \leq .01$, ***$p \leq .001$.

HR be a business partner as well since it can free HR professionals from doing administrative work.

There is a relatively low rating of the degree to which HR practices vary across business units. Moreover, it is lower in 2013 than it was in 1995. This finding suggests that while there may be dedicated HR leaders who are supporting businesses, their role is not to tailor HR practices to those businesses, but rather to work with centers of excellence and HR service units in order to deliver common services to their parts of the organization.

The use of common practices most likely reflects efforts to simplify and achieve scale leverage in HR activities and the tendency for companies to engage in fewer unrelated businesses. There are economies of scale to be gained when corporations use the same HR practices in all their units, particularly in the case of transactions and the creation of self-service HR activities based on information technology.

The HR talent management practices are the least used ones shown in table 6.1. Employee rotation into and out of HR in particular is infrequent and in fact has declined over the years. The lack of rotation is potentially a major problem for the HR function because it means that its members are likely to remain a separate group with a limited perspective on how their organization operates. Furthermore, they are unlikely to be involved in or deeply knowledgeable about the business. There also appears to be relatively little rotation within HR, a practice that creates silo careers and does little to help HR employees develop an understanding of the total HR function.

There are multiple significant relationships between the way that HR is organized and the role it plays in strategy. HR talent development and HR service units are significantly related to HR's role in strategy. This result confirms the point that HR needs to have good talent, perform its own operations effectively, and have expertise and services that meet the needs of the business.

Having decentralized HR generalists has a low but positive relationship to HR's role in strategy. This finding provides weak support for the view that the best way to make HR more of a strategy contributor is to put it close to the business. However, the significant negative correlation with having HR practices that vary across business units suggests that this works against having HR playing a role in strategy. This most likely is because it typically exists when there is not a strong corporate HR function that can influence corporate strategy.

International Results

The international data on HR organization in table 6.2 show, with a few exceptions, that the results for China are different from those of the other countries. It is a low user of almost all of the organization structures and practices.

:The largest difference between China and the other countries is in HR service units. China uses centers of excellence much less frequently than the other countries in the study do. It also uses administrative processing service units less frequently than the other countries do, a difference that is statistically significant with respect to four countries. India has the highest use rate of rotational talent development in HR. It also more frequently than other countries puts individuals with an HR background into the CHRO job (84.9 percent). These two findings suggest that companies in India develop their HR executives so that they do not have to go outside the function for a CHRO.

Strategic Focuses

Table 6.3 shows the relationships between the strategic focuses and the HR organization. The use of service units is significantly associated with most of the strategic focuses. HR talent development is also strongly

Table 6.2. HR organization, by country							
	Means						
HR Organization	United States[1]	Canada[2]	Australia[3]	Europe[4]	United Kingdom[5]	India[6]	China[7]
HR service units	**3.4**[7]	**3.1**[7]	**3.1**[7]	**3.5**[7]	**3.7**[7]	**3.4**[7]	**2.2**[1,2,3,4,5,6]
Centers of excellence provide specialized expertise.	3.5[7]	3.1[7]	3.1[7]	3.4[7]	3.7[7]	3.2[7]	1.9[1,2,3,4,5,6]
Administrative processing is centralized in shared services units.	3.4[7]	3.1	3.0	3.6[7]	3.5[7]	3.6[7]	2.5[1,4,5,6]
Decentralization	**3.0**[2,7]	**2.4**[1,3,4,5,6]	**3.1**[2]	**3.0**[2]	**3.0**[2]	**3.0**[2]	**2.6**[1]
Decentralized HR generalists support business units.	3.6[2,7]	2.8[1,6]	3.7[7]	3.6[7]	3.6	3.6[2,7]	2.8[1,3,4,6]
HR practices vary across business units.	2.4	2.0	2.4	2.4	2.5	2.5	2.3
HR talent development	**2.0**[6]	**1.6**[6]	**2.1**	**2.1**	**2.0**	**2.5**[1,2,7]	**1.7**[6]
People rotate within HR.	2.7[7]	2.1[6]	2.6	2.7[7]	2.7	3.1[2,7]	1.9[1,4,6]
People rotate into HR.	1.7[6]	1.4[4,6]	1.8[6]	2.0[2,6]	1.7[6]	2.5[1,2,3,4,5,7]	1.6[6]
People rotate out of HR to other functions.	1.6	1.4[6]	1.8	1.6	1.6	1.9[2]	1.7

Response scale: 1 = little or no extent, 2 = some extent, 3 = moderate extent, 4 = great extent, 5 = very great extent.

[1,2,3,4,5,6,7] Significant differences ($p \leq .05$) between years.

Table 6.3. Relationship of the HR organization to strategic focuses					
	Strategic Focuses				
HR Organization	Growth	Information-Based Strategies	Knowledge-Based Strategies	Sustainability	Innovation
HR service units	−.09	.31***	.26***	.13	.23**
Decentralization	.29***	.02	−.04	−.13	.08
HR talent development	.11	.27***	.21*	.19*	.32***

Response scale: 1 = little or no extent; 2 = some extent; 3 = moderate extent; 4 = great extent; 5 = very great extent.
Significance level: [†]$p \leq .10$, *$p \leq .05$, **$p \leq .01$, ***$p \leq .001$.

associated with multiple strategic focuses. Only decentralization is not related to multiple strategic focuses. Thus, it seems safe to conclude that the HR organizational designs in table 6.3 fit the strategic focuses of most organizations.

Three of the strategic focuses are significantly associated with multiple HR organization practices: knowledge-based information, information-based strategies, and innovation strategies. Given their reliance on talent, this is hardly surprising since these practices are supportive of good talent management.

Table 6.4. Relationship of the HR organization to management approaches					
	Management Approaches				
HR Organization	**Bureaucratic**	**Low–Cost Operator**	**High Involvement**	**Global Competitor**	**Sustainable**
HR service units	–.07	–.27***	.12	.01	.16^t
Decentralization	.02	.28***	–.04	.24**	–.01
HR talent development	–.19*	–.08	.28***	.23**	.26**

Response scale: 1 = little or no extent; 2 = some extent; 3 = moderate extent; 4 = great extent; 5 = very great extent.
Significance level: $^t p \le .10$, $^* p \le .05$, $^{**} p \le .01$, $^{***} p \le .001$.

Management Approaches

There are significant relationships between an organization's management approach and the structure of its HR organization (table 6.4). Not surprising, the high-involvement approach is related to the development of HR talent , as are the global competitor and sustainable approaches. This is not surprising since these management approaches rely heavily on talent as a source of competitive advantage. The low-cost-operator approach shows strong correlations, suggesting that it creates a clear mandate for how HR organization should be designed.

Future Organizational Design

In 2004 and again in 2007, HR executives were asked to indicate how they see the HR function operating in the future (this was not asked in 2010 or 2013; see Lawler and Boudreau 2012 for data). The data suggested that some important shifts would occur in the way HR operates in the future. In both 2004 and 2007, service units received the highest ratings, indicating that these were viewed as likely and important practices for the future.

Plans to shift toward the greater use of centers of excellence, teams, and a greater emphasis on talent development in 2004 and 2007 were all associated a more strategic role for HR. The significant relationship with HR talent rotation probably indicates that when HR is involved in strategy, it recognizes the importance of developing people with a broad understanding of HR. The expected growth in the use of centers of excellence fits with the importance of having corporate expertise that can support the strategy development process. Growth in the use of joint task teams is one way to be sure that in the future, HR systems will support the business strategy. Given the correlation of these practices with strategic involvement, it is particularly disappointing that HR has not moved ahead with changes it said it would make in 2004 and 2007. They seem to be the right moves but not the ones that HR has made.

Conclusion

Overall the results show some change in the use of the HR organizational design approaches studied: significant growth in service units and centers of excellence, which are related to HR's being more of a strategic partner, and trends toward less use of HR practices that vary across business units. But we do not see greater adoption of career movement of individuals into and out of HR.

A number of important relationships between the characteristics of the HR organization and HR's role in strategy suggest what HR needs to do to become more of a strategic partner: establish centers of excellence, use joint task forces, and develop HR talent. In the past, HR organizations said they planned to use more teams and improve their efficiency, but so far they do not appear to have done either of these.

CHAPTER 7

Changes in HR Activity

- HR executives report focusing more on every HR issue and activity except union relations.

- HR executives who are involved in strategy development report greater involvement in organizational design and development.

- Chinese HR executives are the only ones to report no increase in developing social networks.

- High-involvement management is associated with an increasing focus on employee development as well as recruitment and selection.

To get an in-depth look at the changes that are occurring in the role of HR, we asked whether the focus on and attention to a number of HR activities has increased, stayed the same, or decreased over the past five to seven years. Our expectation when we began this research in 1995 was that there would be an increase in the focus on a number of HR activities, particularly those related to HR being more of a business strategic partner and strategic contributor.

HR Activity Levels

Data analyses showed four clusters of HR activities, with five activity items that did not cluster with any others: executive compensation, HR metrics, HR information systems, social networks, and union relations. Table 7.1 shows these activities and how HR executives responded in 1995, 1998, 2001, 2004, 2007, 2010, and 2013. Just as they have in our previous surveys, in 2013 our respondents reported increasing their focus on all the items but one (those in the table with scores higher than 3.0). As was true in 1998, 2001, 2004, 2007 and 2010, in 2013 HR executives report not increasing their organization's focus on union relations. This is understandable since the union movement continues to decline in the United States, particularly in the private sector. All other areas show a relatively similar amount of rated increase in 2013 (3.5 is the low and 3.9 the high). It is hard to see how HR can continuously increase the focus in all these areas. Perhaps our respondents are feeling a bit overwhelmed by the multiple demands they face, including more demands for performance, in all of these areas.

A comparison of our 2007, 2010, and 2013 data does show an interesting difference in the amount of increase reported in one area. In 2010, in comparison to 2007, recruitment showed a significantly lower rating, undoubtedly driven by the recession that began in 2008 and the end of the war for talent. Our 2013 data show a reversal that is undoubtedly due to the economic recovery. Recruitment is now one of the activities that is expected to increase the most.

Table 7.1 also shows the correlations between the changes in focus on HR activities and HR's role in strategy. Not surprisingly, the highest single correlation in 2010 was between human capital forecasting and planning and HR's role in strategy. In 2013, this relationship once again is strong, as is the relationship of organizational design and development with HR's role in strategy. It suggests that these two HR activities very much go together with strategy, although it does not tell us what the causal direction is. It could be that when HR is involved in strategy

Table 7.1. Change in focus on HR activities, United States								
	Means							Correlation with HR Role in Strategy
HR Activities	1995[1]	1998[2]	2001[3]	2004[4]	2007[5]	2010[6]	2013[7]	
Design and organizational development	—	3.8	3.9	3.9	3.9[6]	3.7[5]	3.8	**.44*****
Human capital forecasting and planning[a]	4.1[6]	3.9	4.0	4.1[6,7]	4.1	3.8[1,4]	3.8[4]	**.33*****
Organizational development	4.0[6]	3.8	3.9	3.8	4.0	3.7[1]	3.8	**.38*****
Organizational design	—	3.6	3.7	3.6	3.7	3.6	3.7	**.37*****
Compensation and benefits	3.9[6,7]	3.7[4]	3.8	4.0[2,6,7]	3.8[6]	3.5[1,4,5]	3.6[1,4]	**−.01**
Compensation	3.9[6]	3.8	3.9[6]	3.9[6]	3.9	3.6[1,3,4]	3.7	**−.00**
Benefits	3.9[2,6,7]	3.6[1,4]	3.6[4]	4.0[2,3,6,7]	3.7	3.5[1,4]	3.5[1,4]	**−.01**
Executive compensation	—	—	—	—	—	3.8	3.9	**.15[t]**
Employee development	—	—	3.6	3.8	3.8	3.6	3.7	**.14[t]**
Training and education	3.8[6]	3.5	3.7	3.7	3.7	3.5[1]	3.5	**.06**
Management development	3.9	3.8	3.8	4.0	3.9	3.7	3.9	**.12**
Performance appraisal	3.8	3.5[4]	3.7	3.9[2]	3.8	3.7	3.6	**−.05**
Career planning	3.3	3.4	3.3	3.3	3.4	3.4	3.5	**.21***
Competency/talent assessment	—	—	3.7	3.8	4.0	3.8	3.8	**.19***
Recruitment and selection	3.4[2,3,4,5,7]	3.9[1]	3.8[1,5]	3.8[1]	4.1[1,3,6]	3.6[5]	3.9[1]	**.13**
Recruitment	3.3[2,3,4,5,6,7]	3.9[1]	3.8[1,5]	3.8[1,5]	4.2[1,3,4,6]	3.6[1,5,7]	3.9[1,6]	**.06**
Selection	3.5[5]	3.8	3.7	3.8	4.0[1,6]	3.6[5]	3.8	**.19***
HR metrics and analytics	—	—	—	3.8	3.9	3.8	3.9	**.27*****
HR information systems	4.1	4.1[6]	4.0	4.0	3.9	3.8[2]	3.8	**−.12**
Union relations	3.1	2.9	2.7	3.0	2.8	2.9	2.8	**−.16[t]**
Developing social networks	—	—	—	—	—	—	3.6	**.26****

Response scale: 1 = greatly decreased; 2 = decreased; 3 = stayed the same; 4 = increased; 5 = greatly increased. Empty cells indicate that the item was not asked in that year.

[a]HR planning prior to 2007.

[1,2,3,4,5,6,7] Significant differences ($p \le .05$) between years.

Significance level: [t]$p \le .10$, *$p \le .05$, ** $p \le .01$, *** $p \le .001$.

formulation, it is because it is involved in human capital planning and organizational development and design or the reverse. One possibility is that in some organizations, the direction goes one way, and in others it goes the reverse. Our guess is that the most prevalent is involvement in strategy that leads to more emphasis on human capital and organizational development and design. Regardless of which causal direction exists in most companies, if HR wants to be an effective strategic partner, the existence of this relationship makes a strong case for HR developing a high level of competence in organizational design, organizational development, forecasting, and strategic planning.

The question on HR metrics and analytics, which was new in 2004, provides interesting data in 2013 as it did in 2010. It shows a relatively high level of increased focus and a relatively strong correlation with HR's role in strategy. The finding of a positive relationship supports the point that metrics and analytics can be key inputs to both the development and assessment of strategy. They also often provide a signal of rigor to leaders outside HR that may result in more HR involvement in strategy and business processes in the future.

International Results

The international data, in table 7.2, are very similar to the US data, as they were in 2010.Nationality does not seem to make a great deal of difference, with three exceptions in the 2013 data: China reports significantly less change in focus than other countries do in a few areas: developing social networks, management development, and talent assessment.

Strategic Focuses

Table 7.3 shows the correlations between HR activities and the five strategic focuses. There are some interesting and important relationships here. Strategies that focus on knowledge are significantly related to an increased focus on five of the HR activities. Not surprisingly, the strongest relationships are with social networks and employee development. There is also a strong relationship with organizational development.

The results for innovation-based strategies are generally similar to those for knowledge-based ones: both are strongly related to employee development activities. The most logical explanation for this relationship is that it exists because human capital is a particularly key aspect of an organization's performance capability. In order to execute either of these types of strategic focuses, an organization needs to build its human capital. Thus, successful efforts that focus on these strategies require increased attention to human capital.

Table 7.2. Change in focus on HR activities, by country

HR Activities	Means						
	United States[1]	Canada[2]	Australia[3]	Europe[4]	United Kingdom[5]	India[6]	China[7]
Design and organizational development	**3.8[7]**	**3.6**	**3.9**	**3.7**	**3.9**	**3.9[7]**	**3.5[1,6]**
Human capital forecasting and planning[a]	3.8[7]	3.6	3.9	3.7	3.8	3.9	3.4[1]
Organizational development	3.8	3.7	4.0	3.8	3.9	3.9	3.5
Organizational design	3.7	3.4	3.9	3.7	3.9	3.8	3.5
Compensation and benefits	**3.6**	**3.7**	**3.5**	**3.3[6]**	**3.6**	**3.8[4]**	**3.5**
Compensation	3.7	3.8	3.8	3.5	3.7	3.9	3.6
Benefits	3.5	3.6[4]	3.3	3.1[2,6]	3.5	3.7[4]	3.4
Executive compensation	**3.9**	**3.5**	**3.9**	**3.5**	**3.6**	**3.9**	**3.7**
Employee development	**3.7**	**3.7**	**3.8**	**3.7**	**3.6**	**3.9[7]**	**3.4[6]**
Training and education	3.5[6]	3.7	3.5	3.5	3.5	4.0[1]	3.6
Management development	3.9[7]	3.8	4.1[7]	3.8	3.7	3.9[7]	3.4[1,3,6]
Performance appraisal	3.6[4]	3.7	4.0	4.1[1,7]	3.6	3.9	3.6[4]
Career planning	3.5	3.6	3.8	3.5	3.5	3.7	3.3
Competency/talent assessment	3.8[7]	3.6	3.7	3.8[7]	3.6	3.8[7]	3.2[1,4,6]
Recruitment and selection	**3.9[4]**	**3.8**	**3.6**	**3.4[1]**	**3.5**	**3.9**	**3.6**
Recruitment	3.9[4]	3.8	3.6	3.4[1]	3.6	3.9	3.7
Selection	3.8	3.7	3.6	3.4	3.4	3.8	3.6
HR metrics and analytics	**3.9[7]**	**3.6**	**3.6**	**3.7**	**3.8**	**3.8**	**3.5[1]**
HR information systems	**3.8**	**3.6**	**3.6**	**3.8**	**3.8**	**3.9**	**3.6**
Union relations	**2.8**	**2.8**	**3.3**	**3.2**	**2.6**	**2.8**	**3.0**
Developing social networks[a]	**3.6[7]**	**3.6[7]**	**3.6[7]**	**3.7[7]**	**3.8[7]**	**—**	**2.9[1,2,3,4,5]**

Response scale: 1 = greatly decreased; 2 = decreased; 3 = stayed the same; 4 = increased; 5 = greatly increased. Empty cells indicate that the item was not asked in that year.

[a]India was not asked to respond to this question.

[1,2,3,4,5,6,7] Significant differences between countries ($p \leq .05$).

Sustainability and innovation are both related to employee development and organizational design and development. This follows logically from the need these strategies create for talent and performance. Both require HR organizations that develop talent and focus on organizational development (Lawler and Worley 2011).

It is somewhat surprising that as was true in 2010, the growth focus is not strongly related to an increase in any of the HR activities. Growth, in particular, creates a number of challenges for HR and might be expected to be related to recruitment and selection. It is weakly related to employee development and recruitment, which may reflect the need to develop competencies, particularly management and leadership skills,

Table 7.3. Relationship of HR activities change to strategic focuses					
HR Activities	**Strategic Focuses**				
	Growth	**Information-Based Strategies**	**Knowledge-Based Strategies**	**Sustainability**	**Innovation**
Design and organizational development	.08	.09	.29***	.10	.21*
Compensation and benefits	.02	−.05	.20*	.16^t	−.01
Executive compensation	.05	−.11	.15^t	−.09	.17^t
Employee development	.14^t	.16^t	.33***	.22**	.17*
Recruitment and selection	.19*	.12	.24**	.11	.20*
HR metrics and analytics	−.05	.09	.10	−.05	.20*
HR information systems	.16^t	.12	.10	.10	.07
Union relations	−.04	−.16^t	.02	.11	−.16^t
Social networks	.04	.29***	.38***	.18*	.33***

Response scale: 1 = greatly decreased; 2 = decreased; 3 = stayed the same; 4 = increased; 5 = greatly increased.
Significance level: $^t p \leq .10$, $^* p \leq .05$, $^{**} p \leq .01$, $^{***} p \leq .001$.

more quickly in a growing organization. Apparently these two business strategies do not entail the kinds of changes that create the need for increased HR focuses.

All of the HR activities show some significant positive relationships to the strategic focuses except for union relations, which is not significantly related to any of them except information and innovation, and those relationships are negative. This suggests that any strategic focus is likely to affect much of what HR does, once again affirming the important relationship between people and strategy.

Design and organizational development are significantly related to two strategic focuses and employee development to three of them. The most likely cause of these relationships is that they are key HR activities regardless of the strategy adopted. They need to support these strategies in order for them to be effective. In some respects, they are strategically neutral; they are likely to receive a decreasing focus only if there is no clear strategy.

Management Approaches

Table 7.4 shows that there are some significant relationships between changes in HR activities and a company's management approach. Not surprisingly, the bureaucratic and low-cost-operator approaches show a negative relationship to almost all of the activities except union relations. Employees simply are not a major focus in these two approaches

Table 7.4. Relationship of HR activities change to management approaches					
	Management Approaches				
HR Activities	**Bureaucratic**	**Low-Cost Operator**	**High Involvement**	**Global Competitor**	**Sustainable**
Design and organizational development	–.19*	–.03	.26**	–.01	.16†
Compensation and benefits	–.09	–.01	.08	.04	.12
Executive compensation	–.18*	–.03	.09	.06	.11
Employee development	–.06	–.06	.30***	.02	.23**
Recruitment and selection	–.15†	–.08	.31***	.10	.11
HR metrics and analytics	.04	–.04	.11	.01	.11
HR information systems	.01	–.07	–.01	.04	–.10
Union relations	.28***	.17*	–.08	–.13	.01
Social networks	–.06	–.07	.19*	–.01	.25**
Response scale: 1 = greatly decreased; 2 = decreased; 3 = stayed the same; 4 = increased; 5 = greatly increased. Significance level: †$p \le .10$, *$p \le .05$, **$p \le .01$, ***$p \le .001$.					

unless they are disruptive. Also note the union relations correlation. The high-involvement approach shows a positive relationship to four of the HR activities, also not surprising. High-involvement organizations are talent focused and thus require HR functions that are broadly supportive of high-quality talent management.

Conclusion

It is not surprising that HR executives report increases in the focus of their organizations on almost all HR activities. This suggests that HR is increasingly being seen as a key determinant of organizational effectiveness and a source of competitive advantage. It argues for an increased HR role in strategy formulation and implementation.

In every survey we have done, HR executives have reported that they are more focused on organizational design and development, and the data show that the more they are, the more likely they are to be involved in strategy. Particularly interesting is the increased activity in design and organizational development when the strategic focuses of knowledge and innovation are present. Organizational design and development is an area that has not always been a focus of HR. It is, however, closely tied to organizational performance and business strategy, so providing expertise in this area appears to be a way for HR to become more of a business partner, particularly in information- and knowledge-based businesses. These same business focuses are related to increased activity in employee development.

Once again, our results point to what is associated with HR being a strategic contributor. This time it is organizational design and development activity. Our data cannot establish a causal relationship, but it seems reasonable that at least some of the relationship may be that the activity leads HR to play more of a strategic role.

CHAPTER 8

Measuring Efficiency,
Effectiveness,
and Impact

- Measurement use patterns have generally changed little compared to the 2007 and 2010 surveys.

- The most common HR measures reflect efficiency, but rarely effectiveness or impact.

- Use of effectiveness and impact measures has increased slowly, but it is still relatively rare.

- Measuring efficiency and effectiveness, but not impact, is related to HR's strategic role.

- Measurement use is less common in Chinese organizations.

- Bureaucratic and low-cost-operator approaches have a negative association with measurement use, while the high-involvement approach has a positive association.

Two comments are frequently used when HR measurement is discussed: "What's measured gets managed" and "Not everything that counts can be counted, and not everything that can be counted actually counts." The first has led business and HR leaders to strive for more measurement in a belief that measures will produce increased attention and understanding of HR issues. The second caution is a key one: simply because something can be measured does not mean that it should be a major focus. In fact, it may not count in terms of organizational goals.

A key decision for HR and business leaders is what to measure and how to use those measures in decision making. The emergence of big data as a topic in human capital signals the latest development in a continuing dilemma: the amount and variety of data available to organizations about their people typically outstrip the ability of leaders to digest, make sense of, and make decisions using such data. This chapter examines the focus of HR measures in terms of three key areas: efficiency, effectiveness, and impact (Boudreau and Ramstad 2007; Cascio and Boudreau 2011). (Chapter 9 examines the outcomes that result from using HR measures.) Efficiency refers to the amount of resources that HR programs use, such as cost-per-hire. Effectiveness refers to the outcomes produced by HR activities, such as learning from training. Impact refers to the business or strategic value created by the HR activities, such as higher sales. All three of these can be useful, and indeed measuring all three is often required to fully understand how HR investments affect organizational performance. Each calls for somewhat different metrics and analytics. They can complement each other when they are used together.

Efficiency measures the resources that are devoted to HR and the functional processes delivered, such as cost-per-hire. Cost-benefit analysis most resembles efficiency and has often been referred to as the holy grail of HR measurement. It certainly has drawn the attention of many HR leaders and consultants. Effectiveness measures the immediate effects of HR processes, such as whether training produces learning and whether a recruitment program increases the number of applicants. Understanding the return on investment of HR programs is similar to effectiveness and is highly useful. Still, neither efficiency nor effectiveness reveals the ultimate business outcomes of HR investments, or whether those investments enhance the most pivotal human capital, or synergies among HR programs, or how measures contribute to decisions about human capital. We refer to these ultimate outcomes, pivotal targets, synergies, and decision effects as impact. A combination of efficiency, effectiveness, and impact measures is likely to be the most effective approach, yet this combination does not exist in most organizations.

Efficiency measures are basic to the HR function, and they connect readily to the existing accounting system. Increasing attention is being given to measuring effectiveness by focusing on such things as turnover, attitudes, and bench strength. Indeed a great deal of emerging attention to big data stems from their ability to better predict who will leave and when. However, organizations rarely consider impact (e.g., the relative effect of improving the quality of different talent pools on organizational effectiveness, or the effects of a measurement on improved human capital decisions). HR measurement and analysis is typically applied across the board, such as reporting turnover or engagement for everyone, and not specifically directed to the most pivotal talent segments (positions, roles, or demographic groups) where decisions are most important. This is unfortunate because our evidence suggests that the evolution of HR measurement toward more comprehensive and analytically rigorous approaches based on a science for human capital is likely a requirement for HR to progress in such areas as strategic partnership, HR information systems, and measurement and analytics.

Metrics and Analytics Use

Table 8.1 shows the pattern of HR's use of metrics and analytics for the US sample. The results in the first three columns show the percentage of HR executives saying that they now have those measures. These results suggest that most of the measurement and analytics elements remain relatively rare, with only four of them rated as "Yes, have now," by

Table 8.1. HR analytics and metrics use, United States

Measures	Yes, Have Now (%)			Means			2013 Correlation with HR Role in Strategy
	2007	2010	2013	2007[1]	2010[2]	2013[3]	
Efficiency							
Measure the financial efficiency of HR operations (e.g., cost-per-hire, time-to-fill, training costs)?	50.5	53.8	48.9	3.1	3.1	3.1	**.35***
Collect metrics that measure the cost of providing HR programs and processes?	39.8	43.3	41.6	3.0	3.0	2.9	**.38***
Benchmark analytics and measures against data from outside organizations (e.g., Saratoga, Mercer, Hewitt)?	48.5	54.9	48.5	3.0	3.0	3.0	**.17***
Effectiveness							
Use HR dashboards or scorecards?	37.8	51.6	46.7	2.9	3.2	3.1	**.31***
Measure the specific effects of HR programs (e.g., learning from training, motivation from rewards, validity of tests)?	19.2	32.4	17.5	2.4	2.6[3]	2.3[2]	**.17***
Have the capability to conduct cost-benefit analyses (also called utility analyses) of HR programs?	18.4	26.4	25.0	2.3	2.5	2.3	**.28***
Impact							
Measure the business impact of HR programs and processes?	20.4	27.6	21.9	2.6	2.7	2.5	**.34***
Measure the quality of the talent decisions made by non-HR leaders?	10.1	18.1	10.9	1.9	2.1	1.9	**.10**
Measure the business impact of high versus low performance in jobs?	12.1	18.1	10.9	2.0	2.1	1.9	**.13**

Response scale: 4 = yes, have now; 3 = being built; 2 = planning for; 1 = not currently being considered.

[1,2,3] No significant differences ($p \le .05$) between years.

Significance level: [1]$p \le .10$, *$p \le .05$, ** $p \le .01$, *** $p \le .001$.

more than 40 percent of organizations. Three of these are clearly in the efficiency category: the financial efficiency of HR operations, the costs of HR programs, and creating traditional HR data benchmarks, which we include in efficiency because the vast majority of such benchmarks reflect costs and activity levels.

The percentage of organizations that report having the three efficiency measures is slightly lower in 2013 than in 2010, but the results from 2007 to 2013 suggest a consistent level of use. The fourth item, rated as "have now" by 46.7 percent of organizations, is dashboards or scorecards. We label this "effectiveness," though dashboards and scorecards contain mostly efficiency measures, because they often also contain information on program outcomes or workforce behaviors such as skill levels, engagement, and turnover. Other measures of effectiveness are much rarer than efficiency measures. Beyond scorecards, the other effectiveness measures are used by less than 25 percent of organizations, including the ability to measure the effects of specific HR programs and the ability to do cost-benefit analyses of HR programs.

Perhaps predictably, measures of impact are the least frequently used, as shown at the bottom of table 8.1. Although about 21.9 percent of organizations report having measures of the business impact of HR programs and processes, only about one in ten have measures of the business impact of performance differences in jobs and actually measure the quality of talent decisions. The latter finding reinforces our results in chapter 5 that while HR leaders believe they are moderately good at talent decisions, HR systems generally do not educate non-HR managers about their decision quality. Indeed, even 21.9 percent may be an overestimate of the use of business impact measures. Our experience suggests that when HR executives are asked if they "measure business impact," they often interpret it to mean effectiveness (the effects of specific programs on workforce changes such as skills, competencies, and attitudes) or efficiency (the effects of programs on cost savings) rather than the effects of such programs on business outcomes such as financial performance and sustainable effectiveness.

The results in table 8.1 generally depict a decline in the use of the impact measures compared to earlier years. Every percentage in 2013 is lower than in 2010, with some even lower than in 2007. The largest decrease is in measuring the effects of specific HR programs (32.4 percent to 17.5 percent). This drop is also statistically significant, as indicated by the columns reflecting the averages across the three years. Thus, when it comes to HR measurement, progress appears at best slow; at worst, it is possible things are moving backward.

Use and Role in Strategy

Is the use of measures important to HR's strategic role? The relationship between the use of HR metrics and HR's role in strategy is shown in the far-right column of table 8.1. All except two of the measurement items are significantly positively correlated with greater HR involvement in strategy. The nonsignificant measurement elements are two impact measures shown at the bottom of the table: the quality of talent decisions and the business impact of performance variations.

Measures of efficiency and program cost are strongly correlated with HR's strategic role. They often draw on information from accounting reports. Measures of specific HR program effects are easy to understand because they associate particular programs with tangible outcomes such as performance ratings, turnover levels, or engagement scores. As a result, they help to establish HR as business focused and a credible contributor to business strategy decisions. Overall, organizations that have efficiency measures rate HR's strategic role more highly. This was also true in the 2010 sample, though the correlations between the three efficiency measures and HR's strategic role were higher in the 2013 sample.

All three of the effectiveness measurement types are significantly related to HR's role in strategy, yet only 46.7 percent of companies use scorecards; the other two are used by 25 percent or less. These proportions are actually lower than in 2010, when more than 50 percent of companies used dashboards and the other two measures were in use by more than 25 percent. This is interesting because the correlations between having such measures and HR's strategic role were somewhat higher in 2010 than in 2007. While correlations do not imply causation, it is nonetheless a paradox that the use of these measures seems to have declined even as their association with HR's strategic role has increased. It may be that if few organizations have such measures, they become a greater distinguishing factor for HR in organizations that actually have them.

We cannot say definitively that increased use of measures leads to higher HR strategy involvement, but there may be significant opportunities for HR to enhance its strategic involvement through greater use of efficiency and effectiveness measures. Such measures are fundamental to the development of a more sophisticated decision science, as the development of marketing and finance has shown (Boudreau and Ramstad 2007). We believe that impact metrics can be both a precursor and a result of HR strategic involvement, yet they remain in use by less than 50 percent of the organizations in our sample.

With regard to measuring impact, only the measure of the business impact of HR programs is significantly related to HR's role in strategy in table 8.1. The percentages of "have now" for all three impact measures are again somewhat lower in 2013 than in 2010. Measuring the quality of talent decisions and the value of performance differences in jobs is used by less than 11 percent of the companies, the lowest-rated measurement items. This pattern has been true since we began asking these questions in 2007, when less than 15 percent of companies reported using these measures.

Considering the nonsignificant correlation with HR's role in strategy for the two types of measures, it is not surprising that we have seen a decline in their use since 2007. That said, such measures are often vital to developing a decision science for HR. It may be, however, that the capability of HR to use such measures effectively or the receptivity of HR's constituents to such measures gives them far less of an impact than more traditional measures. For example, if an organization measures the business impact of performance differences, they will likely discover that some positions are more pivotal than others, but leaders are often ill equipped to explain such differences to employees, and even less prepared to act on them, if that means providing differentiated rewards or development. Similarly, if HR systems track the quality of talent decisions made by leaders, that may cast lower-quality leaders in a bad light, and many HR and non-HR leaders are ill equipped or reluctant to confront the need to address those shortcomings.

The 2013 results continue a trend since 2007 in which the association with HR's strategic role has decreased for measures of the quality of non-HR leader talent decisions and understanding where performance differences are pivotal to strategic success. This may reflect the effects of the economic downturn, which appears to have generally increased the association with HR's role in strategy of more traditional HR roles such as compliance and service delivery. Yet the fact that this trend has continued from 2007 to 2013 suggests it may be more general and not just a reaction to the economic downturn.

At least one measure in each measurement category has a statistically significant relationship with HR's involvement in business strategy. This supports the proposition that the most effective measurement systems combine impact, effectiveness, and efficiency. The more common measurement elements (financial efficiency, cost, and dashboards) have high correlations, suggesting that they have credibility with business leaders. They may represent an attractive first step in the measurement journey. HR leaders can then become more strategically effective by using and communicating the value of the less common HR measures such as the quality of talent decisions. Notably, the correlation with HR's strategic role for an impact measure "the business impact of HR programs," is similar to the more traditional measures of financial efficiency, cost, and dashboards. This suggests that there is a value for HR in developing impact measures and educating HR's constituents so they understand and use them.

International Results

Table 8.2 shows the results for the use of HR metrics and analytics for the different national samples. All countries reflect the general pattern seen in the United States that efficiency measures are more frequently used than effectiveness and impact measures, though the pattern is less pronounced in Australia, Europe, and the United Kingdom. This pattern occurs in the United States primarily due to the significantly higher frequency of use for efficiency measures. It occurs in Canada, Australia, Europe, and the United Kingdom due to the lower frequency of use of the impact measures. The difference between efficiency and impact

Table 8.2. HR analytics and metrics use, by country

Measures	Means						
	United States[1]	Canada[2]	Australia[3]	Europe[4]	United Kingdom[5]	India[6]	China[7]
Efficiency							
Measure the financial efficiency of HR operations (e.g., cost-per-hire, time-to-fill, training costs)?	3.1[7]	2.8	3.0[7]	2.7	3.1[7]	3.1[7]	2.3[1,3,5,6]
Collect metrics that measure the cost of providing HR programs and processes?	2.9[7]	2.5	2.6	2.6	2.6	3.1[7]	2.4[1,6]
Benchmark analytics and measures against data from outside organizations (e.g. Saratoga, Mercer, Hewitt)?	3.0[7]	2.9[7]	3.1[7]	2.7	2.8	3.0[7]	2.2[1,2,3,6]
Effectiveness							
Use HR dashboards or scorecards?	3.1[7]	3.0[7]	3.2[7]	2.9[7]	3.3[7]	3.1[7]	1.8[1,2,3,4,5,6]
Measure the specific effects of HR programs (e.g., learning from training, motivation from rewards, validity of tests)?	2.3	2.0[6]	2.5	2.2	2.4	2.7[2]	2.4
Have the capability to conduct cost-benefit analyses (also called utility analyses) of HR programs?	2.3	1.9[6]	2.2	2.0	2.5	2.7[2]	2.2
Impact							
Measure the business impact of HR programs and processes?	2.5	2.0[6]	2.8	2.3	2.5	2.8[2]	2.4
Measure the quality of the talent decisions made by non-HR leaders?	1.9[6]	1.5[6]	2.0	2.0	1.7	2.4[1,2]	1.9
Measure the business impact of high versus low performance in jobs?	1.9[6]	1.8[6]	1.8[6]	1.8[6]	1.6[6]	2.6[1,2,3,4,5,7]	2.0[6]

Response scale: 4 = yes, have now; 3 = being built; 2 = planning for; 1 = not currently being considered.

[1,2,3,4,5,6,7] Significant differences between countries ($p \le .05$).

measurement frequency is least pronounced in China, where the averages are much more similar across the three measurement types. This appears to be due to low levels of efficiency and effectiveness measures, as well as the same low level of impact measures as in other regions.

The use of dashboards or scorecards as well as financial efficiency and benchmarking is significantly less developed in China relative to other countries. Measures of the business impact of HR programs are rated as most developed in the United States and Australia, particularly when compared to Europe and Canada. As with other elements of our study, the Indian HR leaders in the sample tend to rate themselves somewhat higher than other regions. This is particularly true for the measure of the impact of performance differences in jobs.

Overall the average ratings are almost all less than 3.0, suggesting that for the most part, HR measures are in the planning or building stages on a global basis. The most pronounced cross-country pattern difference is that China has very similar ratings for all three types of HR measures, at roughly 2.5 on the four-point scale, while other countries showed a pattern of more use of measures of efficiency, less use of effectiveness measures, and the least use of impact measures. This may be due to the fact that HR in China has emerged more recently, and so progress on effectiveness and impact measures has been similar to efficiency, while in other countries, the efficiency measures may have emerged earlier, before many of the current impact measurement technologies and frameworks were widespread.

Use and Strategic Focuses

Table 8.3 shows the relationship between the use of HR measurement systems and the strategic focuses of organizations. The pattern suggests that two of the strategic focuses (knowledge based and innovation) are significantly associated with HR measurement in all three areas, while growth and sustainability strategies are not associated with any of the three. Information-based strategies are moderately related to financial efficiency, dashboards, and cost-benefit analysis but not the others.

Table 8.3. Correlations of HR analytics and metrics use to strategic focuses					
	Strategic Focuses				
Measures	**Growth**	**Information-Based Strategies**	**Knowledge-Based Strategies**	**Sustainability**	**Innovation**
Efficiency					
Measure the financial efficiency of HR operations (e.g., cost-per-hire, time-to-fill, training costs)?	−.15^t	.21*	.24**	.10	.21*
Collect metrics that measure the cost of providing HR programs and processes?	−.13	.14	.27**	.11	.10
Benchmark analytics and measures against data from outside organizations (e.g., Saratoga, Mercer, Hewitt)?	−.10	.06	.11	.13	.09
Effectiveness					
Use HR dashboards or scorecards?	−.13	.26**	.34***	.16^t	.22**
Measure the specific effects of HR programs (e.g., learning from training, motivation from rewards, validity of tests)?	−.09	.15^t	.20*	.14	.18*
Have the capability to conduct cost-benefit analyses (also called utility analyses) of HR programs?	−.07	.19*	.26**	.09	.21*
Impact					
Measure the business impact of HR programs and processes?	−.05	.15^t	.20*	.15^t	.19*
Measure the quality of the talent decisions made by non-HR leaders?	−.02	.11	.21*	.15^t	.18*
Measure the business impact of high versus low performance in jobs?	.01	.22*	.30***	.13	.24**
Response scale: 4 = yes, have now; 3 = being built; 2 = planning for; 1 = not currently being considered. Significance level: $^t p \le .10$, * $p \le .05$, ** $p \le .01$, *** $p \le .001$.					

The results for the knowledge-based and innovation strategies show that all three categories of HR measures are about equally correlated with the emphasis on these strategies, suggesting that a broadly balanced HR measurement approach characterizes these organizations. The extent to which organizations pursue a strategy of growth is not significantly related to the HR measurement items. This was also true in the 2007 study. This finding reinforces the earlier observation that growth-focused strategic pursuit tends to have somewhat lower correlations with decision science elements generally. It may be that growth-focused organizations are at an earlier stage of development or focused on traditional measures of financial growth.

The sustainability strategy shows differences when the 2010 and 2013 results are compared. In the 2010 results, the degree to which sustainability is pursued showed nonsignificant correlations for all of the efficiency and most of the effectiveness measures, but relatively strong correlations for the use of cost-benefit analysis and all of the impact measures. This pattern is apparent in the 2013 data shown in table 8.3 but less pronounced. It may be that a sustainability focus typically carries with it a stronger focus on nonfinancial outcomes, making traditional efficiency measures less emphasized. It may also be that this focus on nontraditional outcomes extends to a greater focus and accountability for the employment relationship as an outcome in itself, leading to greater use of impact measures that focus on the talent decisions of leaders.

Use and Management Approaches

Table 8.4 shows the correlations between measurement use and the degree to which organizations pursue different organization and management approaches. The pattern is similar to what we found in 2010 but somewhat more pronounced. The bureaucratic and low-cost-operator approaches are not associated with the use of most measurement categories. There are significant negative associations for the low-cost-operator approach with measures of HR program cost and dashboards. The global competitor approach and the sustainable approach are generally unrelated to these measures.

Only the high-involvement approach shows significant positive correlations with HR measures, in particular for five of the nine measurement uses: measuring HR costs, using dashboards, conducting cost-benefit analysis, measuring the quality of leaders' talent decisions, and the impact of performance differences. Similar to findings in other areas of the survey, this suggests that a high-involvement approach is generally positively associated with advanced HR practices. In particular, such an approach seems friendlier to a focus on leader talent decisions

Table 8.4. Correlations of HR analytics and metrics use to management approaches

Measures	Management Approaches				
	Bureaucratic	Low-Cost Operator	High Involvement	Global Competitor	Sustainable
Efficiency					
Measure the financial efficiency of HR operations (e.g., cost-per-hire, time-to-fill, training costs)?	.00	−.13	.14	−.01	.07
Collect metrics that measure the cost of providing HR programs and processes?	−.05	−.23**	.19*	−.03	.05
Benchmark analytics and measures against data from outside organizations (e.g. Saratoga, Mercer, Hewitt)?	−.09	−.10	.09	−.20*	−.16†
Effectiveness					
Use HR dashboards or scorecards?	.03	−.17*	.21*	−.01	.12
Measure the specific effects of HR programs (e.g., learning from training, motivation from rewards, validity of tests)?	.05	−.08	.16†	−.02	.03
Have the capability to conduct cost-benefit analyses (also called utility analyses) of HR programs?	.02	−.06	.26**	.04	.08
Impact					
Measure the business impact of HR programs and processes?	−.03	−.09	.11	−.03	.14
Measure the quality of the talent decisions made by non–HR leaders?	.03	−.07	.21*	.01	.09
Measure the business impact of high versus low performance in jobs?	−.16†	−.12	.22*	.08	.17*

Responses scored: 4 = yes, have now; 3 = being built; 2 = planning for; 1 = not currently being considered.

Significance level: †$p \leq .10$, *$p \leq .05$, **$p \leq .01$, ***$p \leq .001$.

and performance impact, which are relatively rare impact measures. It may be that pursuing a high-involvement approach naturally reveals and creates discussions about leader talent decisions and the relative impact of performance differences in different roles because of the high involvement of workers. In such situations, the operating approach creates a culture and management mind-set that is more prepared for the challenges that come with such measurement.

Conclusion

There is significant variability in how much organizations use different types of HR measures. Efficiency measures are used the most, effectiveness measures next, and impact measures the least. Overall, no measurement type is used by over 50 percent of all companies. This pattern holds across different national samples, with the United States showing greater implementation of efficiency measures and China showing consistent moderate use of measures across all three categories. Compared to the 2010 survey, there has been a general decrease in the percentages of organizations that report they now have measures in each of the categories. Clearly there is room for HR to do more measurement and reason to believe that it would have a positive impact.

The use of HR measures and analytics is significantly related to HR's role in strategy. It is also important to note that all measurement elements are not equal when it comes to strategy. In the 2013 and 2010 data, in contrast to the 2007 results, impact measures reflecting non-HR leaders' talent decisions and the difference in pivotal impact of job performance between roles were not significantly related to HR's role in strategy. More traditional measures such as benchmarks and scorecards were more strongly related to HR's strategic role in 2010 and 2013 than in 2007. This may suggest a return to more traditional measures.

This is understandable, as the tidal wave of data and the increasing ability of HR information systems to deliver those data through cloud-based applications is daunting. Organizations can be forgiven for retreating to measurement approaches that reflect the tried-and-true emphasis on saving money or producing an immediate program effect. It is, however, also paradoxical, because this same tidal wave of big data is uniformly expected to create a demand for more sophistication and differentiation in human capital decisions. It is the impact measures that form the basis for such sophistication.

Overall the results present tantalizing evidence that there may be systematic variations in how HR measures are used and that the pattern of use significantly relates to the strategies and management approaches of organizations, as well as HR's strategic role. There is no doubt that HR metrics and analytics remain underdeveloped and underused. Increasing the attention given to HR metrics and analytics seems to be called for considering the potential for improvement and the added value it will bring. That said, at the moment, it appears that the best way to increase HR's strategic role is to create and use traditional efficiency and effectiveness measures. It may be wise for HR to start in traditional areas and work toward more advanced impact measures as its constituents develop their understanding of HR metrics. Notably, an emphasis on high-involvement management approaches has a strong association with impact measures, suggesting an organization's management approach can create a friendly environment for HR measurement information.

CHAPTER 9

The Outcomes of HR Metrics and Analytics

- Strategic and functional HR contributions received similar measurement effectiveness ratings, at the midpoint of the scale, and changed little from earlier years.

- Using advanced data analysis and big data were the lowest rated for effectiveness.

- Measurement effectiveness is consistently and positively correlated with HR's role in strategy.

- Measurement effectiveness is rated higher in China and India than in Western countries.

- Measurement effectiveness is higher in organizations with a stronger focus on information-based, knowledge-based, and innovation strategies.

- Measurement effectiveness is higher the more organizations pursue a high-involvement approach, and lower the more they pursue low-cost-operator and bureaucratic approaches

The previous chapter examined the use of HR measures; here the focus is on the outcomes that result from the use of HR metrics and analytics by organizations. First, we examine two broad areas of effectiveness: strategic contributions (such as contributing to strategy decisions, identifying where talent makes the greatest strategic impact, connecting human capital practices to organizational performance, and supporting organization change) and HR functional and operational strategies (such as improving HR department operations and evaluating and investing in HR practices).

Second, we focus on four elements that contribute to the effectiveness of measures as catalysts for organizational change:

Logic (frameworks that articulate the connections between talent and strategic success, as well as the principles and conditions that predict individual and organizational behavior)

Analytics (tools and techniques to transform data into rigorous and relevant insights, e.g., statistical analysis, research design)

Measures (numbers and indices calculated from data system)

Process (communication and knowledge transfer mechanisms through which the information becomes accepted and acted on by key organization decision makers)

These four elements comprise the LAMP framework, which identifies these four vital features of measurement systems for driving strategic change (Boudreau and Ramstad 2007; Cascio and Boudreau 2011). In the 2013 survey, we added an item, "using big data," to examine if this is an area where HR measurement effectiveness is emerging.

HR Metrics and Analytics Effectiveness

Table 9.1 shows the results regarding how HR leaders rated the effectiveness of HR information measurement and analysis systems in contributing to outcomes related to HR strategic contributions, HR functional and operational contributions, and the four LAMP elements. Overall the picture shows consistent average effectiveness ratings,

Table 9.1. HR analytics and metrics effectiveness, United States								
	2013 Percentages					**Means**		**Correlation with HR Role in Strategy**
Outcomes	**Very Ineffective**	**Ineffective**	**Somewhat Effective**	**Effective**	**Very Effective**	**2010**	**2013ᵃ**	
Strategy contributions								
Contributing to decisions about business strategy and human capital management	7.0	21.9	26.6	41.4	3.1	3.1	3.1	.54***
Identifying where talent has the greatest potential for strategic impact	7.0	28.1	27.3	35.9	1.6	2.8	3.0	.37***
Connecting human capital practices to organizational performance	8.6	39.8	29.7	21.1	0.8	2.6	2.7	.32***
Supporting organizational change efforts	5.5	19.5	25.8	42.2	7.0	3.2	3.3	.38***
HR functional and operational contributions								
Assessing and improving HR department operations	7.0	17.1	24.0	47.3	4.7	3.1	3.3	.44***
Predicting the effects of HR programs before implementation	10.1	37.2	32.6	20.2	0.0	2.6	2.6	.29***
Pinpointing HR programs that should be discontinued	11.8	34.6	28.3	24.4	0.8	2.6	2.7	.38***
Logic, analysis, measurement, and process (LAMP)								
Using logical principles that clearly connect talent to organization success	6.2	30.2	25.6	34.9	3.1	3.0	3.0	.43***
Using advanced data analysis and statistics	14.1	38.3	30.5	15.6	1.6	2.6	2.5	.27**
Providing high-quality (complete, timely, accessible) talent measurements	7.8	32.6	31.8	26.4	1.6	2.7	2.8	.40***
Motivating users to take appropriate action	9.3	30.2	32.6	27.1	0.8	2.9	2.8	.40***
Using big data	21.1	38.3	25.0	14.1	1.6	—	2.4	.24**
Significance level: ᵗp ≤ .10, *p ≤ .05, ** p ≤ .01, *** p ≤ .001.								
ᵃNo significant differences (p ≤ .05) between years.								

hovering around 3.0, with many below 3.0. The averages are not very different from 2010, and they are also quite similar to 2007. Thus, progress is slow at best. Nevertheless, there appears to be some progress. In 2010, none of these outcomes were rated effective or very effective by more than 40 percent of respondents, but in 2013, three the items were rated at that level.

Two of the highest- rated outcomes are related to strategic contributions: "supporting organizational change efforts" and "contributing to decisions about business strategy and human capital management." These were also highly rated in the 2010 sample. A third strategic outcome, "identifying where talent has the greatest potential for strategic impact," showed a significant increase in the proportion of those rating it effective in 2013 as compared to 2010. The other two highly rated items concern assessing and improving HR department operations and using logical principles that clearly connect talent to organizational success.

It is encouraging that some strategically related items are relatively effective, but again this is in the context of rather low effectiveness ratings overall. The effectiveness ratings fall at or are slightly below the midpoint (3.0 = somewhat effective) of the five-point scale, suggesting improvement is possible in all areas. Although there has been some progress, the results are largely similar to those from as far back as 2004. Indeed, none of the ratings in 2013 was significantly different from the 2010 levels.

The four items reflecting the LAMP framework show the highest effectiveness ratings for the logic element, high-quality measures, and motivating users to take action, with slightly lower ratings for the elements of advanced data analysis and big data. The results concerning advanced data analysis are interesting in that they contradict much of the anecdotal evidence we encounter. Most organizations report that their ability to generate measurements is well developed and they have good data analysis capabilities. Failure to effectively use measures is usually attributed to the fact that those receiving the information lack the cognitive frameworks to make sense of the information (such as understanding how an engagement score or a turnover rate connects to business success) or failing to convey the information in ways that motivate and direct the right decisions and actions. Still, we would not make too much of the relatively higher effectiveness ratings of some of the LAMP categories, considering that the effectiveness ratings in table 9.1 are low for all four LAMP areas, leaving significant opportunity for improvement in the HR measures and analyses and on the part of managers using the data.

The ratings for the outcome of "using big data" are the lowest in table 9.1. This is not surprising given the relatively recent emergence of big data as a significant objective for HR analytics, but it does suggest that HR has a lot of work to do in order for it to capitalize on its availability.

Role in Strategy

All of the effectiveness ratings in table 9.1 are significantly associated with HR's role in strategy. This was also true in 2010, and the pattern of correlations is similar to 2010 too. The highest correlation is for "contributing to decisions about business strategy and human capital management." Thus, the uniformly high correlations suggest that effectively measuring both HR's strategic and functional/operational outcomes relates to HR's strategic role. Similarly, it is notable that measurement effectiveness in all four elements of the LAMP framework is positively related to HR's role in strategy. This suggests that the four elements may work together to support or to help advance HR's strategic role, as Boudreau and Ramstad (2007) and Cascio and Boudreau (2011) suggested.

Notably, although big data appear to still be an emerging area, effectiveness in using these data still generated a significant correlation with HR's strategic role, albeit somewhat less than other areas. Thus, it appears that when HR organizations are effective in this emerging arena, they also play a stronger strategic role.

Overall the main conclusion is that all the correlations between measurement effectiveness with HR's role in strategy are relatively high and statistically significant. Compared to the 2004 and 2007 results, the 2013 correlations are higher and more frequently statistically significant. This suggests that over time, the level of the effectiveness of these measurement areas has increased, as has their association with HR's strategic role.

We often encounter HR and business leaders who believe that the HR profession must first get its own house in order by improving its measurement capability and achieving functional effectiveness and that only after doing so should it focus on its strategic effectiveness. The results reported here suggest that both strategy and HR functional measurement effectiveness contribute to a strong strategic role. Thus, they support the idea of developing measurement systems that are effective at strategic outcomes, even if HR functional and operational outcomes are not yet perfect.

International Results

The international results for measurement effectiveness are shown in table 9.2. The results are quite similar to those for the United States in terms of both the level of effectiveness and the relative effectiveness across the different measures.

Table 9.2. HR analytics and metrics effectiveness, by country

Outcomes	Means						
	United States[1]	Canada[2]	Australia[3]	Europe[4]	United Kingdom[5]	India[6]	China[7]
Strategy contributions							
Contributing to decisions about business strategy and human capital management	3.1	3.1	3.4	3.1	3.0	3.3	3.2
Identifying where talent has the greatest potential for strategic impact	3.0	2.8[6]	3.0	2.9	2.6[6]	3.4[2,5]	3.1
Connecting human capital practices to organizational performance	2.7[6]	2.6[6]	2.7	2.8	2.2[6,7]	3.4[1,2,5]	3.0[5]
Supporting organizational change efforts	3.3	3.2	3.4	3.2	3.3	3.5	3.3
HR functional and operational contributions							
Assessing and improving HR department operations	3.3	3.0	3.4	3.3	3.3	3.5	3.4
Predicting the effects of HR programs before implementation	2.6[6,7]	2.6[6]	2.5	2.6	2.5[6]	3.2[1,2,5]	3.1[1]
Pinpointing HR programs that should be discontinued	2.7	2.8	2.6	2.5	2.9	3.1	2.8
Logic, analysis, measurement, and process (LAMP)							
Using logical principles that clearly connect talent to organization success	3.0	2.9	3.0	2.9	2.7	3.3	3.2
Using advanced data analysis and statistics	2.5[6]	2.5	2.5	2.5	2.5	3.1[1]	2.9
Providing high-quality (complete, timely, accessible) talent measurements	2.8	2.6	2.8	2.8	2.4[6,7]	3.2[5]	3.1[5]
Motivating users to take appropriate action	2.8[6,7]	2.7[6,7]	2.9	2.8	2.7[7]	3.3[1,2]	3.3[1,2,5]
Using big data[a]	2.4[7]	2.4	2.2[7]	2.5	2.2[7]	—	3.0[1,3,5]

Response scale: 1 = very ineffective; 2 = ineffective; 3 = neither; 4 = effective; 5 = very effective.

[a]India was not asked to respond to this question.

[1,2,3,4,5,6,7] Significant differences between countries ($p \leq .05$).

The notable exceptions to the pattern of similar results are those from China and India, where the ratings are generally higher. The Chinese and Indian HR executives consistently rate the effectiveness of their metrics slightly above the scale midpoint on almost all items. In the other countries, the ratings are more varied, with some items receiving lower effectiveness ratings. From our data, we cannot determine if the companies in China and India are more effective at HR measurement in more areas, or if this is a response difference that is due to the recency with which HR measurement systems have been implemented in these two countries and thus may carry a novelty effect. In other countries, these systems have a longer history, and as a result, HR executives may have developed higher standards for effectiveness levels. It may also be that in China and India, the more recently emerged HR functions could immediately use the increasingly efficient measurement systems that are embedded in modern technology platforms and HR information systems. This may be because there are fewer legacy systems in China and India to hold back such adoption.

Strategic Focuses

Table 9.3 shows the relationship between the effectiveness of HR metrics and analytics and the different strategic focuses. Once again, the growth strategy focus shows no significant correlations with any of the measurement effectiveness areas. Apparently a focus on organizational growth does not lead to the systemic enhancements of HR effectiveness generally—and in this case, the effectiveness of HR measures.

In marked contrast to the correlations for growth are the correlations with information-based, knowledge-based, and innovation strategic focuses, which show a large number of significant correlations. While the sustainability focus exhibits somewhat fewer significant correlations, it is often positively associated with measurement effectiveness. With the exception of the growth strategy, it appears that enhanced measurement effectiveness may support pursuit of the other strategies, albeit to different degrees.

The data do not explain why the correlations for the knowledge-based and information-based strategic focuses are particularly strong. It may

Table 9.3. HR analytics and metrics effectiveness to strategic focuses					
	Strategic Focuses				
Outcomes	**Growth**	**Information-Based Strategies**	**Knowledge-Based Strategies**	**Sustainability**	**Innovation**
Strategy contributions					
Contributing to decisions about business strategy and human capital management	−.09	.34***	.35***	.15^t	.25**
Identifying where talent has the greatest potential for strategic impact	−.07	.22*	.38***	.19*	.16^t
Connecting human capital practices to organizational performance	−.04	.22*	.30***	.14	.12
Supporting organizational change efforts	−.14	.21*	.21*	.29***	.25**
HR functional and operational contributions					
Assessing and improving HR department operations	.03	.25**	.27**	.19*	.21*
Predicting the effects of HR programs before implementation	−.10	.06	.19*	.13	.02
Pinpointing HR programs that should be discontinued	−.16^t	.07	.17^t	.06	.06
Logic, analysis, measurement, and process (LAMP)					
Using logical principles that clearly connect talent to organization success	−.03	.30***	.30***	.13	.21*
Using advanced data analysis and statistics	−.15^t	.11	.13	.04	.09
Providing high-quality (complete, timely, accessible) talent measurements	−.07	.16^t	.26**	.19*	.21*
Motivating users to take appropriate action	−.08	.16^t	.20*	.10	.18*
Using big data	−.09	.27**	.24**	.05	.31***
Significance level: $^tp ≤ .10$, $*p ≤ .05$, $**p ≤ .01$, $***p ≤ .001$.					

be that these strategies rely more on organizational integration and employee understanding and involvement than the others and because of this, they put more of an emphasis on metrics and analytics to enhance that understanding and involvement. It may also be that knowledge-based and information-based strategies create a general culture and capability that make the organization more facile and comfortable with measurement. Both strategies are somewhat unique in their emphasis on information and knowledge. In an organization that is already generally predisposed toward knowledge and information, it may be that effective HR measures are more easily justified and developed.

Management Approaches

The correlations between the five management approaches and the effectiveness of HR measures and analytics are shown in table 9.4. The high-involvement approach shows strong correlations with the effectiveness of HR measures, as it did in 2010. As in 2010, the global competitor focus does not show any significant associations with the effectiveness of HR measures. The biggest difference between the 2010 and 2013 samples is for the focus on sustainability, which showed many significant correlations in the 2010 sample but only a few in the 2013 sample.

The other two strategic focuses, bureaucratic and low-cost operator, show an interesting pattern that parallels prior results for the development of the HR decision science and for measurement use. Specifically, both focuses show negative correlations with most elements of measurement effectiveness, and some of these negative correlations are statistically significant. These results are consistent with results of our previous studies and suggest a meaningful relationship.

It appears that when organizations emphasize a bureaucratic or low-cost-operator management approach, they are significantly less likely to find that measurement effectiveness contributes to strategic decisions, supports organizational change efforts, improves HR department operations, encourages using logical principles, and motivates action. The causal direction could go either way, but it seems most likely that pursuit of the bureaucratic or the low-cost-operator approach simply and directly leads to less attention to HR measurement and thus less effective HR measures. Considering the strong association between HR measurement effectiveness and HR's role in strategy (see table 9.1), this suggests that HR leaders wishing to pursue state-of-the-art measures might need to avoid organizations emphasizing bureaucratic or low-cost-operator approaches, or shift the management approach to one that is more HR friendly, or find creative ways to demonstrate the value of a more strategic approach to HR measurement and HR more generally.

Table 9.4. HR analytics and metrics effectiveness to management approaches

Outcomes	Management Approaches				
	Bureaucratic	Low-Cost Operator	High Involvement	Global Competitor	Sustainable
Strategy contributions					
Contributing to decisions about business strategy and human capital management	–.14	–.13	.29***	–.02	.17ᵗ
Identifying where talent has the greatest potential for strategic impact	–.11	–.25**	.35***	–.01	.18*
Connecting human capital practices to organizational performance	–.05	–.16ᵗ	.20*	–.06	.11
Supporting organizational change efforts	–.27**	–.27**	.34***	–.12	–.03
HR functional and operational contributions					
Assessing and improving HR department operations	–.26**	–.08	.27**	.04	.14
Predicting the effects of HR programs before implementation	–.19*	–.28**	.27**	–.06	.03
Pinpointing HR programs that should be discontinued	–.24**	–.20*	.29***	–.13	.10
Logic, analysis, measurement, and process (LAMP)					
Using logical principles that clearly connect talent to organization success	–.18*	–.04	.30***	.06	.19*
Using advanced data analysis and statistics	.00	–.08	.12	.03	.16ᵗ
Providing high-quality (complete, timely, accessible) talent measurements	–.12	–.06	.30***	.11	.21*
Motivating users to take appropriate action	–.14	–.08	.22*	.00	.07
Using big data	–.04	–.13	.19*	–.03	.15ᵗ

Significance level: ᵗ$p \leq .10$, *$p \leq .05$, **$p \leq .01$, ***$p \leq .001$.

The stronger relationship between the high-involvement approach and HR measurement outcomes across virtually all items is an important finding. It appears that the focus of high-involvement organizations on making employees and the employment relationship a key element of competitive success and on the employment relationship as a key performance driver leads to investing in effective HR measurement.

Conclusion

The results for HR measurement system effectiveness indicate moderate effectiveness and a slight improvement since our 2007 study. The outcomes of HR measurement continue to show consistently strong relationships with HR's strategic role, an important area for HR and one where improvement is needed in order for HR to have a meaningful role in determining business strategy. The results for the effectiveness of HR measures and analytics in many ways reinforce the findings from chapter 9 on measure use and strategy. Not only does measurement effectiveness generally relate to HR's strategic role, but effectiveness in

HR functional and operational areas relates particularly significantly with the strength of HR's strategic role.

Our results show a strong relationship between the four LAMP elements and HR's strategic role, supporting the point that all four elements are necessary for a strategically effective measurement system. Of course, the causal direction cannot be discerned from our data, so it may be that as HR organizations become more strategically involved and relevant, organizations perceive and support more effective HR measures and create them. It seems plausible, however, that at least some of the causal effect may be because effective measures lead to a greater strategic contribution from HR.

The results for strategic focuses suggest that organizations pursuing knowledge-, information-, sustainability-, and innovation-based strategies are likely to have measurement effectiveness across a wide array of outcomes, particularly for knowledge and information-based strategic focuses. Although these results are not definitive, they suggest that effective HR measurement may be more readily accepted and used in organizations that rely on broad-based talent understanding and involvement to achieve competitive advantage, innovation or sustainability. They may also suggest that when organizations pursue general strategies that are measurement and data-centric, there is a more welcoming environment for more advanced HR measurement and it is more effective.

It appears that some management approaches, such as the bureaucratic and low-cost-operator ones, may actually discourage HR measurement excellence. Just the opposite appears to be true of the high-involvement and sustainable management approaches. They are associated with higher HR measurement excellence, a finding that fits their focus on the importance of human capital.

Overall, the findings reinforce the conclusion from our prior surveys: the potential for HR metrics and analytics to contribute to HR's strategic value is significant, while the perceived effectiveness levels remain stubbornly moderate. Our results also suggest that leaders both inside and outside HR can find great value in pursuing HR measurement effectiveness at the strategic and functional levels. They further suggest doing it through a balanced approach of logic, analytics, measures, and process.

CHAPTER 10

HR's Role in Sustainability

- HR does not have a major role in most companies' sustainability activities.

- HR executives believe that HR should play a larger role in the sustainability programs of companies than it currently does.

- HR executives think that sustainability should be built into HR processes such as selection and training, but they report that it is not.

- HR executives report that HR should be much more active in the design of sustainability programs, providing change management support, and organizational design expertise than it currently is.

- The more involved HR is in sustainability activities, the larger its role in corporate strategy.

The future of corporations increasingly depends on their addressing the social and environmental challenges that affect their economic activity. Corporate social and environmental responsibilities need to shift from being a peripheral add-on focus and risk-avoidance activity to being integrated into how companies operate and into their business strategies (Mohrman and Lawler 2014).

Society is increasingly demanding that corporations develop sustainably and operate in ways that meet the needs of the present, without compromising the ability of future generations to meet their needs. This definition of sustainable performance was originally articulated in a 1987 United Nations report, *Our Common Future* (Brundtland 1987), and has become the dominant definition of sustainability.

Leading companies have made strides in embedding the triple bottom line of financial, environmental, and social sustainability in their operating and reporting practices. However, it is not clear how many companies have fully incorporated social and environmental responsibility into their business strategy, financial decision making, performance goals, reward systems, or employment processes (Mohrman and Lawler 2014).

Companies are finding that corporate social responsibility is now a major factor in being able to attract, hire, and retain top talent. Some organizations have created an employer brand that addresses this need and are providing employees with meaningful ways to participate in the transition to sustainability. HR functions can play a major role in implementing corporate sustainability by building it into HR strategy, policy, and practices. They also can help organizations manage the changes that are required in order for them to be sustainably effective. Human resource professionals can play a central role in change management, culture change, organizational design, and competency building, all of which are critical components of a sustainable business strategy.

In many respects, sustainability is not new turf for HR. It has always been active in organizations' community and charitable activities. HR has also had a major role in determining and assessing how its organization's employees are treated, a key part of an organization's social sustainability.

HR Role in Sustainability Activities

The responses to the survey's questions about HR's role in sustainability activities show that HR does not play a major or leadership role in the sustainability activities of most corporations. As can be seen in figure 10.1, most HR executives say that they play either a minor role or an active support role; less than 15 percent say they play a major support or leader role.

The roles that HR executives say they play are dramatically different from the ones they say they should play. Most HR executives believe that HR should at least be in an active support role, and close to a majority say that they should be either a major supporter or a leader of sustainability.

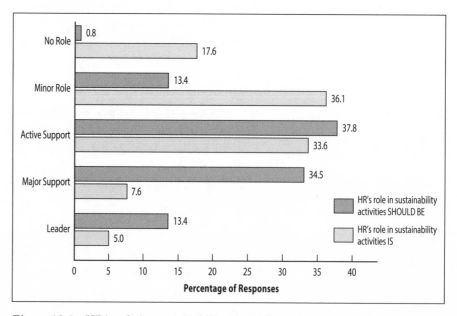

Figure 10.1. HR's role in sustainability activities

Table 10.1. Sustainability activities, United States							
	2013 Percentages					2013 Means	Correlation with HR Role in Strategy
Sustainability activities	Strongly Disagree	Somewhat Disagree	Neither Disagree nor Agree	Somewhat Agree	Strongly Agree		
Sustainability performance and competences *are* explicitly built into HR processes such as selection, rewards, and development.	16.7	29.2	20.8	27.5	5.8	2.8	**.25****
Sustainability performance and competences *should be* explicitly built into HR processes such as selection, rewards, and development.	0.0	11.7	22.5	40.8	25.0	3.8	**−.12**
HR *is involved* in the design of sustainability initiatives and programs.	13.3	20.8	22.5	31.7	11.7	3.1	**.41*****
HR *should be involved* in the design of sustainability initiatives and programs.	0.8	12.5	18.3	40.8	27.5	3.8	**.03**
HR *provides* support and expertise in organizational design issues that have an impact on sustainability.	10.0	14.2	21.7	40.0	14.2	3.3	**.48*****
HR *should provide* support and expertise in organizational design issues that have an impact on sustainability.	0.8	3.3	12.5	44.2	39.2	4.2	**−.01**
HR *provides* change management support for building sustainability into the way my company does business.	10.8	14.2	24.2	39.2	11.7	3.3	**.52*****
HR *should provide* change management support for building sustainability into the way my company does business.	0.8	3.3	13.3	40.8	41.7	4.2	**−.11**
Significance level: $^\dagger p \le .10$, $^* p \le .05$, $^{**} p \le .01$, $^{***} p \le .001$.							

Table 10.1 provides data on the kind of role HR plays in sustainability activities and how much it directly supports the sustainability performance objectives of the company. The statements in the table are paired so we can compare what HR does and what HR thinks it should do. On all questions, the gap between what HR feels it should do with respect to sustainability and what it actually does is very large in the direction of HR not doing enough.

The scores for what it does average around the middle of the scale (neither agree nor disagree). They consistently fall short of doing what is needed to make HR a positive force when it comes to sustainability. For example, the first statement refers to whether sustainability performance and competencies are explicitly built into HR processes. Only a little over 30 percent of the executives believe that is true of their company. But when it comes to whether they feel that it should be true, almost 70 percent feel that it should be true.

Although the gap between "should be" and "is" is not as large as it is for building sustainability into HR programs, there is also a gap with respect to whether HR is involved in the design of the sustainability initiatives, whether it provides support and expertise in organizational design relative to sustainability, and whether it provides change management support for building sustainability into the way the company operates.

Perhaps the best way of summarizing the data presented in figure 10.1 and table 10.1 is that HR executives believe that HR should play a significant role in the design and implementation of sustainability activities and sustainability should be a key part of the company's HR systems. However, when it comes to whether that is currently true of HR organizations, the answer is no: HR does not play the major role that it should when it comes to sustainability. It is particularly telling that the lowest score in table 10.1 is on sustainability being built into HR processes, the area where HR has the best chance to influence sustainability practices and results.

The correlations in table 10.1 between HR's role in sustainability activities and HR's role in strategy are all positive and quite high. It appears that when HR plays a major role in sustainability, it is also a player in corporate strategy. In many respects, this is not surprising since a key issue in many organizations' corporate strategy is sustainability. Therefore, if HR is involved in sustainability activities, this work naturally will lead to HR being involved in corporate strategy. Similarly, if it is involved in corporate strategy, it is likely to be involved in discussions about sustainability because it can be a key piece of an organization's business strategy.

Overall, the data on HR and sustainability clearly show that HR is not the player in sustainability that it would like to be and feels that it should be. It has a lot to offer if it has expertise in change management, organizational design, and the design of HR systems that support sustainability. Clearly sustainability expertise and activities go hand-in-hand with HR being a more powerful and involved strategic partner in corporations. It does not appear that HR has to give up anything when it comes to being a strategic partner by being heavily involved in a corporation's sustainability activities. Indeed, quite the contrary appears to be true: they go together and represent a positive opportunity for HR. Given the low level of activity that HR currently reports with respect to sustainability, this appears to be an area where HR can move forward and not only improve how the company functions but also position itself to be a stronger business strategy contributor.

Table 10.2. Sustainability activities, by country

Sustainability Activities	Means						
	United States[1]	Canada[2]	Australia[3]	Europe[4]	United Kingdom[5]	India[6]	China[7]
Sustainability performance and competences *are* explicitly built into HR processes such as selection, rewards, and development.	2.8	3.0	3.1	2.9	2.7	—	3.2
Sustainability performance and competences *should be* explicitly built into HR processes such as selection, rewards, and development.	3.8	4.1	4.0	4.1	3.9	—	3.8
HR *is involved* in the design of sustainability initiatives and programs.	3.1	3.3	3.1	3.2	3.3	—	3.4
HR *should be involved* in the design of sustainability initiatives and programs.	3.8	4.1	4.0	4.0	3.9	—	4.1
HR *provides* support and expertise in organization design issues that have an impact on sustainability.	3.3	3.1	3.4	3.3	3.7	—	3.6
HR *should provide* support and expertise in organization design issues that have an impact on sustainability.	4.2	4.2	4.2	4.1	4.2	—	4.1
HR *provides* change management support for building sustainability into the way my company does business.	3.3	3.3	3.4	3.3	3.2	—	3.5
HR *should provide* change management support for building sustainability into the way my company does business.	4.2	4.0	4.1	4.3	4.1	—	4.1

Note: India was not asked to respond to any of these questions.

Response scale: 1 = strongly disagree; 2 = somewhat disagree; 3 = neither disagree nor agree; 4 = somewhat agree; 5 = strongly agree.

[1,2,3,4,5,6,7] No significant differences between countries ($p \leq .05$).

International Results

HR's role in sustainability does not vary significantly in the countries surveyed (table 10.2). There are no significant differences between countries with respect to HR sustainability activities and not many nearly significant differences either. We expected the activity scores in China to be lower than in Europe and the United States, where there is more environmental regulation and legislation, but they are not.

Strategic Focuses and HR Sustainability Activities

The relationship between the role of HR in sustainability and the strategic focuses of organizations are shown in table 10.3. The highest correlations in the table are with the sustainability focus. Not surprisingly, HR is more involved in sustainability activities when a company

Table 10.3. Relationship of sustainability activities to strategic focuses

Sustainability	Strategic Focuses				
	Growth	Information-Based Strategies	Knowledge-Based Strategies	Sustainability	Innovation
Sustainability performance and competences *are* explicitly built into HR processes such as selection, rewards, and development.	.15	.21*	.23*	.38***	.30***
Sustainability performance and competences *should be* explicitly built into HR processes such as selection, rewards, and development.	.02	.01	-.02	.27**	.01
HR *is involved* in the design of sustainability initiatives and programs.	.03	.11	.18*	.24**	.17^t
HR *should be involved* in the design of sustainability initiatives and programs.	.05	.03	-.01	.21*	-.06
HR *provides* support and expertise in organization design issues that have an impact on sustainability.	.08	.16^t	.23**	.29**	.18^t
HR *should provide* support and expertise in organization design issues that have an impact on sustainability.	.03	.04	.01	.14	-.09
HR *provides* change management support for building sustainability into the way my company does business.	.03	.13	.24**	.30***	.23*
HR *should provide* change management support for building sustainability into the way my company does business.	.03	-.05	-.04	.18*	-.14

Response scale: 1 = strongly disagree; 2 = somewhat disagree; 3 = neither disagree nor agree; 4 = somewhat agree; 5 = strongly agree.
Significance level: $^tp ≤ .10$, $^*p ≤ .05$, $^{**}p ≤ .01$, $^{***}p ≤ .001$.

Table 10.4. Relationship of HR's role in sustainability to management approaches

Sustainability	Management Approaches				
	Bureaucratic	Low-Cost Operator	High Involvement	Global Competitor	Sustainable
HR's role *is*	-.18^t	-.13	.26**	.08	.23*
HR's role *should be*	.14	.20*	-.12	-.09	.05

Response scale: 1 = no role; 2 = minor role; 3 = active support; 4 = major support; 5 = leader.
Significance level: $^tp ≤ .10$, $^*p ≤ .05$, $^{**}p ≤ .01$, $^{***}p ≤ .001$.

has a major strategic focus on it. Apparently organizations that have a strong strategic focus on sustainability find a greater opportunity for HR's role to be a strongly supportive one when it comes to sustainability activities.

In table 10.3, all of the correlations between HR's role in sustainability activities and the degree to which an organization has a sustainability focus are significant though not particularly high. The highest correlation is between sustainability performance competencies being explicitly built in to HR processes and the degree to which a company focuses on sustainability. This is an obvious connection point, and it shows that HR has somewhat adjusted its activities to fit the business strategy of a sustainability-oriented organization.

Sustainability and Management Approach

The correlations shown in table 10.4 between HR's role in sustainability activities and the management approach of the organization are surprisingly low. There is a low but significant correlation between the degree to which an organization's management approach focuses on sustainable performance and the degree to which HR plays a role in the organization's sustainability activities. There is also a low nonsignificant correlation between what HR executives say HR's role should be and the use of the sustainable management approach. This is a particularly surprising finding given that a management approach that focuses on sustainability should send a message to the HR function that it should be a major player in the organization's sustainability activities. The fact that this does not seem to be true may be a significant contributor to HR's not being the business partner that it would like to be. Clearly it needs to play a role in the organization that supports the way that it is managed if it wants to be seen as a strategically relevant part of the organization.

As can be seen in table 10.5, there are no significant relationships between HR's belief that it should engage in various sustainability support activities and the degree to which an organization has a sustainable management approach. This is surprising, but it appears that HR executives believe HR should participate in sustainability activities and support it regardless of their organization's strategy.

There is a positive correlation in table 10.5 between the degree to which an organization has a management approach that focuses on sustainable performance and the degree to which sustainability is part of HR processes. Here, there is an alignment between what HR is doing and the way the organization is being managed. However, this correlation is relatively low compared to what might be expected if an organization's HR function was committed to a sustainable management approach.

The results in table 10.5 do show a number of significant correlations between the high-involvement management approach and HR's role in sustainability. The more an organization takes this approach, the more HR seems to be involved in sustainability initiatives and programs. In some respects, this is not surprising and probably reflects the people side of the triple bottom line. High-involvement management focuses

Table 10.5. Relationship of sustainability activities to management approaches

Sustainability	Management Approaches				
	Bureaucratic	Low-Cost Operator	High Involvement	Global Competitor	Sustainable
Sustainability performance and competences *are* explicitly built into HR processes such as selection, rewards, and development.	−.19*	−.04	.33***	.20*	.32***
Sustainability performance and competences *should be* explicitly built into HR processes such as selection, rewards, and development.	.07	.03	−.02	−.02	.01
HR *is involved* in the design of sustainability initiatives and programs.	−.18ᵗ	−.19*	.30***	.05	.23*
HR *should be involved* in the design of sustainability initiatives and programs.	.18ᵗ	.02	.01	−.11	.01
HR *provides* support and expertise in organization design issues that have an impact on sustainability.	−.15	−.17ᵗ	.32***	.02	.23*
HR *should provide* support and expertise in organization design issues that have an impact on sustainability.	.22*	.03	−.11	−.16ᵗ	−.07
HR *provides* change management support for building sustainability into the way my company does business.	−.20*	−.18*	.39***	.03	.18ᵗ
HR *should provide* change management support for building sustainability into the way my company does business.	.20*	.03	−.05	−.14	−.09

Response scale: 1 = strongly disagree; 2 = somewhat disagree; 3 = neither disagree nor agree; 4 = somewhat agree; 5 = strongly agree.
Significance level: ᵗ$p \leq .10$, *$p \leq .05$, **$p \leq .01$, ***$p \leq .001$.

on the people side of organizations. Thus, in an organization with a high-involvement management approach, it is not surprising that HR would be engaged in sustainability practice installation and change management design.

What is surprising in table 10.5 is that there is not a stronger relationship between the "should be" items and the high-involvement approach to management. None of these correlations are significant. Apparently the HR executives surveyed do not necessarily think that HR should emphasize sustainability in their HR systems simply because their organization has a high-involvement approach to management. And as we noted earlier, even when organizations have a sustainable management approach, HR executives do not necessarily think that HR should be more active in the design of sustainability activities.

Conclusion

In most companies, HR is not very active in sustainability activities, although HR executives feel it should be significantly more active. This is true in all the countries studied. The areas where HR executives think it should provide more support are the design of sustainability programs, organizational design, change management, and the way business is conducted. HR executives also believe that sustainability should be built into such HR processes as selection, rewards, and development. Not surprising, HR is more involved in sustainability activities when an organization has a strategic focus. Finally, it is important to note that when HR is active in sustainability, it is much more likely to play a significant role in strategy. This once again makes the point that HR can be a contributor to strategy if it does the right things.

CHAPTER 11

Outsourcing HR

- There is no evidence that outsourcing of HR is in a growth mode.

- By a large margin, the area of HR most likely to be outsourced is employee assistance.

- Benefits is the area that is second with respect to frequency of outsourcing.

- In Europe, the United Kingdom, and China, employee assistance is less likely to be outsourced than in other countries.

- Less than 20 percent of U.S. firms have multiprocess HR outsourcing contracts.

- HR executives rate moderate outsourcing as the most effective approach to outsourcing.

- HR executives rate SAAS (hosted in cloud) as effective.

Outsourcing transactional work is a possible way to improve the effectiveness of an HR function and make it more strategic by reducing the workload of HR organizations, increasing quality, and reducing costs (Lawler, Ulrich, Fitz-enz, and Madden 2004). In the best-case scenario, transaction-outsourcing companies can provide better and cheaper services because they focus on a particular process or area of expertise that is their core competency. In addition, when they provide transaction services, they can capture economies of scale by servicing multiple organizations. They also can improve the processes of organizations because of the knowledge they have.

At the very least, outsourcing can reduce the number of employees who are on the HR department payroll and can create a flexible cost structure when services are needed occasionally or for short periods of time. They also can allow companies to relatively easily increase or decrease the number of people working on their HR programs.

By outsourcing professional and knowledge work, organizations can acquire expertise and strategic information that may not be available internally. Here the hoped-for advantages are not as much related to scale as they are to expertise in areas like HR strategy, organizational development, and training. Particularly in the case of the large consulting firms, they can provide a depth of expertise in their areas of specialization that most companies cannot hope to achieve.

Use of Outsourcing

Table 11.1 shows the degree to which eighteen HR activities were being outsourced in the United States in 2010 (no data were collected in 2013). Activities are grouped by the three factors that our statistical analysis produced; ten items did not group. In 1995, 1998, 2001, 2004, 2007, and 2010, the use of outsourcing varied widely among the activities, but in no case were any of these activities even close to being completely outsourced by a majority of the companies.

Table 11.1. HR outsourcing use, United States					
	Percentages			Means	Correlation with HR Role in Strategy, 2010
Type of Outsourcing	Not at All	Partially	Completely	2010	
Overall outsourcing (mean for all items except union relations)	—	—	—	1.4	.15^t
Human capital forecasting and planning[a]	98.3	1.7	0.0	1.0	.05
Organizational design/ development	—	—	—	1.2	.01
Organizational development	81.5	18.5	0.0	1.2	.12
Organizational design	89.1	10.3	0.6	1.1	−.11
Training	—	—	—	1.5	.19*
Training/education	39.0	59.9	1.1	1.6	.15^t
Management development	56.0	42.3	1.7	1.5	.16*
HR information systems	54.5	41.5	4.0	1.5	.07
Staffing and career development	—	—	—	1.2	.08
Performance appraisal	84.2	15.3	0.6	1.2	.04
Recruitment	48.9	51.1	0.0	1.5	.07
Selection	78.3	21.7	0.0	1.2	.04
Career planning	92.0	8.0	0.0	1.1	−.05
HR metrics and analysis	86.7	13.3	0.0	1.1	.15^t
Benefits	27.0	65.7	7.3	1.8	.08
Compensation	74.4	25.6	0.0	1.3	.09
Legal affairs	48.6	51.4	0.0	1.5	.20**
Executive compensation	67.4	31.4	1.1	1.3	.11
Employee assistance	25.8	34.8	39.3	2.1	.00
Competency/talent assessment	74.7	24.1	1.1	1.3	.14^t
Union relations	90.8	8.0	1.2	1.1	−.01

[a]This item was worded as "HR Planning" prior to 2007.

Significance level: $^t p \leq .10$, $^* p \leq .05$, $^{**} p \leq .01$, $^{***} p \leq .001$.

At one extreme in 2010, over 90 percent of the companies did not outsource human capital forecasting, career planning, or organizational design, all areas in which HR can add considerable strategic value and act as a strategic contributor. However, they are not all areas where HR is particularly active (strategic planning and organizational design) and as a result represent areas of opportunity for HR given their importance.

By a large margin, the most likely area to be completely outsourced is employee assistance, with 39.3 percent of the companies completely outsourcing it in 2010. This is hardly surprising given its personal and confidential nature. Benefits was the next most likely to be outsourced: 73 percent of the companies partially or completely outsourced it. The frequency of outsourcing benefits probably reflects the combination of transactional and specialized knowledge work that it involves. In over 50 percent of companies, training, recruitment, and legal were partially or completely outsourced. Management development was partially outsourced by almost 40 percent of the companies.

Overall, outsourcing occurs in areas where specialized expertise is involved, such as legal affairs, and areas where primarily transactional work occurs, such as benefits administration. This result provides confirmation that organizations are outsourcing to gain both transactional efficiency and expertise.

A comparison between the 1995 and 2010 results shows some areas where there was a small increase in the use of outsourcing: HR information systems, compensation, recruitment, performance appraisal, and legal affairs. Organizational development was less likely to be outsourced in 2010 than in 1995.

A comparison between the 2004 and 2010 data shows essentially no change in the frequency of outsourcing. Thus, although outsourcing has increased slightly since 1995, our data show little evidence of the increased use of outsourcing; the obvious conclusion is that there has been no trend in this direction.

Clearly the opportunity exists for more outsourcing to take place since few companies completely outsource any of their HR activities and many HR activities are barely outsourced. This finding raises the question of whether there will be a new wave of outsourcing that will lead to a significant increase in the amount of outsourcing that takes place.

One possibility is that outsourcing will increase because more and more organizations will decide to outsource their HR administration to the growing number of HR business process outsourcing (BPO) firms that exist. To check on this for the first time, in 2007, we asked whether the companies had a multiple-process HR outsourcing contract: 21 percent said they did, and another 10 percent said they were considering it. We asked this question again in 2010 and got slightly lower answers. Apparently multiprocess outsourcing is not growing even though it promises to reduce costs, and the period from 2007 to 2010 was one during which many companies tried to reduce their costs. Overall, there is little reason to believe there will be a significant increase in most of the types of outsourcing that are shown in table 11.1.

Table 11.1 also shows the relationship between outsourcing and the role that HR plays in strategy. There is little indication that these two issues are related. Only the correlations with management development and legal efforts are significant.

International Results

The amount of outsourcing does not vary greatly among the countries in our international survey (see Lawler and Boudreau 2012 for data). Only three areas show a significant difference: executive compensation, employee assistance, and benefits. All are areas where national laws and practices differ, so it is not surprising there is a difference in the degree to which they are outsourced. For example, China is low in outsourcing benefits and employee assistance in part because suppliers do not exist in these areas.

Strategic Focuses and Management Approaches

There are very few significant relationships between the strategic focuses and outsourcing, a result that is not surprising. The strongest relationship is with growth. Growth puts a stress on the HR delivery capabilities of an organization, and outsourcing can provide a quick way to acquire additional support for a function that is under pressure to serve a larger organization.

There is also little relationship between outsourcing and the management approaches of organizations. This is not surprising, since the five management approaches do not differ in how appropriate outsourcing is.

Impact of HR Outsourcing

In 2007, questions were asked about the impact of outsourcing; they were not asked in 2010 or 2013. Table 11.2 presents the results for 2007. In general, outsourcing does seem to help HR be a business partner, contribute to strategy, or perform high-value-added activities. It seems to have only a small positive impact in virtually every area. The most positive responses are to questions concerned with HR being more strategic and a business partner. Apparently to a limited extent, it does free

Table 11.2. Impact of outsourcing HR services, 2007 (percentages)						
Effect of Outsourcing	Greatly Decreased	Decreased	Stayed the Same	Increased	Greatly Increased	Mean
Overall effectiveness of the HR function	1.2	9.5	31.0	52.4	6.0	3.5
Ability of HR to be a business partner	0.0	8.3	31.0	52.4	8.3	3.6
Ability of HR to contribute to business strategy	0.0	3.7	42.7	47.6	6.1	3.6
Cost of HR services	0.0	32.9	40.2	20.7	6.1	3.0
Quality of HR services	3.6	15.7	34.9	37.3	8.4	3.3
The value HR adds to the organization	0.0	7.0	36.0	47.7	9.3	3.6
Satisfaction of company employees with HR services	1.2	23.8	39.3	26.2	9.5	3.2
Satisfaction of HR staff	2.4	19.0	34.5	36.9	7.1	3.3
Commitment of HR staff	1.2	14.1	47.1	27.1	10.6	3.3
Mining of employee data by HR	0.0	12.7	60.8	20.3	6.3	3.2
Time spent on HR strategy	0.0	4.8	40.5	50.0	4.8	3.5
Use of metrics by HR	1.3	1.3	54.4	38.0	5.1	3.4
Time spent on business strategy by HR	0.0	2.5	43.2	46.9	7.4	3.6
Availability of HR metrics	0.0	9.0	46.2	35.9	9.0	3.4
Use of HR analytical models	1.3	7.9	63.2	23.7	3.9	3.2

up HR to be more strategic and perhaps provide HR with the expertise it needs to be a strategic partner. Overall, 60 percent of the HR executives surveyed report it has a positive impact, only 10 percent report it has a negative impact, and 30 percent report no change.

Outsourcing Effectiveness

A new question in 2007 asked about the effectiveness of different amounts of outsourcing. Table 11.3 presents the US results for 2013, and table 11.4 presents the international results for the same year. The clear winners in the opinion of HR executives are moderate outs–ourcing to a single vendor and software as a service. The worst option is perceived to be no outsourcing. Somewhat surprising are the low effectiveness ratings for substantial outsourcing. The high rating for software as a service is interesting. This question was first asked in 2013, and this approach to outsourcing is relatively new but seems to be quite powerful and effective. If it is used properly, it can provide numerous services and analytical capabilities. Software as a service is rated highly. This clearly is a growth area, and so far in the United States at least, it seems to be producing positive results.

Table 11.3. Effectiveness of outsourcing HR services, 2013 (percentages)						
Amount of Outsourcing	Very Ineffective	Ineffective	Neither	Effective	Very Effective	Mean
No outsourcing	29.5	36.7	25.2	7.9	0.7	2.1
Very limited—only a few transactional services (e.g., payroll)	3.7	29.4	27.2	36.8	2.9	3.1
Moderate outsourcing	1.4	10.8	25.9	56.1	5.8	3.5
Substantial outsourcing	11.6	31.2	33.3	21.0	2.9	2.7
Software as a service (hosted in cloud)	1.4	4.3	31.9	42.8	19.6	3.7

Table 11.4. HR outsourcing approaches, by country							
	2013 Means						
Effectiveness of Outsourcing	United States[1]	Canada[2]	Australia[3]	Europe[4]	United Kingdom[5]	India[6]	China[7]
No outsourcing	2.1	2.5	2.3	2.4	2.1	2.5	2.5
Very limited—only a few transactional services (e.g., payroll)	3.1	3.3	3.5	3.3	3.2	3.5	3.0
Moderate outsourcing	3.5	3.2	3.7	3.3	3.6	3.3	3.5
Substantial outsourcing	2.7	2.3	2.5	2.5	2.7	2.9	2.8
Software as a service (hosted in cloud)[a]	3.7[7]	3.6	3.8	3.7	3.7	—	3.2[1]

Response scale: 1 = very ineffective; 2 = ineffective; 3 = neither; 4 = effective; 5 = very effective.

[a]India was not asked to respond to this question.

[1,2,3,4,5,6,7]Significant differences between countries ($p \leq .05$).

HR Outsourcing Approaches

In order to better understand HR outsourcing, we asked about multi-process HR outsourcing contracts (HRBPO) for the first time in 2007, again in 2010, but not in 2013. As can be seen in table 11.5, less than 20 percent of US firms had one, a slight drop from 2007. Almost 75 percent said they were not considering one. China, like the United States, shows a relatively high adoption rate, with 23 percent reporting they had a contract and a very high percent (32 percent) saying they were considering one.

The satisfaction with HRBPO data in table 11.6 shows a mixed picture. In all the countries except Canada, where only four organizations have a contract, at least 20 percent of all organizations reported they were dissatisfied with their HRBPO relationship. In the United States, 24 percent said they

Table 11.5. Use of HRBPO, by country (percentages)							
	United States[1]		Canada[2]	Australia[3]	Europe[4]	United Kingdom[5]	China[6]
Use of HRBPO	2007	2010					
Yes	22.1	18.9[6]	10.0[6]	11.1[6]	7.5[6]	10.5[6]	23.0[1,2,3,4,5]
No, but seriously considering	9.6	7.0	5.0	0.0	9.4	15.8	32.4
No, not seriously considering	68.3	74.1	85.0	88.9	83.0	73.7	44.6

[1,2,3,4,5,6] Significant differences between countries ($p \leq .05$).

Table 11.6. Satisfaction with HRBPO, by country (percentages)							
	United States[1]		Canada[2]	Australia[3]	Europe[4]	United Kingdom[5]	China[6]
Satisfaction Level	2007	2010					
Very dissatisfied	9.1	8.0[2]	0.0[16]	0.0	0.0	0.0	0.0[2]
Dissatisfied	0.0	8.0	0.0	0.0	25.0	25.0	8.3
Somewhat dissatisfied	13.6	8.0	0.0	33.3	0.0	25.0	27.1
Neither satisfied nor dissatisfied	22.7	8.0	0.0	33.3	25.0	0.0	22.9
Somewhat satisfied	27.3	44.0	0.0	0.0	25.0	25.0	27.1
Satisfied	27.3	20.0	25.0	33.3	25.0	25.0	14.6
Very satisfied	0.0	4.0	75.0	0.0	0.0	0.0	0.0

[1,2,3,4,5,6] Significant differences between countries ($p \leq .05$).

were dissatisfied. It is clear that most firms that do not have an HRBPO contract may be a hard sell for an industry that is committed to growth.

Conclusion

Overall, there is little evidence that outsourcing is in a strong growth mode. As a result, organizations may be missing an opportunity to improve their HR activities. Outsourcing can allow them to access knowledge and expertise that they lack and are not in a good position to develop. They may also be missing a chance to realize economies of scale.

An obstacle to the growth of outsourcing may be the number of problems associated with it, including the apparent difficulty of getting sustained cost and quality advantages. The evidence is mixed on whether it helps HR to be more of a strategic partner. HR executives say it can, but the amount of it is only slightly correlated with the degree to which HR plays a role in strategy. There remains the possibility that outsourcing will grow in the future, but given its failure to do so during the recession, it is not clear what could happen that would cause an increase. One possibility is strong economic growth, which is slightly correlated with the degree to which firms have a growth strategy.

CHAPTER 12

Information Technology in HR

- Human resource information systems (HRIS) are used for most HR processes in all countries, with the exception of China.

- HRIS did not receive very high performance ratings. The highest ratings are in speed, costs, and service.

- HRIS systems are most likely to be effective in companies that have knowledge- and information-based strategies.

- The more activities an HRIS can do, the more effective it is perceived to be.

- HRIS systems are doing little to create social and knowledge networks.

- India's HRIS systems received the highest marks among the countries surveyed.

- System integration and automation increase over time.

- Integration and automation show slight positive relationships to HR's role in strategy and organizational performance.

- Positive HRIS outcomes (efficiency, cost/head count reduction, employee satisfaction, speed) are frequent but not often related to HR's strategic role and organization performance.

- Strategic HRIS outcomes (improving decisions, creating social/ knowledge networks, strategic information, measuring HR impact) are not common.

Information technology (IT) is potentially a way to accomplish HR record keeping, HR transactions, and many other administrative tasks more quickly, efficiently, and accurately. It can enable HR to save money and spend more time on strategic business support, but IT can do more than just serve as an administrative tool. It can be a way to deliver expert advice to managers and employees in areas such as selection, career development, talent management, and compensation. It can analyze data in ways that can guide and support evidence-driven HR practices and policies. It can also facilitate change efforts by assessing the capabilities of the workforce and providing information and training that support change. Finally, it can support the development and implementation of business strategy by providing important information about the capabilities and core competencies of the organization, as well as creating transparency with respect to organizational performance.

Amount of Use

Table 12.1 shows the state of IT-based HR processes from 1995 to 2013. In 2013, 63 percent of companies report using human resource information systems (HRIS) for most or all of their HR processes, a relatively high level of use. Although there is not a consistent pattern of significant increases from 1995 to 2013, there are some increases in comparison to 1995, 1998, and 2001. This is not surprising, particularly in light of the great amount of activity occurring in the HRIS world. In many respects, the increase almost had to occur given the increased popularity of business software and the fact that the major business software companies (e.g., SAP, Oracle, Workday) have HR applications. It is somewhat surprising, given the growth in the use of IT by companies, that there has not been a greater increase in use from 2004 to 2013, and that in 2013, only 63 percent of US companies report that most or all of their processes are IT based.

Table 12.1. State of HRIS, United States							
	Percentages						
State of Information System	1995[1]	1998[2]	2001[3]	2004[4]	2007[5]	2010[6]	2013[7]
Little or no information technology present in the HR function	6.3	8.4	8.3	6.1	7.8	3.8	7.4
Some HR processes are information technology based	45.3	40.3	48.3	32.3	32.0	30.1	29.4
Most processes are information technology based but not fully integrated	40.6	42.9	35.9	48.5	51.5	49.7	55.9
Completely integrated HR information technology system	7.8	8.4	7.6	13.1	8.7	16.4	7.4
Mean[a]	3.50[6]	3.50[6]	3.41[6]	3.69	3.59	3.79[1,2,3]	3.63

[a]Response scale: 1 = no information technology; 2 = little information technology; 3 = some processes integrated; 4 = most processes integrated; 5 = completely integrated.
[1,2,3,4,5,6,7]Significant differences ($p \le .05$). between years.

Table 12.2. State of HRIS, by country							
	Percentages						
State of Information System	United States[1]	Canada[2]	Australia[3]	Europe[4]	United Kingdom[5]	India[6]	China[7]
Little or no information technology present in the HR function	7.4	17.1	18.2	9.8	0.0	15.1	50.7
Some HR processes are information technology based	29.4	39.0	31.8	24.4	57.1	22.6	34.8
Most processes are information technology based but not fully integrated	55.9	41.5	50.0	46.3	39.3	49.1	11.6
Completely integrated HR information technology system	7.4	2.4	0.0	19.5	3.6	13.2	2.9
Mean[a]	3.63[7]	3.27[7]	3.32[7]	3.76[7]	3.46[7]	3.60[7]	2.54[1,2,3,4,5,6]

[a]Response scale: 1 = no information technology; 2 = little information technology; 3 = some processes integrated; 4 = most processes integrated; 5 = completely integrated.
[1,2,3,4,5,6,7]Significant differences between countries ($p \le .05$).

International Results

The international results in table 12.2 show some significant differences in the state of HRISs. China has by far the lowest rate of use. This low rate is not surprising; China lags somewhat behind in the adoption of information technology for most business processes. The rest of the countries have relatively similar rates in 2013. As was true in 2010, Australia has the lowest rate among them. In 2010, the United States had the highest rate, but this is no longer true; Europe is higher.

Type of Use

Data on some of the many uses of IT are presented in table 12.3. In general, these show moderate to low use rates. One change worth noting is an increase in the degree to which HR transactional activities are done on a self-service basis. This most likely is because the greater availability of HRIS allows web-based self-service and it can deliver cost savings.

Overall, these uses of information technology do not show high use rates. All the uses except transactional activities are rated lower than "moderate extent." This is surprising given the growth in the use of information technology and the growing popularity of the cloud and big data. It may be that these uses are being written and talked about more than they are occurring. There are some situations where the use rate is relatively high. Organizations with information-, knowledge-, and

Table 12.3. Use of information technology, United States							
	Means						Correlation with HR Role in Strategy
	1998[1]	2001[2]	2004[3]	2007[4]	2010[5]	2013[6]	
Information Technology	—	—	—	—	—	2.6	**.33***
Transactional HR work is outsourced	2.3	2.3	2.5	2.4	2.3	2.2	**.13**
Some transactional activities that used to be done by HR are done by employees on a self-service basis	2.3[3,4,5,6]	2.5[3,4,5,6]	2.9[1,2]	3.0[1,2]	2.9[1,2]	3.1[1,2]	**.18***
HR advice is available online for managers and employees	—	—	2.5	2.7	2.6	2.5	**.16[t]**
Uses social networks for HR activities such as recruiting, performance management, and work assignments.	—	—	—	—	—	2.7	**.33***
Uses mobile technology to support HR activities such as recruiting, self-service, and communication	—	—	—	—	—	2.3	**.26****
Uses software-as-a-service model (subscription based, hosted in the cloud).	—	—	—	—	—	2.5	**.19***

Response scale: 1 = little or no extent, 2 = some extent, 3 = moderate extent, 4 = great extent, 5 = very great extent. Empty cells indicate that the item was not asked in that year.

[1,2,3,4,5,6,7] Significant differences ($p \le .05$) between years.

Significance level: [t] $p \le .10$, * $p \le .05$, ** $p \le .01$, *** $p \le .001$.

innovation-based strategies are larger users of these information technology approaches.

In addition to an overall significant relationship, there are some individual significant relationships between the use of information technology and HR's role in strategy. The use of social networks and mobile technology is significantly related to the role of HR in strategy. Thus, it appears that the selective use of information technology is yet another way that can help HR play a more significant role in strategy.

IT System Effectiveness

Because of the relative newness of HRISs, relatively little information is available about their overall effectiveness or about their impact on the effectiveness of organizations and their HR systems. In order to measure effectiveness, beginning in 2001 we asked questions about both the effectiveness of HRISs in general and their effectiveness in key areas (table 12.4). We asked some questions starting in 2001; others are new in 2010 and 2013.

As was true in 2001, 2004, 2007, and 2010, the HRISs did not receive very high performance ratings on any of the outcomes. The highest ratings are in the areas of speed, cost, and service, but even there, the highest-rated item received a rating in the middle of the five-point scale. It is hardly surprising that high ratings came in the efficiency area (costs, speed, and service level), since efficiency is an area where IT systems should achieve short-term payoffs. Nevertheless, it is significant that we now have longitudinal data confirming that the systems do, to some extent, improve HR services, reduce costs, and increase speed.

The ratings concerned with business effectiveness are among the lowest. HR executives do not see their HRISs strongly affecting organizational performance, strategic decision making, HR's impact on the business, or human capital decision making. Improving human capital decisions and measuring HR's impact get low ratings. Overall it is clear that HRISs are not yet doing a good job of providing the information that HR executives need to be strategic business partners. Furthermore, there is no sign of improvement; the 2001 results are very similar to the 2013 results. This is disappointing since there are good reasons to believe that HRIS can have a big impact in these areas. The failure of HRISs to have an impact may be in part due to the newness of some of the systems and the fact that organizations are just beginning to learn how to use HRIS as a strategic tool.

We added two new "networks" items in 2010. Both received very low effectiveness ratings in 2010 and 2013. It is clear that HRIS systems are

Table 12.4. HRIS outcomes, United States						
	Means					Correlation with HR Role in Strategy 2013
HRIS Outcomes	2001[1]	2004[2]	2007[3]	2010[4]	2013[5]	
Overall effectiveness[a]	**2.6**	**2.8**	**2.7**	**2.7**	**2.6**	**.16[t]**
Employee satisfaction	**2.4**	**2.7**	**2.6**	**2.7**	**2.5**	**.14**
Efficiency	**2.9**	**3.0**	**2.8**	**2.8**	**2.7**	**.15[t]**
Improve HR services	3.0	3.0	2.9	3.0	2.9	**.26****
Reduce HR transaction costs	2.9	3.0	2.8	3.0	2.8	**.07**
Speed up HR processes	3.1	3.2	3.0	3.0	2.9	**.18***
Reduce the number of employees in HR	2.4	2.6	2.4	2.3	2.4	**.03**
Business effectiveness	**2.2**	**2.3**	**2.5**	**2.5**	**2.5**	**.15[t]**
Provide new strategic information	2.1[4,5]	2.3	2.5	2.5[1]	2.5[1]	**.16[t]**
Integrate HR processes (e.g., training, compensation)	2.4	2.4	2.5	2.4	2.5	**.11**
Measure HR's impact on the business	—	**2.1**	**2.3**	**2.3**	**2.2**	**.20***
Improve human capital decisions of managers outside HR	—	—	**2.4**	**2.3**	**2.3**	**.17***
Effective	—	—	**2.9**	**3.0**	**2.8**	**.16[t]**
Create knowledge networks	—	—	—	**1.9**	**1.9**	**.21***
Build social networks that help get work done	—	—	—	**1.7**	**1.8**	**.20***
Offer a positive user experience	—	—	—	—	**2.5**	**.15[t]**
Represent a state-of-the-art solution	—	—	—	—	**2.2**	**.14**
Use the most advanced technology	—	—	—	—	**2.1**	**.12**

[a]Includes items from Employee Satisfaction, Efficiency, and Business Effectiveness scales only.

Response scale: 1 = little or not extent; 2 = some extent; 3 = moderate extent; 4 = great extent; 5 = very great extent. Empty cells indicate that the item was not asked in that year.

[1,2,3,4,5] Significant difference ($p \le .05$) between years.

Significance level: [t]$p \le .10$, *$p \le .05$, **$p \le .01$, ***$p \le .001$.

not doing much to create networks that help employees share knowledge and facilitate getting work done.

The three items added in 2013 show results that are very similar to the data for the other items. The scores are relatively low. The highest is for user experience; the results for the level of technology being used are lowest.

The relationships between the effectiveness of HRISs and the role of HR in strategy are shown in table 12.4. Most are statistically significant, although the correlations are relatively low. It is somewhat surprising that the highest correlation is with "improve HR services." Except for improving the credibility of HR, it is hard to see how this can do much to help HR be a strategic contributor. Nevertheless, the existence of positive correlations does suggest that HRIS systems can lead to a more important role for HR in strategy.

Only time will tell what impact HRISs will have on HR and organizations. As Boudreau and Ramstad (2003) have noted, a decision science for HR remains elusive, yet it is essential for guiding decision makers through the increasingly daunting amount of information available in HRIS systems. They note that having such a decision science is one reason that data systems in finance, marketing, supply chains, and other areas have been so influential. As the HR profession develops a deeper and more precise decision science, HRISs may become more effective in the HR arena.

International Results

There are some differences among the countries in our international sample. As can be seen in table 12.5, Canada and the United Kingdom have the lowest scores. In the case of the United Kingdom, this is not surprising; it also is a low user of HRISs. Canada's low score is somewhat surprising since it is not one of the lowest HRIS users. The highest scores are those for the United States, Europe, and India. Given the high adoption rate in these countries, this result is not surprising. Finally, China's results are interesting: it is a low user, but its scores are relatively positive, particularly with respect to networks. The high score for networks most likely is the result of a translation problem with the questions wording in Mandarin. After the survey was complete, we were told that these two items were not clear.

Strategic Focuses and Management Approaches

In table 12.6, we see a number of significant relationships between HRIS effectiveness and the strategic focuses. All of the strategic focuses show some significant relationships, with the strongest ones involving knowledge-based and information-based strategies. The next strongest set is with sustainability and innovation. These results are not surprising since all four of these can be aided by an effective HRIS. Only a weak relationship with growth exists, and it fits the pattern we have seen with respect to growth. It seems to be a strategic focus that is quite different from the other four.

There are only a few significant correlations between the management approach items and the HRIS effectiveness items. The global competitor approach scores higher on networks and state-of-the-art solutions. Given their need to manage a dispersed workforce, they most likely put more emphasis on building an effective HRIS.

Table 12.5. HRIS outcomes, by country							
HRIS Outcomes	**Means**						
	United States[1]	**Canada[2]**	**Australia[3]**	**Europe[4]**	**United Kingdom[5]**	**India[6]**	**China[7]**
Overall effectiveness[a]	**2.6[6]**	**2.3[6]**	**2.4[6]**	**2.8**	**2.4[6]**	**3.2[1,2,3,5,7]**	**2.5[6]**
Employee satisfaction	**2.5[6]**	**2.1[6]**	**2.4[6]**	**2.6[6]**	**2.2[6]**	**3.3[1,2,3,5,7]**	**2.4[6]**
Efficiency	**2.7[6]**	**2.3[6]**	**2.6**	**2.8**	**2.5[6]**	**3.3[1,2,5,7]**	**2.6[6]**
Improve HR services	2.9[6]	2.5[6]	2.5[6]	3.0	2.5[6]	3.4[1,2,3,5,7]	2.7[6]
Reduce HR transaction costs	2.8[6]	2.4[6]	2.8	2.8[6]	2.6[6]	3.4[1,2,4,57,]	2.7[6]
Speed up HR processes	2.9[6]	2.5[6]	2.8	3.0	2.7[6]	3.5[1,2,5,7]	2.7[6]
Reduce the number of employees in HR	2.4	1.9[6]	2.3	2.5	2.4	2.7[2]	2.3
Business effectiveness	**2.5[6]**	**2.3[6]**	**2.1[6]**	**2.7**	**2.3[6]**	**3.2[1,2,3,5,7]**	**2.4[6]**
Provide new strategic information	2.5[6]	2.3[6]	2.1[6]	2.7	2.5	3.1[1,2,3,7]	2.3[6]
Integrate HR processes (e.g. training, compensation)	2.5[6]	2.3[6]	2.1[6]	2.8	2.1[6]	3.2[1,2,3,5,7]	2.5[6]
Measure HR's impact on the business	**2.2[6]**	**2.0[6]**	**2.5**	**2.3[6]**	**2.0[6]**	**3.1[1,2,4,5,7]**	**2.3[6]**
Improve human capital decisions of managers outside HR	**2.3[6]**	**2.2[6]**	**2.3[6]**	**2.4[6]**	**2.3[6]**	**3.2[1,2,3,4,5,7]**	**2.3[6]**
Effective	**2.8[6]**	**2.6[6]**	**2.7**	**3.0**	**2.5[6]**	**3.3[1,2,5,7]**	**2.6[6]**
Create knowledge networks	**1.9[6]**	**1.7[6]**	**1.8[6]**	**2.0[6]**	**1.8[6]**	**3.2[1,2,3,4,5,7]**	**2.1[6]**
Build social networks that help get work done	**1.8[6]**	**1.6[6]**	**1.8[6]**	**2.1[6]**	**2.0[6]**	**3.0[1,2,3,4,5,7]**	**2.0[6]**
Offer a positive user experience[b]	**2.5[7]**	**2.2**	**2.3**	**2.5**	**2.3**	**—**	**2.0[1]**
Represent a state-of-the-art solution[b]	**2.2[5]**	**1.7[4]**	**1.9**	**2.5[2,5,7]**	**1.6[1,4]**	**—**	**1.9[4]**
Use the most advanced technology[b]	**2.1[5]**	**1.7[4]**	**2.0**	**2.4[2,5]**	**1.5[1,4]**	**—**	**1.9**

Response scale: 1 = little or no extent; 2 = some extent; 3 = moderate extent; 4 = great extent; 5 = very great extent.

[a] Includes items from Employee Satisfaction, Efficiency, and Business Effectiveness scales only.

[b] India was not asked to respond to this question.

[1,2,3,4,5,6,7] Significant differences between countries ($p \leq .05$).

Effectiveness and Use

Table 12.7 shows the relationship of HRIS system effectiveness and the use of information technology (see table 12.1). There clearly is a strong relationship here, as there was in 2001, 2004, 2007, and 2010. Completely integrated HRISs are rated much higher in all areas. Less strongly related, but still significantly related, are the two network items. This

Table 12.6. Relationship of HRIS outcomes to strategic focuses					
HRIS Outcomes	**Strategic Focuses**				
	Growth	**Information-Based Strategies**	**Knowledge-Based Strategies**	**Sustainability**	**Innovation**
Overall effectiveness[a]	–.01	.15^t	.29***	–.00	.11
Employee satisfaction	–.00	.19*	.34***	.08	.14
Efficiency	–.00	.21*	.32***	.00	.12
Improve HR services	.03	.11	.27***	.05	.13
Reduce HR transaction costs	–.02	.16^t	.26**	.00	.07
Speed up HR processes	.01	.15^t	.29***	–.02	.10
Reduce the number of employees in HR	–.03	.28***	.28***	–.02	.13
Business effectiveness	.02	.04	.17*	–.01	.10
Provide new strategic information	.03	.07	.17*	–.00	.13
Integrate HR processes (e.g. training, compensation)	.03	.03	.15^t	–.02	.06
Measure HR's impact on the business	–.06	.13	.27**	.05	.10
Improve human capital decisions of managers outside HR	.07	.12	.21*	.06	.13
Effective	.09	.17*	.29***	.02	.07
Create knowledge networks	.08	.17*	.26**	.19*	.25**
Build social networks that help get work done	.08	.16^t	.19*	.09	.22*
Offer a positive user experience	.07	.11	.28***	.07	.13
Represent a state-of-the-art solution	.06	.12	.24**	.05	.08
Use the most advanced technology	.08	.09	.22**	.02	.10

[a]Includes items from Employee Satisfaction, Efficiency, and Business Effectiveness scales only.

Response scale: 1 = little or no extent; 2 = some extent; 3 = moderate extent; 4 = great extent; 5 = very great extent.

Significance level: $^t p \le .10$, $^* p \le .05$, $^{**} p \le .01$, $^{***} p \le .001$.

is not surprising since networks can be created without an integrated HRIS system and most systems are not designed to facilitate the development of networks.

The strong relationships between HRIS outcomes and use undoubtedly reflect the power that integrated systems have. They offer the opportunity to do many things, including analyses related to business effectiveness and strategy. For example, it is possible to assess the practicality of a business strategy by determining whether the organization has the

Table 12.7. Relationship of HRIS outcomes to use	
HRIS Outcomes	**HRIS[b]**
Overall effectiveness[a]	**.46*****
Employee satisfaction	**.43*****
Efficiency	**.47*****
Improve HR services	.46***
Reduce HR transaction costs	.46***
Speed up HR processes	.36***
Reduce the number of employees in HR	.31***
Business effectiveness	**.39*****
Provide new strategic information	.35***
Integrate HR processes (e.g., training, compensation)	.39***
Measure HR's impact on the business	**.32*****
Improve human capital decisions of managers outside HR	**.32*****
Effective	**.48*****
Create knowledge networks	**.18***
Build social networks that help get work done	**.14**
Offer a positive user experience	**.36*****
Represent a state-of-the-art solution	**.43*****
Use the most advanced technology	**.43*****

[a]Includes items from Employee Satisfaction, Efficiency, and Business Effectiveness scales only.
[b]HRIS amount of use.
Significance level: [†]$p \leq .10$, *$p \leq .05$, **$p \leq .01$, ***$p \leq .001$.

capability to execute it. It is also possible to determine the impacts of HR programs and more effectively develop and place employees.

Conclusion

Our findings show that HRISs are most effective at providing transactional tools for HR administration. When combined with the data we collected on use, we can see that HRISs are used the most to do what they do best: administration. There is a slow but sure movement toward companies having integrated HR information systems that improve decision making and organizational performances, but there is a long way to go.

HRISs are not rated as more effective in 2013 than they were in 2001. They also are not rated as very effective in an absolute sense. There are many possible reasons for this result, including the fact that they are relatively new and that companies and managers are just beginning to learn how to use them effectively. The technology is advancing rapidly, and many companies may be experiencing difficulties dealing with a technology that is not well developed. Expectations about what HRIS can and should deliver may be rising, and as a result, great improvement is needed just to maintain an existing satisfaction level.

The evidence is quite clear that HRISs are most effective when they fit the strategy of an organization. They are particularly likely to be perceived as successful when used by companies with knowledge- and information-based strategies. Perhaps the strongest finding is that the more activities an HRIS can do and the more services it performs, the more effective it is perceived to be. Thus, in the future, HR should focus on developing comprehensive HRISs.

CHAPTER 13

HR Skills

- HR professionals suffer from a skills deficit that limits their role in business strategy development and implementation.

- The highest-rated skills in importance for HR managers are business understanding and those related to interpersonal dynamics and change management.

- Ratings of HR skills show a moderate level of satisfaction.

- Satisfaction with the skills of HR staff has increased in only a few areas since 1995.

- Satisfaction with HR skills is lowest in China.

- HR skills satisfaction is closely related to HR's involvement in business strategy.

- HR skill satisfaction is highest in organizations that have knowledge-based strategies.

The skills and knowledge of the members of an organization's HR function are perhaps the most important determinant of what it does and how well it performs (Ulrich, Brockbank, Johnson, Sandholtz, and Younger 2008). Much of the high-value-added work HR does is knowledge work that requires considerable expertise in a wide variety of areas. In today's rapidly changing global economy, the knowledge and skill requirements for the members of an organization's staff functions are continuing to evolve just as they are for the firm's core business and technical units. The key issues for HR are what skills and knowledge HR professionals need and what the current level of their skills and knowledge is.

Skill Importance

In 2007, we asked HR executives and managers to rate the importance of a variety of HR skills and knowledge (Lawler and Boudreau 2009). For survey length reasons, we did not ask this question in 2010 or 2013. Table 13.1 shows the results of a statistical analysis that yielded four factors and one item. There is some similarity between our factors and the HR competencies that Ulrich and his partners have identified (Ulrich et al. 2008, 2012). However, ours are more focused on the content knowledge that HR executives need, while theirs include personal traits (e.g., "credible activist"), and as a result there are significant differences.

Although there is some variation in how highly they are rated, most of the skills are rated high in importance. The skills that are rated

Table 13.1. Importance of HR skills, 2007					
	Percentages			Means	
Skills	Not Important	Somewhat Important	Very Important	HR Executives	Managers
HR skills				**2.7**	**2.7**
HR technical skills	1.0	26.8	72.2	2.7	2.9[1]
Process execution and analysis	2.1	29.2	68.8	2.7	2.5[1]
Interpersonal dynamics				**2.8**	**2.7[1]**
Team skills	0.0	12.4	87.6	2.9	2.7
Interpersonal skills	0.0	14.4	85.6	2.9	2.8
Consultation skills	1.0	20.6	78.4	2.8	2.6
Coaching and facilitation	1.0	22.7	76.3	2.8	2.7
Leadership/management	1.0	15.5	83.5	2.8	2.7
Business partner skills				**2.6**	**2.6**
Business understanding	0.0	7.2	92.8	2.9	2.8
Strategic planning	0.0	38.1	61.9	2.6	2.4[1]
Organizational design	3.1	53.6	43.3	2.4	2.7[1]
Change management	0.0	20.6	79.4	2.8	2.8
Cross-functional experience	8.2	51.5	40.2	2.3	2.2
Global understanding	18.6	39.2	42.3	2.2	2.2
Communications	0.0	19.6	80.4	2.8	2.9
Metric skills				**2.4**	**2.3**
Information technology	9.3	55.7	35.1	2.3	2.0[1]
Metrics development	5.2	48.5	46.4	2.4	2.4
Data analysis and mining	6.2	48.5	45.4	2.4	2.3
Managing contractors/vendors	12.4	58.8	28.9	**2.2**	**2.1**

[1]Significant difference ($p \leq .05$) between HR executives and managers.

particularly high include business understanding and skills having to do with interpersonal dynamics and change management. HR executives rate business understanding, team skills and interpersonal skills highest and metrics skills and managing contractor skills lowest in importance. The relatively low rating for managing contractor/vendors is not surprising or concerning. The relatively low rating of metrics skills is another story, however, because it is an area of growing importance and certainly is one that HR functions need to have. Or course, these data were collected in 2007. In the years since then, much more attention has been focused on metrics and big data. As a result, if we had collected data in 2013, we might have seen metrics skills rated higher.

Overall, it is clear that these results support the argument that HR professionals need to have a range of business skills; it is not enough for them to just be good HR technicians. They need to understand the business and what makes it effective. Furthermore, they need to be able to help design the organization, develop teams and leaders, and support change efforts.

Skills Satisfaction

Table 13.2 shows the level of satisfaction with the skills of the HR staff as rated by HR executives in 2013. Not surprisingly, as was true in past surveys, one of the two highest levels of satisfaction is with HR technical skills. The other highest level of satisfaction is with skills that pertain to interpersonal dynamics: team skills, interpersonal skills, consultation skills, and leadership/management skills. This is the only area where

Table 13.2. Satisfaction with skills of HR staff, United States

Skills and Knowledge	Means							Correlation with HR Role in Strategy
	1995[1]	1998[2]	2001[3]	2004[4]	2007[5]	2010[6]	2013[7]	
HR technical	—	—	—	4.0[7]	3.7	3.8	3.7[4]	.40***
Interpersonal dynamics	3.3[3,4,5,6,7]	3.1[3,4,5,6,7]	3.6[1,2]	3.7[1,2]	3.6[1,2]	3.6[1,2]	3.5[1,2]	.54***
Team skills	3.3[3,4,5,6,7]	3.2[3,4,5,6,7]	3.7[1,2]	3.7[1,2]	3.7[1,2]	3.6[1,2]	3.7[1,2]	.36***
Interpersonal skills	3.7[3,4,5]	3.5[3,4,5,6,7]	4.0[1,2]	4.1[1,2]	4.0[1,2]	3.9[2]	3.9[2]	.40***
Consultation skills	3.0[4]	2.9[3,4,5,6]	3.3[2]	3.4[1,2]	3.3[2]	3.3[2]	3.1	.43***
Leadership/management skills	3.0[4,5,6,7]	2.9[3,4,5,6,7]	3.3[2]	3.5[1,2]	3.5[1,2]	3.5[1,2]	3.4[1,2]	.52***
Business partner	—	—	—	3.0	3.0	3.1	2.9	.53***
Business understanding	3.0[3,4,5,6,7]	2.9[3,4,5,6,7]	3.3[1,2]	3.3[1,2]	3.3[1,2]	3.4[1,2]	3.3[1,2]	.38***
Cross-functional experience	2.9	2.8	2.9	2.9	2.8	3.0	2.8	.33***
Strategic planning	—	2.8	2.9	3.0	2.9	3.0	2.7	.42***
Organizational design	—	2.7[4,6]	2.8	3.1[2]	3.0	3.0[2]	2.9	.31***
Global understanding	—	2.6	2.7	2.8	2.8	2.9	2.9	.33***
Change management	—	—	3.1	3.3	3.2	3.2	3.1	.47***
Metrics	—	—	—	2.8	2.7	2.9	2.7	.32***
Information technology	—	—	3.1	3.0	2.9	3.0	3.0	.17[1]
Metrics development	—	—	—	2.7	2.7	2.9[7]	2.6[6]	.36***
Data analysis and mining	—	—	—	2.8	2.5	2.8	2.6	.26**
Sustainability	—	—	—	—	—	—	2.8	.28***
Social media	—	—	—	—	—	—	2.8	.23**
Globalization	—	—	—	—	—	—	2.8	.24**
Risk management	—	—	—	—	—	—	3.0	.20*

Response scale: 1 = very dissatisfied; 2 = dissatisfied; 3 = neither; 4 = satisfied; 5 = very satisfied. Empty cells indicate that the item was not asked in that year.

[1,2,3,4,5,6,7] Significant difference ($p \leq .05$) between years.

Significance level: [1]$p \leq .10$, *$p \leq .05$, **$p \leq .01$, ***$p \leq .001$.

the individual skills show an increased level of satisfaction when the 2010 and 2013 data are compared to earlier data. Business understanding is the only other individual skill that shows a significant increase in satisfaction , clearly a positive for HR. HR must have these skills if it is going to be a business partner. The data would be even more positive for HR if the satisfaction level was continuing to increase, but it is not. The high level of satisfaction with interpersonal skills is positive, but it may reflect HR being an eager-to-please "nice guy" when it could add more value by being an effective business partner and/or metrics expert.

A relatively low area of satisfaction is business partner skills. A comparison of the data from 1998 with those from 2013 shows a significant increase in satisfaction with business understanding. However, there still is not a positive level of satisfaction with the substantive business support areas of strategic planning, organizational design, and global understanding. Satisfaction with change management skills remains slightly above the neutral point. Finally, the HR staff continues to have a low level of cross-functional experience, a factor that may well contribute to the relatively low scores in the business partner area.

It is encouraging that HR professionals understand the business better than they did in 1998. However, they still do not appear to bring substantive business expertise to the table. This deficit clearly has to change if HR is to influence an organization's strategic direction. It is a critical weakness with respect to HR's performing as an effective strategic contributor. Fixing this deficit requires going well beyond simple business acumen to being able to create a truly unique perspective on strategy through the lens of HR and human capital.

As in 2004, 2007, and 2010, the lowest satisfaction level is with metrics and information technology skills and there was no increase in the level from 2004 to 2013. Apparently HR managers are not improving their skills in this critical area. Metrics skills are particularly critical in terms of the ability of the HR function to play a major business strategy role. Bringing data and performing data analyses are critical in many business decisions; thus, it is particularly important that HR executives have good skills in these areas.

The four new items added to the 2013 survey—sustainability, social media, globalization, and risk management—are all areas of increased importance in today's business environment. None of them have received high satisfaction ratings despite the fact that a great deal of attention has been focused on their importance. In chapter 10, we presented data suggesting that HR is not active in the sustainability area, so this result is not surprising. The same cannot be said for social media, globalization, and risk management. They are important issues for most organizations and areas where human capital issues are front and center. HR executives need to improve the skills in them.

International Results

Except for China, the skills satisfaction results for the other countries are very similar to those for the United States (see table 13.3). With one exception, no other country stands out as having a particularly high or low level of skills satisfaction in all areas. India does show a higher level of skills satisfaction with metrics skills. This, combined with India's higher score on information technology use, suggests that the large

Table 13.3. Satisfaction with skills of HR staff, by country							
	Means						
Skills and Knowledge	**United States[1]**	**Canada[2]**	**Australia[3]**	**Europe[4]**	**United Kingdom[5]**	**India[6]**	**China[7]**
HR technical skills	**3.7[7]**	**3.6[7]**	**3.8[7]**	**3.4**	**3.7[7]**	**3.3**	**2.9[1,2,3,5]**
Interpersonal dynamics	**3.5[7]**	**3.7[7]**	**3.5[7]**	**3.4[7]**	**3.5[7]**	**3.4[7]**	**2.8[1,2,3,4,5,6]**
Team skills	3.7[7]	3.6[7]	3.6[7]	3.5[7]	3.7[7]	3.5[7]	2.9[1,2,3,4,5,6]
Interpersonal skills	3.9[7]	4.0[7]	3.9[7]	3.8[7]	3.7	3.7[7]	3.2[1,2,3,4,6]
Consultation skills	3.1[7]	3.6[7]	3.3	3.0	3.2	3.1	2.6[1,2]
Leadership/management skills	3.4[7]	3.5[7]	3.4	3.3	3.2	3.3[7]	2.6[1,2,6]
Business partner skills	**2.9[7]**	**3.1[7]**	**3.2**	**2.9**	**3.0**	**3.2[7]**	**2.6[1,2,6]**
Business understanding	3.3	3.2	3.5	3.2	3.4	3.4	2.9
Cross-functional experience	2.8[2]	3.3[1]	3.0	2.7	2.7	3.1	2.8
Strategic planning	2.7	3.1[7]	3.1	2.6	2.6	3.2[7]	2.5[2,6]
Organizational design	2.9	3.0	3.2	2.9	3.1	3.2[7]	2.6[6]
Global understanding	2.9[7]	2.8[7]	2.8	3.0[7]	3.0[7]	3.0[7]	2.1[1,2,4,5,6]
Change management	3.1[7]	3.2[7]	3.3[7]	3.0	3.3[7]	3.2[7]	2.4[1,2,3,5,6]
Metrics skills	**2.7[6]**	**2.8**	**2.8**	**2.6[6]**	**2.7**	**3.2[14]**	**2.7**
Information technology	3.0	3.1	3.0	2.9	2.7	3.4[7]	2.8[6]
Metrics development	2.6[6]	2.5	2.9	2.5	2.7	3.1[1]	2.8
Data analysis and mining	2.6[6]	2.6	2.6	2.4[6]	2.6	3.1[14]	2.6
Sustainability[a]	**2.8**	**3.0**	**2.8**	**3.1**	**2.9**	**—**	**2.7**
Social media[a]	**2.8**	**2.9**	**2.8**	**2.7**	**2.6**	**—**	**2.5**
Globalization[a]	**2.8[7]**	**2.7**	**2.8**	**3.0[7]**	**2.9**	**—**	**2.3[1,4]**
Risk management[a]	**3.0[7]**	**2.9**	**3.4[7]**	**2.7**	**3.0**	**—**	**2.5[1,3]**

Response scale: 1 = very dissatisfied; 2 = dissatisfied; 3 = neither; 4 = satisfied; 5 = very satisfied.

[a]India was not asked to respond to this question.

[1,2,3,4,5,6,7] Significant differences between countries ($p \leq .05$).

companies we surveyed in India are at least equal to their global competitors when it comes to HR information systems.

China has lower satisfaction levels with HR technical skills, interpersonal dynamics skills, and business partner skills. As was true in 2010, it has similar satisfaction levels with respect to metrics skills. There is one positive: China scores well on cross-functional experience.

Overall, the satisfaction with skills scores are low for all countries on an absolute basis. This is particularly true for business partner skills and metrics skills, clearly areas that HR professionals in all countries need to improve.

Managers' Satisfaction with Skills

In 2010, we collected satisfaction data comparing the responses of HR executives with those of other managers on skill satisfaction (Lawler and Boudreau 2012). The result was surprising: in every skill area, HR executives were actually less satisfied with the skills of the HR staff than are other managers. Interestingly, this trend was also found in our 2004 and 2007 surveys, the first ones that gathered data from managers on skill satisfaction. We have no data in our survey that identify the cause of this pattern, but it may be that HR suffers from a bit of an inferiority complex, because it is often on the defensive and criticized by others in organizations and in the press.

The differences between the views of HR executives and managers were particularly striking in the area of metrics and business partner skills. In the 2010 data, managers rated HR as significantly more skillful in metrics development and data analysis and mining than did HR executives. We suspect that this result may arise in part because managers have low expectations and may be impressed with the mere existence of HR measures, data, and scorecards. HR executives, in contrast, may be better able to see the untapped potential in such systems.

All of the business partner skill areas were rated considerably lower by HR executives than they were by managers. This appears to be one area where HR underestimates its skills. What may need to happen for HR to become more of a business partner is for it to realize that it often has something to contribute in this area and that others see it as capable of adding value. Perhaps it needs to knock on its business partner's door more often; our data suggest that if it does, it is likely to find a more favorable reception than it expects.

Despite the fact that HR executives and managers differ in just how satisfied they are with certain HR skills, they are in general agreement when it comes to which skills they are most and least satisfied with.

When we correlated the mean satisfaction levels for managers and HR executives, we found a very high correlation ($r = .88$, $p \leq .001$). Thus, it seems that HR executives and managers are in general agreement about what HR can do well and what it cannot do well.

Role in Strategy

The relationship between HR skills satisfaction and HR's role in strategy is shown in table 13.2. The correlations for HR technical skills, interpersonal dynamics, business partner skills, and metrics skills are statistically significant. The four business partner areas (sustainability, social media, globalization, and risk management) are related to HR's role in strategy but at a lower level. The significant correlations between HR technical skills and HR's role in strategy support the view that HR technical skills are required in order to get involved in business strategy. The correlations of role in strategy with interpersonal dynamics and business partner skills were expected to be high, given that they are truly the foundation for contributing to business strategy from both an implementation and a development point of view. The correlations with metrics skills are not as high as the others, but they are significant. These skills certainly are potentially useful in strategy development and implementation, so it is not surprising that they are related.

The relatively low correlations for sustainability, social media, globalization, and risk management are not surprising. Although they are important factors in strategy development, they are not core HR issues and as a result are most likely not key to HR playing a role in strategy development. However, the fact that they are related suggests that HR can play a larger role in strategy development by developing them.

In 2010, a similar picture of the relationship of HR skills and HR's role in strategy existed in the data from managers. All the skills areas were significantly related to managers' perception of HR, and the relationships were stronger than they were for HR executives. Not surprisingly, business partner skills were strongly related to managers' perceptions of HR being involved with strategy. Metrics skills also were strongly related to HR's role in strategy. Overall, our findings about the relationship of HR skill satisfaction and the strategic role of HR strongly suggest that technical, interpersonal, metrics, and business partner skills are all critical to HR's role in strategy. This is not surprising since, with the exception of HR technical skills, these are skills that are related to the development and implementation of business strategies.

Overall Skill Levels

Despite the improvement in satisfaction with skills in some areas, as we see in table 13.4, the percentage of HR professionals with the necessary overall skills has not changed significantly from 1995 to 2013 in the judgment of HR executives. Very few HR executives report that over 80 percent of their staff have the necessary skills. This disappointing rating suggests that the HR function in many companies is staffed with many individuals who lack the skills they need in order to perform well.

International Results

The international results on skill sets are shown in table 13.5. All but two countries, Australia and China, show the same result. Australia shows that a slightly higher percentage of HR professionals have the necessary skill set, while China shows a much lower percentage of professionals with the necessary skill set. This is not surprising given the low skill satisfaction scores in table 13.3 for China. Together they provide strong evidence that HR professionals in China need to greatly improve their skills.

Strategic Focuses

The relationship between the strategic focuses and HR skill satisfaction as rated by HR executives is shown in table 13.6. All the correlations are positive except for those with growth.

Overall, organizations with stronger strategic focuses have HR functions with better skill sets. It is easy to see why having information, knowledge, sustainability, and innovation focuses would lead to better skills in the HR area. They often require HR functions that are able not only to do HR technical work, but are able to design systems and develop talent that supports organizational performance and knowledge development. The results for social media are interesting. Satisfaction with the skills of HR in this area is correlated with the three strategic focuses (information, knowledge, and innovation) that are most likely to gain from having a social media capability.

Management Approaches

The pattern of correlation between HR skills satisfaction and the five management approaches shown in table 13.7 is very interesting. The bureaucratic and low-cost-operator approaches are negatively related to all the skills. This most likely is due to the low importance these approaches place on human capital, which leads to having HR functions with low skill levels.

The management approach that focuses the most on human capital, high involvement, has significant positive relationships with all types of HR skills satisfaction. This is not surprising since they place a major emphasis on talent and talent management, and therefore need skilled HR managers.

Table 13.4. HR professionals with necessary skill set, United States

Have Skills	Percentages						
	1995	1998	2001	2004	2007	2010	2013
None	0.0	0.0	0.0	0.0	0.0	0.0	0.9
1–20%	0.0	1.7	4.7	2.1	2.0	6.3	1.8
21–40%	18.6	15.1	18.9	12.4	17.3	16.0	17.7
41–60%	34.9	38.7	33.1	37.1	33.7	29.7	37.2
61–80%	37.2	40.3	33.1	34.0	36.7	35.4	36.3
81–99%	8.5	4.2	10.1	11.3	10.2	11.4	6.2
100%	0.8	0.0	0.0	3.1	0.0	1.1	0.0
Mean	4.38	4.30	4.25	4.49	4.36	4.33	4.25

Response scale: 1 = none; 2 = 1–20 percent; 3 = 21–40 percent; 4 = 41–60 percent; 5 = 61–80 percent; 6 = 81–99 percent; 7 = 100 percent.

No significant differences ($p \leq .05$) between years.

Table 13.5. HR professionals with necessary skill set, by country

Have Skills	Means						
	United States[1]	Canada[2]	Australia[3]	Europe[4]	United Kingdom[5]	India[6]	China[7]
None	0.9	0.0	0.0	0.0	0.0	0.0	0.0
1–20%	1.8	6.1	10.0	0.0	7.4	8.0	18.2
21–40%	17.7	15.2	0.0	34.4	14.8	22.0	47.3
41–60%	37.2	27.3	35.0	40.6	25.9	22.0	21.8
61–80%	36.3	42.4	35.0	25.0	40.7	38.0	12.7
81–99%	6.2	9.1	20.0	0.0	11.1	10.0	0.0
100%	0.0	0.0	0.0	0.0	0.0	0.0	0.0
Mean	4.25[7]	4.33[7]	4.55[7]	3.91	4.33[7]	4.20[7]	3.29[1,2,3,5,6]

Response scale: 1 = none; 2 = 1–20 percent; 3 = 21–40 percent; 4 = 41–60 percent; 5 = 61–80 percent; 6 = 81–99 percent; 7 = 100 percent.

[1,2,3,4,5,6,7] Significant differences between countries ($p \leq .05$).

Table 13.6. Relationship of HR skills satisfaction to strategic focuses

Skills	Strategic Focuses				
	Growth	Information-Based Strategies	Knowledge-Based Strategies	Sustainability	Innovation
HR technical	−.07	.08	.15[t]	.05	.11
Interpersonal dynamics	−.14	.16[t]	.24**	.23*	.22*
Business partner	−.14	.16[t]	.24**	.18*	.28**
Metrics	−.22*	.25**	.29***	.15	.25**
Sustainability	−.02	.02	.09	.38***	.12
Social media	−.02	.26**	.20*	.04	.25**
Globalization	.09	.10	.11	.05	.16[t]
Risk management	−.23*	.08	.07	−.10	.06

Significance level: [t] $p \leq .10$, * $p \leq .05$, ** $p \leq .01$, *** $p \leq .001$.

	Management Approaches				
Skills	**Bureaucratic**	**Low-Cost Operator**	**High Involvement**	**Global Competitor**	**Sustainable**
HR technical	–.14	–.22*	.20*	–.17†	–.02
Interpersonal dynamics	–.18*	–.27**	.38***	–.11	.11
Business partner	–.22*	–.23*	.30***	–.06	.07
Metrics	–.04	–.18*	.22*	–.12	.01
Sustainability	–.24**	–.24**	.33***	–.11	.19*
Social media	–.21*	–.22*	.25**	–.04	.02
Globalization	–.19*	–.13	.14	.13	.01
Risk management	.02	–.07	.06	–.07	.05

Table 13.7. Relationship of HR skills satisfaction to management approaches

Significance level: †$p \leq .10$, *$p \leq .05$, ** $\leq .01$, *** $p \leq .001$.

It is surprising that globalization and risk management are not related to any of the management approaches. This may be due to their not being traditional HR skill areas and, as a result, not a focus of HR that is influenced by the management approach.

Conclusion

The results suggest that HR professionals suffer from a skills deficit that limits their role in business strategy development and implementation. It is notable that there is at best only moderate satisfaction with all HR skills: no rating by HR executives was higher than a mean of 3.9 on a five-point scale, and that was on interpersonal skills. Most ratings in the countries studied fall around the neutral point. Of particular concern are the relatively low ratings given to business partner skills, since they are related to HR playing a significant role in strategy. On the encouraging side, there has been an improvement in some business partner skills. Still, much work remains to be done on enhancing HR skills, as well as developing a common understanding about the level those skills need to be at in order to have an effective HR organization.

CHAPTER 14

Effectiveness of the HR Organization

- HR is rated most effective at delivering HR services.

- HR is rated least effective at analyzing HR and business metrics; also low is helping to develop business strategies.

- HR services are rated as very important, as are contributions to the business and strategy.

- Chinese HR executives attach low importance to making contributions to the business and strategy.

- The effectiveness of HR organizations is strongly related to their role in strategy.

Determining the effectiveness of an HR organization must be based on an assessment of its performance in a number of areas. The most obvious area is service delivery, but good service delivery is not enough. To be an effective contributor to organizational performance effectiveness, HR also has to support current business performance by contributing to effective employment relationships and good staffing and strategic talent management decisions. In addition, it needs to deliver value with respect to business strategy, organizational change, and organizational design.

HR Effectiveness

HR executives were asked to judge the overall effectiveness of their HR organizations and their effectiveness in performing twelve activities. (In 2010 only, non-HR managers were also asked to judge the effectiveness of HR. See Lawler and Boudreau 2012.). As shown in table 14.1, our statistical analysis produced three groups of effectiveness items: services, corporate roles, and business and strategy

The results for HR executives show ratings for 2013 that are generally at the same level as the 2007 and 2010 ratings and slightly lower than the 2004 ratings. Many of the ratings are higher than they were in 1998 and 2001. Given these results, the best conclusion is that HR's performance has not improved since 2004 in the opinion of HR executives.

The effectiveness ratings from 2001, 2004, 2007, 2010, and 2013 are highest for the HR services area. The highest-rated items in the survey are providing HR services and being an employee advocate. This is consistent with other studies, which have found that HR tends to be rated particularly high when it comes to the delivery of basic HR services (Csoka and Hackett 1998).

HR receives its lowest effectiveness ratings in the business and strategy area. The ratings by both HR executives in this survey and managers in past surveys are lowest on developing business strategy. However, being a business partner is rated relatively high. This finding supports the point made in chapter 1 that there is a difference between being a business partner and having an active role in strategy development. When managers and HR executives consider what a successful business partnership is, they do not seem to see it as synonymous with playing an active role in developing and implementing business strategies.

Table 14.1. Effectiveness of the HR organization, United States								
				Means				Correlation with HR Role in Strategy
Activities	1995[1]	1998[2]	2001[3]	2004[4]	2007[5]	2010[6]	2013[7]	
Overall effectiveness (all items)	—	—	—	**6.8**	**6.4**	**6.4**	**6.4**	**.60*****
HR services	—	—	—	**7.0**	**6.7**	**6.9**	**6.6**	**.51*****
Providing HR services	7.1[4,6]	7.0[4,6]	7.3	7.8[1,2]	7.4	7.7[1,2]	7.4	**.42*****
Being an employee advocate	—	6.8	7.2	7.4	7.3	7.1	7.4	**.37*****
Analyzing HR and business metrics	—	—	—	5.9	5.3	5.9	5.3	**.32*****
Preparing talent for the future	—	—	—	—	—	—	6.4	**.48*****
Corporate roles	—	—	—	**6.9[6]**	**6.5**	**6.2[4]**	**6.3**	**.51*****
Managing outsourcing	—	—	—	7.3[5,6,7]	6.1[4]	5.9[4]	6.1[4]	**.34*****
Operating HR centers of excellence	—	5.5[4,5,6,7]	5.6[4,5,7]	6.8[2,3]	6.7[2,3]	6.3[2]	6.4[2,3]	**.49*****
Operating HR shared service units	—	5.7[4,6]	6.0	6.9[2]	6.3	6.6[2]	6.4	**.33*****
Working with the corporate board	—	—	—	7.1[6]	6.8	6.2[4]	6.7	**.43*****
Business and strategy	—	—	—	**6.5**	**6.1**	**6.4**	**6.1**	**.59*****
Providing change consulting services	5.8	5.5[4]	5.7	6.5[2]	5.9	6.1	5.8	**.45*****
Being a business partner	6.3	6.5	6.4	7.1	6.8	6.9	6.8	**.50*****
Helping to develop business strategies	—	6.2	5.8	6.0	5.8	5.9	5.6	**.64*****
Improving decisions about human capital	—	—	—	6.7	6.1	6.4	6.3	**.47*****

Response scale: 1 = not meeting needs, 10 = all needs met. Empty cells indicate that the item was not asked in that year.

[1,2,3,4,5,6,7] Significant difference ($p \leq .05$) between years.

Significance level: [†]$p \leq .10$, *$p \leq .05$, ** $p \leq .01$, *** $p \leq .001$.

The ratings of HR's performance in its corporate roles are mixed. HR gets low ratings on managing outsourcing. It gets higher ratings on work with the board, but as we discussed in chapter 4, it has a limited role with respect to boards.

In order to better understand the overall performance ratings that HR executives gave to the HR function, we analyzed these ratings further. We did a regression analysis in order to see how their ratings of specific activities were related to those of overall performance. The most important determinant of HR executives' overall rating is their rating of HR's performance in delivering services. Next in line was change consulting services. When we ran these analyses on the 2010 data that we gathered from nonmanagers, we got a different result. For the nonmanagers, the best predictors were being a business partner and developing business strategies (Lawler and Boudreau 2012). Put together, these findings suggest that when it comes to the effectiveness of HR, HR executives think of how it does as a service deliverer, while managers think of how it does as a business partner. One clear implication is that in order to be seen by others as effective, HR needs to perform better as a strategic partner, currently a relatively low performance area for it.

One final way to look at the scores on effectiveness concerns their absolute level. The ratings are on a ten-point scale; thus, even the highest average rating of 7.4 in 2013 falls significantly short of the top of the scale. Particularly low is the rating for analyzing HR and business metrics, an area of growing importance. Also low are developing business strategies and change consulting. Clearly there is still plenty of room for HR to improve its effectiveness, particularly in activities related to the business and strategy.

International Results

The international data show some significant differences in HR organization effectiveness ratings, most of which concern China (table 14.2). In all three effectiveness areas (services, corporate roles, and strategy) and overall effectiveness, the results are much lower for China. This is not surprising given the low ratings of the skills of the HR managers in China. That said, the ratings are somewhat lower for China than might have been expected. Overall, the difference between China and the other countries is larger here than anywhere else, and this is the most important area since it is concerned with the effectiveness of the function.

The United States and India show the most positive data overall, but the rest of the countries are very close. Europe and Australia are rated lower on the average of all items, and Europe is rated much lower in three

Table 14.2. Effectiveness of the HR organization, by country							
	Means						
Activities	United States[1]	Canada[2]	Australia[3]	Europe[4]	United Kingdom[5]	India[6]	China[7]
Overall effectiveness (all items)	**6.4[7]**	**6.4[7]**	**5.9**	**5.6**	**6.2[7]**	**6.4[7]**	**4.9[1,2,5,6]**
HR services	**6.6[7]**	**6.7[7]**	**6.1**	**6.2**	**6.6[7]**	**6.6[7]**	**5.4[1,2,5,6]**
Providing HR services	7.4[7]	7.5[7]	6.7	7.3[7]	7.6[7]	7.3[7]	5.6[1,2,4,5,6]
Being an employee advocate	7.4[7]	7.2[7]	6.3	6.8[7]	7.4[7]	6.5[7]	5.0[1,2,4,5,6]
Analyzing HR and business metrics	5.3	5.8	5.1	4.8	5.1	6.1	5.5
Preparing talent for the future[a]	6.4	6.3	6.1	6.0	6.1	—	5.5
Corporate roles	**6.3[7]**	**5.7**	**5.8**	**5.5**	**6.3[7]**	**6.2[7]**	**4.2[1,5,6]**
Managing outsourcing	6.1[7]	5.9[7]	5.8	4.8	5.5	5.6[7]	4.0[1,2,6]
Operating HR centers of excellence	6.4[7]	6.5[7]	5.8	6.0[7]	6.7[7]	6.7[7]	4.2[1,2,4,5,6]
Operating HR shared service units	6.4[7]	6.4[7]	5.9	5.8	6.1[7]	6.2[7]	4.3[1,2,5,6]
Working with the corporate board	6.7[7]	6.2	6.1	5.5	6.7[7]	6.3[7]	4.7[1,5,6]
Business and strategy	**6.1[7]**	**6.3[7]**	**6.0**	**5.5**	**6.3[7]**	**6.2[7]**	**4.8[1,2,5,6]**
Providing change consulting services	5.8[7]	6.1[7]	5.7	5.3	6.3[7]	5.9[7]	4.3[1,2,5,6]
Being a business partner	6.8[7]	6.7[7]	6.6	6.0	7.1[7]	6.8[7]	5.1[1,2,5,6]
Helping to develop business strategies	5.6	6.3[7]	5.5	4.8	6.0	5.9	4.7[2]
Improving decisions about human capital	6.3[7]	6.3	6.1	5.7	5.9	6.6[7]	5.1[1,6]

Response scale: 1 = not meeting needs, 10 = all needs met.

[a]India was not asked to respond to this question.

[1,2,3,4,5,6,7]Significant differences between countries ($p \le .05$).

areas. As was true in 2010, Europe has a particularly low rating on managing outsourcing. As noted earlier, outsourcing is not especially popular in Europe. It is impossible to determine from our study the degree to which its lack of popularity is due to poor management. All we can say is that it is not as popular or successful elsewhere in the world as it is in the United States.

Role in Strategy

Table 14.1 shows the correlations between the role that HR plays in strategy and its effectiveness. Many of these correlations are high. Not surprisingly, the strongest pattern of relationships has to do with the effectiveness of HR performance in the business and strategy area. The more effective HR is in this area, the more active role it plays in strategy formulation. The implication is clear: if HR wants to play a more important role in strategy formulation, it needs to be more effective when it comes to the business and strategy activities listed in table 14.1.

Effectiveness in providing HR services is significantly related to the strategic role of HR. It is impossible to tell from the data whether the correlations with service effectiveness mean that providing good services is prerequisite to playing a strategic role or simply that effective HR organizations that are doing a good job at service delivery are also partners in strategy. Our view is that it most likely means that delivering high-quality services is imperative if HR wants to be a strategic contributor.

The Importance of HR Performance

The results for the ratings of the importance of HR performance in table 14.3 are generally high for the 2004, 2007, 2010, and 2013 data (asked for the first time in 2004). It is not surprising that HR executives see overall HR performance as very important. The highest importance ratings for 2013 concern improving decisions about human capital and being a business partner, a pattern that is similar to the one found in 2007 and 2010 in the ratings by HR executives and managers. The lowest ratings in 2013 are given to the corporate role items.

In 2013, HR executives rate providing HR services very highly. In our 2010 study, non-HR managers also rated it the highest (Lawler and Boudreau 2012). This finding once again makes the point that HR must not lose sight of the importance of delivering basic HR services. It also reinforces the pattern we saw earlier: business leaders value HR's contribution to human capital management more highly than they do its developing business strategies. One implication of this pattern is that HR leaders may need to do some selling to the non-HR community with respect to what they can contribute to business strategy.

The relatively high importance rating for all the performance areas except managing outsourcing highlights again the challenge HR faces. It needs to provide services as well as contribute to corporate strategy and business effectiveness.

As for the correlations between HR's role in strategy and the HR activity importance ratings, a number of items are statistically significant. Not surprisingly, playing a major role in strategy is associated with placing high importance on the various corporate roles and on the business and strategy items.

Table 14.3. Importance of HR activities, United States					
	Means				**Correlation with HR Role in Strategy**
Activities	**2004**[1]	**2007**[2]	**2010**[3]	**2013**[4]	
Overall Importance (all items)	**8.1**	**8.0**	**7.9**	**8.0**	**.23***
HR services	**8.2**	**8.0**	**8.2**	**8.4**	**.13**
Providing HR services	9.0	8.5	8.7	8.5	.04
Being an employee advocate	7.9	7.5	7.9	7.8	.05
Analyzing HR and business metrics	7.9	8.2	8.2	8.3	.14
Preparing talent for the future	—	—	—	9.2	.12
Corporate roles	**7.6**	**7.3**	**7.2**	**7.4**	**.25***
Managing outsourcing	7.6[2,3,4]	6.6[1]	6.5[1]	6.2[1]	.18[t]
Operating HR centers of excellence	7.7	7.9	7.9	7.9	.27**
Operating HR shared service units	7.6	7.4	7.6	7.8	.20*
Working with the corporate board	8.0[3]	7.2	7.2[1]	7.8	.06
Business and strategy	**8.4**	**8.6**	**8.3**	**8.4**	**.21***
Providing change consulting services	8.2	8.3	7.9	8.0	.26**
Being a business partner	9.0	9.1	8.8	9.0	.13
Helping to develop business strategies	8.0	8.4[4]	7.9	7.7[2]	.09
Improving decisions about human capital	8.3	8.8	8.6	8.8	.22*

Response scale: 1 = not important, 10 = very important. Empty cells indicate that the item was not asked in that year.

[1,2,3,4] Significant difference ($p \le .05$) between years.

Significance level: [t] $p \le .10$, * $p \le .05$, ** $p \le .01$, *** $p \le .001$.

International Results

The ratings of the importance of HR performance show some interesting country differences. As can be seen in table 14.4, the overall importance of HR is rated as least important by China. Particularly striking are the low importance ratings given to the corporate role items. This clearly is an area that HR managers in China do not see as important as other executives feel it is. They do agree with executives from other countries that it is the least important of the three areas.

Table 14.4. Importance of HR activities, by country							
	Means						
Activities	United States[1]	Canada[2]	Australia[3]	Europe[4]	United Kingdom[5]	India[6]	China[7]
Overall Importance (all items)	**8.0[7]**	**8.3**	**8.3**	**7.6**	**8.4[7]**	**7.5**	**7.3[1,5]**
HR services	**8.4[67]**	**8.6[7]**	**8.4**	**8.1**	**8.6**	**7.8[1]**	**7.8[1,2]**
Providing HR services	8.5[7]	9.3[6,7]	8.6	8.4	8.8[7]	8.0[2]	7.6[1,2,5]
Being an employee advocate	7.8	7.8	7.3	7.3	8.2	7.7	7.4
Analyzing HR and business metrics	8.3	8.4	8.6	7.6	8.3	7.6	7.9
Preparing talent for the future[a]	9.2[7]	9.0	8.9	9.0	9.2	—	8.2[1]
Corporate roles	**7.4**	**7.2**	**7.6**	**6.5**	**7.8**	**7.2**	**6.8**
Managing outsourcing	6.2	6.0	6.2	5.6	6.4	6.4	5.6
Operating HR centers of excellence	7.9	8.6[4,7]	8.1	6.9[2,5]	8.6[4]	7.6	7.3[2]
Operating HR shared service units	7.8	8.0	8.3	6.5	8.1	7.3	7.1
Working with the corporate board	7.8	6.9	7.7	7.1	8.1	7.4	7.3
Business and strategy	**8.4[7]**	**8.5[7]**	**8.8[7]**	**8.3**	**8.6[7]**	**7.6**	**7.4[1,2,3,5]**
Providing change consulting services	8.0[7]	8.0	8.2	8.1	8.2	7.4	7.0[1]
Being a business partner	9.0[6,7]	9.0[6,7]	9.2[6,7]	8.8[7]	9.1[6,7]	7.8[1,2,3,5]	7.5[1,2,3,4,5]
Helping to develop business strategies	7.7	8.4	8.5	7.8	8.4	7.5	7.6
Improving decisions about human capital	8.8[6,7]	8.6[7]	9.1[6,7]	8.5[7]	8.5[7]	7.7[1,3]	7.3[1,2,3,4,5]

Response scale: 1 = not important, 10 = very important.

[a]India was not asked to respond to this question.

[1,2,3,4,5,6,7] Significant differences between countries ($p \le .05$).

These results fit with the general tendency for HR to be rated low in China. With respect to effectiveness, it does raise the question of causation: Is HR unimportant because it performs poorly, or does it perform poorly because it is considered to be unimportant? The latter seems like the better explanation.

Effectiveness and Importance

The results of a comparison between the importance assigned to HR activities and their effectiveness are shown in table 14.5. To create this table, the effectiveness ratings were subtracted from the importance ratings. Thus, the larger the number is, the bigger the gap between importance and effectiveness and the greater the cause for concern because it means that HR is doing an important activity poorly.

The results are relatively similar in 2007, 2010, and 2013. For all years, most of the largest numbers are in the business and strategy area, with a small gap in the cases of being an employee advocate and managing outsourcing. There is a very small gap for working with corporate boards.

Table 14.5. HR importance and effectiveness rating differences, United States			
	Mean Differences		
Activities	2007[1]	2010[2]	2013[3]
Overall importance/effectiveness (all items)	**1.6**	**1.5**	**1.7**
HR services	**1.3[3]**	**1.3[3]**	**1.8[1,2]**
Providing HR services	1.0	1.0	1.1
Being an employee advocate	0.1	0.8	0.4
Analyzing HR and business metrics	2.9	2.3	2.9
Preparing talent for the future	—	—	2.8
Corporate roles	**0.8**	**1.1**	**1.2**
Managing outsourcing	0.5	0.5	0.3
Operating HR centers of excellence	1.2	1.6	1.5
Operating HR shared service units	1.1	1.1	1.4
Working with the corporate board	0.5	1.0	1.1
Business and strategy	**2.5**	**2.0**	**2.3**
Providing change consulting services	2.3	1.9	2.3
Being a business partner	2.3	1.9	2.2
Helping to develop business strategies	2.6	2.1	2.1
Improving decisions about human capital	2.8	2.2	2.5

Importance response scale: 1 = not important, 10 = very important.

Effectiveness response scale: 1 = not meeting needs, 10 = all needs met.

Empty cells indicate that the item was not asked in that year.

[1,2,3] Significant difference ($p \leq .05$) between years.

Conclusion

HR executives seem to be in general agreement about where HR is most effective: delivering HR services and being an employee advocate. HR executives also report there are a number of important contribution areas where the function falls short. One is business and strategy. It is an important area where the effectiveness of HR is not rated highly. One contributor to this may be its low rating with respect to analyzing HR and business data.

HR executives say that a strong emphasis needs to be placed on HR's role as a business partner and on improving decisions about human capital. These are areas of relatively low effectiveness for HR, and thus there is a tremendous opportunity for HR improvement. These areas also are related to the strategic involvement of the HR function. Thus, by making improvements in these areas, HR is likely to become much more of a strategic contributor and more effective. Overall, it appears that HR has not improved its effectiveness since 1995.

CHAPTER 15

Determinants of HR Effectiveness

- HR effectiveness is caused by a number of identifiable and changeable design features.

- The effectiveness of HR in an organization is strongly related to how it is organized and the role it takes in an organization.

- HR needs to do administration well, but the best opportunities for improvement are in becoming more strategic and driven by the business.

- Among the major predictors of HR effectiveness are the use of information technology and service units, as well as focusing on organizational design and development.

- The effectiveness of the HR information system and its degree of integration in a company is related to HR's effectiveness.

- The use of HR metrics and analytics is strongly associated with HR effectiveness.

What determines how effective an HR organization is? To answer this question, we look at the relationship between the effectiveness of the organization in companies and the HR strategies, practices, and activities that are likely to influence its effectiveness.

Time Spent

The amount of time spent on HR roles relates significantly to HR effectiveness. Our results for 2013, in table 15.1, show a strong negative relationship between effectiveness and the amount of time HR executives report that their function spends maintaining records, auditing, and controlling. In contrast to this is the strong, positive relationship between the amount of time spent as a strategic business partner and HR effectiveness. These results are consistent with what we found in the 2004, 2007, and 2010 surveys. Despite this, as we saw in chapter 2, the percentage of its time spent on the major HR roles has not changed over the years.

The strong positive correlation between time spent on being a business partner and HR effectiveness is consistent with the positive correlation between HR effectiveness and the role HR plays in strategy, as reported in chapter 14. The more HR is involved in business strategy, the more effective it is seen to be.

Our findings paint a consistent picture that effective HR organizations spend less time on record-keeping and controlling activities and are more involved in human capital and business strategy issues. In table 15.1,

Table 15.1. Relationship of HR time spent to HR effectiveness, United States				
HR Roles[a]	**HR Effectiveness**[b]			
	2004	**2007**	**2010**	**2013**
Maintaining records: Collect, track, and maintain data on employees	–.47***	–.33**	–.42***	–.37***
Auditing/controlling: Ensure compliance with internal operations, regulations, and legal and union requirements	–.04	–.18	–.30***	–.38***
HR service provider: Assist with implementation and administration of HR practices	–.05	.05	–.24**	–.06
Development of HR systems and practices: Develop new HR systems and practices	.24[t]	.02	.12	.15
Strategic business partner: Member of the management team; involved with strategic HR planning, organizational design, and strategic change	.30*	.27*	.54***	.40***

[a]Based on percentage of time spent on HR roles as rated by HR executives.

[b]Based on total score for all twelve effectiveness items as rated by HR executives.

Significance level: $^tp \le .10$, $^*p \le .05$, $^{**}p \le .01$, $^{***}p \le .001$.

the only statistically significant positive correlations are with time spent being a strategic partner: the more time spent, the better.

Business Strategy

HR's activity in the business strategy process is significantly related to the effectiveness of the function as rated by HR executives (see table 15.2). Indeed, when compared to the 2004 and 2007 results, the relationships in 2010 and 2013 are even stronger and more consistent. In 2013, all of the correlations are statistically significant. None of the strategic activities shows a pattern of being consistently more strongly related to effectiveness; all the activities are related to HR effectiveness. The biggest difference between 2004 and 2013 is that the absolute level of the correlations is generally higher in 2013 than in 2004. This suggests that over this time period, the strategy activities of HR have become more important in determining its effectiveness.

HR Strategy

The extent to which the HR function has a well-developed HR strategy is strongly related to HR executives' ratings of HR effectiveness. Table 15.3 shows that all the relationships between the HR strategy items and HR effectiveness are statistically significant in the 2004, 2007, 2010, and 2013 data. The weakest relationship in 2004 concerned analytics support for business decision making. In 2007, 2010, and 2013, however, this correlation is among the highest. This suggests an increasing realization of the value of a decision science paradigm for HR, in which the mandate is extended to the quality of decision support, not just services and compliance.

Table 15.2. Relationship of business strategy activities to HR effectiveness, United States

Activities[a]	HR Effectiveness[b]			
	2004	2007	2010	2013
Help identify or design strategy options	.32*	.31**	.45***	.47***
Help decide among the best strategy options	.45***	.35**	.53***	.48***
Help plan the implementation of strategy	.31*	.35**	.55***	.58***
Help identify new business opportunities	.27*	.28*	.47***	.40***
Assess the organizations readiness to implement strategies	.30*	.32**	.59***	.53***
Help design the organization structure to implement strategy	.42***	.35**	.62***	.58***
Assess possible merger, acquisition or divestiture strategies	.23[t]	.17	.55***	.44***
Work with the corporate board on business strategy	.32*	.19	.51***	.41***

[a]Based on response scale: 1 = little or no extent, 2 = some extent, 3 = moderate extent, 4 = great extent, 5 = very great extent.

[b]Based on total score for all twelve effectiveness items as rated by HR executives.

Significance level: $^{t}p \leq .10$, $^{*}p \leq .05$, $^{**}p \leq .01$, $^{***}p \leq .001$.

Table 15.3. Relationship of HR strategy to HR effectiveness, United States

HR Strategy	HR Effectiveness[a]			
	2004	2007	2010	2013
Data-based talent strategy	.50***	.44***	.50***	.49***
A human capital strategy that is integrated with business strategy	.48***	.51***	.54***	.53***
Provides analytical support for business decision making	.38**	.67***	.58***	.65***
Provides HR data to support change management	.46***	.61***	.60***	.71***
Drives change management	.48***	.59***	.65***	.63***
Makes rigorous data-based decisions about human capital management	.47***	.62***	.60***	.62***

[a]Based on total score for all twelve effectiveness items as rated by HR executives.

Significance level: $^{t}p \leq .10$, $^{*}p \leq .05$, $^{**}p \leq .01$, $^{***}p \leq .001$.

Taken together, the results in tables 15.2 and 15.3 indicate that HR is most effective when it focuses on both contributing to business strategy and developing a robust human capital and HR functional strategy. The best overall conclusion is that HR is most effective when it plays a major role in business strategy development and implementation, as well as having a well-developed HR strategy that is aligned with the business strategy.

Table 15.4. Relationship of HR organization to HR effectiveness, United States					
HR Organization	**HR Effectiveness[c]**				
	2001	**2004**	**2007**	**2010**	**2013**
HR service units[a]	.44***	.43***	.36***	.54***	.59***
Decentralization[a]	−.01	−.09	−.17	−.00	−.22*
Information technology[b]	—	—	—	—	.53***
HR talent development[a]	.32***	−.04	.30**	.51***	.45***

[a]See table 6.1. for items in scale.

[b]See table 12.3. for items in scale.

[c]Based on total score for all twelve effectiveness items as rated by HR executives.

Empty cells indicate that the scale was not asked in that year.

Significance level: $^{\dagger}p \leq .10$, $*p \leq .05$, $**p \leq .01$, $***p \leq .001$.

HR Organization

The effectiveness of the HR organization is clearly related to certain features of how it is organized and managed. As can be seen in table 15.4, the results from 2001, 2004, 2007, 2010, and 2013 are similar. The use of service units is strongly related to HR effectiveness, as is the use of information technology. Service units and information technology show consistently positive relationships with HR's strategic role, so these results reinforce the importance of these approaches to organizing and managing the HR function.

It is somewhat surprising that doing talent development for the HR staff is not related to the effectiveness of the HR organization in 2004. There was a significant relationship in 2007 and a much stronger one in 2010 and 2013, a result that is understandable since HR needs a talented workforce.

It is notable that the decentralization of HR is not positively correlated with HR effectiveness in 2001, 2004, 2007, 2010, or 2013. In fact, in 2013, there is a significant negative correlation. Much has been written advocating locating HR centrally for efficiency and control, and similarly strong positions are often taken in favor of decentralizing it for responsiveness and flexibility. Our results with respect to the positive effects of service units suggest that HR organizations need a strong corporate center, and our result for decentralization suggests that decentralization in general is not a positive approach.

Activity Changes

The relationship between reported HR activity changes in the last five to seven years and HR effectiveness is shown in table 15.5. The results for 2001 and 2004 show no strong relationship. In 2007, HR effectiveness

Table 15.5. Relationship of HR activity changes to HR effectiveness, United States					
	HR Effectiveness[b]				
HR Activities[a]	**2001**	**2004**	**2007**	**2010**	**2013**
Design and organizational development	.20*	.21	.37***	.35***	.36***
Compensation and benefits	.30**	−.08	.11	.23**	.11
Employee development	.13	.17	.22[t]	.38***	.12
Recruitment and selection	.08	.13	.08	.25**	.08
HR metrics and analytics	—	.12	.26*	.34***	.22*
HR information systems	.11	−.14	−.01	.15[t]	−.14
Union relations	−.05	.18	−.12	−.01	−.08
Social networks	—	—	—	—	.23*

[a]See table 7.1. for items in scales.

[b]Based on total score for all twelve effectiveness items as rated by HR executives.

Empty cells indicate that the scale was not asked in that year.

Significance level: [t]$p \le .10$, *$p \le .05$, **$p \le .01$, ***$p \le .001$.

was strongly related to increasing time on design and organizational development and on metrics and analytics. The results for 2010 show five significant relationships, but the results for 2013 show only three significant relationships. Design and organizational development, and metrics show the significant relationships in 2007, 2010, and 2013, suggesting that spending more time on them has created more effective HR organizations.

In 2007, 2010, and 2013, the relationship between increased attention to metrics and HR effectiveness is significant. As we saw earlier, the effectiveness of HR measurement and analytics is related to HR having a strategic role as well. This suggests that metrics have reached the point where increased attention to them makes a significant difference in the impact of the HR function, likely because of an increasing technical capability to develop effective HR information systems (HRIS) and meaningful metrics that tie closely to functional and organizational performance effectiveness.

Outsourcing

Analysis of the data relationship between outsourcing and HR effectiveness showed no statistically significant relationships ($p \le .05$) in 2004 and only one in 2007 and 2010 (not asked in 2013). The degree to which individual activities are outsourced clearly is not a significant predictor or cause of HR effectiveness. Given this result, an organization's decisions about what to outsource probably should be based on its situation with respect to costs, logistics, and internal capabilities. There is no compelling evidence that it is generally best either to outsource or not to outsource.

Information Technology

The results from 2001, 2004, 2007, 2010, and 2013 show a positive relationship between IT use and HR effectiveness. As can be seen in table 15.6, there is a clear trend: the greater the presence of IT and the more HR processes are IT based, the greater is the effectiveness of HR. This finding is consistent with the finding (see chapter 12) that organizations that use information technology for most HR processes tend to be perceived as the most effective.

Table 15.7 provides more detail concerning the relationship between IT and HR effectiveness. In this table, we examine not the use of IT but the outcomes of the HRISs as they relate to HR effectiveness. Here our results show strong positive correlations in 2004, 2007, 2010, and 2013. The more positive the outcomes are in the areas, the more effective HR is judged to be. In 2004, efficiency generated the highest correlation; in 2007, the correlations are very similar (though somewhat lower) across all the outcomes. The correlations in 2010 and 2013 again are high for all HRIS outcomes except reducing number of employees. This suggests that today HRISs contribute to HR effectiveness across a wide spectrum of outcomes, ranging from efficiency to effectiveness and impact.

Two new items in 2010, knowledge networks and social networks, show significant relationships to HR effectiveness in both 2010 and 2013. Apparently creating HRISs that aid networks is positive for most HR functions. One reason may be that it helps individuals in HR deal with aspects of their work.

It is also notable that the new 2007 item reflecting the HRIS's effectiveness in improving human capital decisions among those outside HR shows a positive relationship with HR effectiveness in 2007, 2010, and 2013. This may well be because everyone in an organization needs to make good decision in order to have an effective HR organization.

Metrics and Analytics Use

The use of HR metrics and analytics is significantly related to HR effectiveness. As seen in table 15.8, this is true in 2004, 2007, 2010, and 2013. In 2013, the greater use of HR metrics concerned with efficiency, effectiveness, and impact is significantly associated with greater HR effectiveness. This supports the position that like other disciplines, such as finance and marketing, attention to all three areas is an important determinant of HR effectiveness.

Table 15.6. Relationship of information system use to HR effectiveness, United States

Information System	Mean HR Effectiveness[a]				
	2001*	2004*	2007	2010	2013
Completely integrated HR IT system	6.6	7.7	7.5	7.4	7.2
Most processes are IT based but not fully integrated	6.5	6.9	6.6	6.5	6.6
Some HR processes are IT based	6.0	6.5	5.9	5.4	6.1
Little IT present in the HR function	4.6	6.4	6.0	6.0	4.9
No IT present	5.1	No respondents	4.7	No respondents	No respondents

[a]Based on total score for all twelve effectiveness items as rated by HR executives.

*Significant difference in HR effectiveness ($p \le .05$) among information system use levels.

Table 15.7. Relationship of HRIS outcomes to HR effectiveness, United States

HRIS Outcomes[a]	HR Effectiveness[b]			
	2004	2007	2010	2013
Overall effectiveness	**.61*****	**.47*****	**.49*****	**.40*****
Employee satisfaction	**.55*****	**.40*****	**.34*****	**.44*****
Efficiency	**.63*****	**.46*****	**.48*****	**.36*****
Improve HR services	.56***	.45***	.40***	.42***
Reduce HR transaction costs	.49***	.44***	.45***	.34***
Speed up HR processes	.40**	.37***	.42***	.37***
Reduce the number of employees in HR	.55***	.39***	.36***	.10
Business effectiveness	**.40****	**.42*****	**.47*****	**.36*****
Provide new strategic information	.23[t]	.28*	.41***	.40***
Integrate HR processes (e.g., training, compensation)	.49***	.47***	.43***	.26**
Measure HR's impact on the business	**.49*****	**.41*****	**.41*****	**.35*****
Improve human capital decisions of managers outside HR	—	**.37*****	**.38*****	**.33*****
Effective	**.44*****	**.39*****	**.33*****	**.39*****
Create knowledge networks	—	—	**.40*****	**.34*****
Build social networks that help get work done	—	—	**.34*****	**.29****
Offer a positive user experience	—	—	—	**.36*****
Represent a state-of-the-art solution	—	—	—	**.23***
Use the most advanced technology	—	—	—	**.20***

[a]Includes items from Employee Satisfaction, Efficiency, and Business Effectiveness scales only.

[b]Based on total score for all twelve effectiveness items as rated by HR executives.

Empty cells indicate that the items were not asked in that year.

Significance level: [t]$p \le .10$, *$p \le .05$, **$p \le .01$, ***$p \le .001$.

Table 15.8. Relationship of HR analytics and metrics use to HR effectiveness, United States

Measures[a]	HR Effectiveness[b]			
	2004	2007	2010	2013
Efficiency				
Measure the financial efficiency of HR operations (e.g., cost-per-hire, time-to-fill, training costs)?	.53***	.42***	.39***	.40***
Collect metrics that measure the cost of HR programs and processes?	.45***	.49***	.35***	.41***
Benchmark analytics and measures against data from outside organizations (e.g., Saratoga, Mercer, Hewitt)?	.17	.22[t]	.38***	.26**
Effectiveness				
Use HR dashboards or scorecards?	.37**	.29*	.48***	.41***
Measure the specific effects of HR programs (e.g., learning from training, motivation from rewards, validity of tests)?	—	.32**	.28**	.21*
Have the capability to conduct cost-benefit analyses (also called utility analyses) of HR programs?	.53***	.19[t]	.28***	.30***
Impact				
Measure the business impact of HR programs and processes?	.44***	.24*	.36***	.31***
Measure the quality of the talent decisions made by non-HR leaders?	—	.33**	.18*	.16[t]
Measure the business impact of high versus low performance in jobs?	—	.24*	.34***	.24*

[a]Response scale: 1 = not currently being considered; 2 = planning for; 3 = being built; 4 = yes, have now.

[b]Based on total score for all twelve effectiveness items as rated by HR executives.

Empty cells indicate that the item was not asked in that year.

Significance level: $^{t}p \leq .10$, $^{*}p \leq .05$, $^{**}p \leq .01$, $^{***}p \leq .001$.

The only use that did not show a strong significant relationship in 2004 and 2007 is benchmarking analytics and measures against data from outside organizations. In 2010 and to a degree in 2013, however, it does show a significant relationship, strengthening the case for efficiency as an important measure.

Metrics and Analytics Effectiveness

Table 15.9 examines the relationship between the effectiveness of metrics and analytics and overall HR effectiveness. The results for 2013 are very similar to those for 2004, 2007, and 2010. They show that the effectiveness of HR is strongly related to the effectiveness of an organization's HR metrics and analytics activities. All of the items concerned with the effectiveness of metrics and analytics are strongly related to HR effectiveness, including the strategic and HR functional features. This is also true for all the elements of the logic, analysis, measurement, and process (LAMP) framework.

It is somewhat surprising that there is relatively little difference in the size of the correlations in table 15.9. This suggests that having effective HR analytics and metrics in almost any area is a way to improve the effectiveness of the HR function, possibly because it helps to make the HR organization more strategic. It is also possible that even for metrics that are not used directly to advance strategic decisions (such as those focusing on HR department operations), their existence signals rigor and effectiveness. Perhaps at this point in the evolution of the HR profession, demonstrating the effective use of metrics and analytics in virtually any HR area is a significant contributor to its effectiveness.

Table 15.9. Relationship of HR analytics and metrics effectiveness to HR effectiveness, United States				
	HR Effectiveness[b]			
Effectiveness[a]	2004	2007	2010	2013
Strategy contributions				
Contributing to decisions about business strategy and human capital management	.52***	.55***	.58***	.53***
Identifying where talent has the greatest potential for strategic impact	.47***	.49***	.51***	.52***
Connecting human capital practices to organizational performance	.42***	.57***	.40***	.44***
Supporting organizational change efforts	.47***	.56***	.45***	.65***
HR functional and operational contributions				
Assessing and improving the HR department operations	.61***	.63***	.50***	.55***
Predicting the effects of HR programs before implementation	—	.50***	.43***	.50***
Pinpointing HR programs that should be discontinued	.52***	.52***	.46***	.54***
Logic, analysis, measurement, and process (LAMP)				
Using logical principles that clearly connect talent to organization success	—	.55***	.53***	.44***
Using advanced data analysis and statistics	—	.54***	.52***	.40***
Providing high-quality (complete, timely, accessible) talent measurements	—	.49***	.51***	.46***
Motivating users to take appropriate action	—	.52***	.45***	.54***
Using big data	—	—	—	.44***

[a]Response scale: 1 = very ineffective; 2 = ineffective; 3 = neither; 4 = effective; 5 = very effective.

[b]Based on total score for all twelve effectiveness items as rated by HR executives.

Empty cells indicate that the item was not asked in that year.

Significance level: $^{\dagger}p \le .10$, $^{*}p \le .05$, $^{**}p \le .01$, $^{***}p \le .001$.

The best conclusion concerning the use of metrics and analytics is that effective use is clearly tied to the effectiveness of the HR function and that the HR function needs to make increasing use of them. It is particularly important that HR develop greater effectiveness in metrics and analytics areas considering the relatively low effectiveness ratings the metrics and analytics items received from HR executives (see table 9.1). The typical response was "somewhat effective" to all of these items.

Decision Science

The sophistication of managers' decisions about human capital is clearly and strongly related to HR effectiveness, as was the case in 2004, 2007, and 2010. As can be seen in table 15.10, most of the decision science items are highly correlated with HR effectiveness as rated by HR executives. This was also true in 2010 for HR effectiveness as rated by managers.

For HR executives, all business skill areas (e.g., culture, organization design) are significantly related to their perceptions of HR effectiveness. Two areas, finance and marketing, do have relatively low correlations. Perhaps HR executives, working hard to connect to business decisions, vividly see the difficulty of being effective if business decisions are not well grounded and sophisticated.

One of the highest correlations in table 15.10 is with talent decisions, further confirmation of the importance managers put on talent decisions.

Sustainability

The relationship between HR's role in company sustainability programs and HR effectiveness is shown in tables 15.11 and 15.12. The correlations are positive and high. It is clear that effective HR functions are more likely to be involved in sustainability than are ineffective ones.

It is impossible to tell whether being an effective HR function leads to its being involved in sustainability or reverse. Our guess is that it might be a mutually reinforcing causal relationship that creates a virtuous spiral. When an HR function is effective, it has the credibility and resources to help create effective sustainability activities. As a result, it is seen as more effective and can do even more to create effective sustainability programs and activities.

Skill Satisfaction

Table 15.13 shows the relationships between HR effectiveness and the satisfaction of HR managers, with the HR and business skills of HR professionals. There are strong correlations for all the skills. The strong relationship for all of these skills once again confirms the importance of HR

Table 15.10. Relationship of decision science sophistication to HR effectiveness, United States

Decision Making	HR Effectiveness[a]			
	2004	2007	2010	2013
We excel at competing for and with talent where it matters most to our strategic success.	—	.47***	.58***	.41***
Business leaders' decisions that depend on or affect human capital (e.g., layoffs, rewards) are as rigorous, logical, and strategically relevant as their decisions about resources such as money, technology, and customers.	.44***	.51***	.57***	.38***
Business leaders understand and use sound principles when making decisions about:				
1. Motivation	.45***	.50***	.52***	.36***
2. Development and learning	.44***	.53***	.50***	.40***
3. Culture	.45***	.52***	.37***	.42***
4. Organizational design	.61***	.49***	.36***	.55***
5. Business strategy	.52***	.49***	.35***	.43***
6. Finance	—	.30**	.22*	.15
7. Marketing	—	.39***	.29***	−.01
HR leaders have a good understanding about where and why human capital makes the biggest difference in their business.	.52***	.58***	.61***	.57***
Business leaders have a good understanding about where and why human capital makes the biggest difference in their business.	.44***	.60***	.46***	.45***
HR systems educate business leaders about their talent decisions.	—	.46***	.55***	.42***
HR adds value by ensuring compliance with rules, laws, and guidelines.	—	.20[t]	.34***	.25**
HR adds value by delivering high-quality professional practices and services.	—	.56***	.72***	.63***
HR adds value by improving talent decisions inside and outside the HR function.	—	.56***	.64***	.62***

[a]Based on total score for all twelve effectiveness items as rated by HR executives.

Response scale: 1 = little or no extent; 2 = some extent; 3 = moderate extent; 4 = great extent; 5 = very great extent. Empty cells indicate that the item was not asked in that year.

Significance level: [t]$p \leq .10$, *$p \leq .05$, **$p \leq .01$, ***$p \leq .001$.

Table 15.11. Relationship of HR role in sustainability activities to HR effectiveness, United States

HR Role	HR Effectiveness[a]
HR's role *is*	.52***
HR's role *should be*	−.16

[a]Based on total score for all twelve effectiveness items as rated by HR executives.

Significance level: [t]$p \leq .10$, *$p \leq .05$, **$p \leq .01$, ***$p \leq .001$.

Table 15.12. Relationship of sustainability activities to HR effectiveness, United States	
Sustainability Activities[a]	**HR Effectiveness**[b]
Sustainability performance and competences are explicitly built into HR processes such as selection, rewards, and development.	.37***
HR is involved in the design of sustainability initiatives and programs.	.39***
HR provides support and expertise in organizational design issues that impact sustainability.	.57***
HR provides change management support for building sustainability in the way my company does business	.58***

[a]Response scale: 1 = strongly disagree; 2 = somewhat disagree; 3 = neither disagree nor agree; 4 = somewhat agree; 5 = strongly agree.

[b]Based on total score for all twelve effectiveness items as rated by HR executives.

Significance level: [t]$p \leq .10$, *$p \leq .05$, **$p \leq .01$, ***$p \leq .001$.

Table 15.13. Relationship of HR skill satisfaction to HR effectiveness, United States				
	HR Effectiveness[b]			
HR Skills[a]	**2004**	**2007**	**2010**	**2013**
HR technical skills[c]	.32*	.43***	.52***	.48***
Interpersonal dynamics	.62***	.66***	.65***	.68***
Business partner skills	.65***	.76***	.64***	.72***
Metrics skills	.56***	.68***	.56***	.63***
Sustainability	—	—	—	.45***
Social media	—	—	—	.38***
Globalization	—	—	—	.41***
Risk management	—	—	—	.39***

[a]Response scale: 1 = very dissatisfied; 2 = dissatisfied; 3 = neutral; 4 = satisfied; 5 = very satisfied.

[b]Based on total score for all twelve effectiveness items as rated by HR Executives.

[c]Scale for HR technical skills recalculated for pre-2013 surveys.

Empty cells indicate that the item was not asked in that year.

Significance level: [t]$p \leq .10$, *$p \leq .05$, **$p \leq .01$, ***$p \leq .001$.

professionals having skills beyond just HR technical skills. As we noted earlier, interpersonal, business partner, and metrics skills are rated only moderately present and effective by HR executives. This means that there is a great opportunity to enhance HR effectiveness by improving the skills of HR professionals.

Importance of HR Practices and Activities

In order to determine the relative importance of the many practices, structures, and skills that are associated with HR effectiveness, we performed a final analysis: running a regression analysis using key items from tables 15.1 to 15.13. The following items (in the order of predictive power) were the best predictors of HR effectiveness.

1. Satisfaction with business partner skills

2. Provides analytics support for business decision making

3. HRIS that improves HR operations

4. Increased activity in organization design and development

Once again, our data suggest that HR needs to perform in its administrative activities well and to be an effective business and strategic partner. In terms of relative importance, the data suggest that HR's business and strategic performance are the most important practices and activities.

Conclusion

Our results show a number of strong relationships between the effectiveness of the HR function and the way it is organized, managed, and staffed. Among the most important findings are the following:

- Spending time on maintaining records is negatively related to HR effectiveness; being a strategic partner is positively related.

- Strategic activities such as helping plan the implementation of strategy and choosing strategy options are strongly related to HR effectiveness.

- Using information technology and service units as delivery mechanisms for HR services is strongly related to HR effectiveness.

- Increased focus on organizational design and development is related to HR effectiveness.

- Having a completely integrated HRIS leads to the highest level of HR effectiveness.

- The effectiveness of the HRIS system is strongly related to the overall effectiveness of the HR organization.

- Having a wide array of effective HR metrics and analytics is strongly related to HR effectiveness.

- The decision science sophistication of business leaders is strongly related to the effectiveness of the HR function.

- There is a clear relationship between the skills of HR managers and the effectiveness of the HR function.

Overall, the findings tell an important story. HR effectiveness is associated with a wide array of HR activities, structures, systems, and skills that are within the control of HR. HR can do a lot to make HR more effective. It certainly needs to be sure its administrative processes work well, but its best opportunities for improvement appear to be in the business partner role and in strategy.

CHAPTER 16

Determinants of Organizational Performance

- How HR is organized, managed, and staffed is related to overall organizational effectiveness.

- A key for HR to contribute to organizational effectiveness is having a human capital strategy that is integrated with the business strategy.

- The use of analytics and metrics as well as having an integrated HR information system is associated with organizational performance.

- Decision science sophistication is clearly associated with organizational performance.

- Higher-performing organizations have HR functions that are active in sustainability.

How does the design and operation of HR influence organizational performance? To answer this question, we need to look at the relationship between the performance of organizations and the HR practices and activities that are likely to influence it.

The obvious HR practices and activities to look at are those that influence the effectiveness of HR, the focus of chapter 15. Although they are the best place to look, they may have a different relationship to organizational performance than they have to HR effectiveness.

In our sample of companies, there is only a moderate relationship between the HR executives' ratings of organizational performance and their rating of HR effectiveness ($r = .31$, $p \le .001$). This is not surprising since HR is just one of many determinants of organizational performance. The performance of marketing, finance, operations, and the other groups in a corporation also influences organizational performance. Furthermore, because of its role in companies, some HR practices and activities do not have a direct impact on the bottom line of organizations, and as a result, some HR activities that influence HR effectiveness may not affect organizational performance. Thus, the relationship between organizational performance and HR practices should be much weaker than those between HR effectiveness and HR practices. It is very likely that some HR practices and activities that are significantly related to HR effectiveness will not be related to organizational performance at all.

Time Spent

The results in table 16.1 show that time spent on maintaining records, auditing, controlling, and HR service provision were all negatively related to organizational performance in 2010. Of these, only the HR service provider correlation for 2010 was statistically significant.

Table 16.1. Relationship of time spent and organizational performance, United States	Organizational Performance[b]	
HR Time Spent[a]	2010	2013
Maintaining records: Collect, track, and maintain data on employees.	–.12	.01
Auditing/controlling: Ensure compliance with internal operations, regulations, and legal and union requirements	–.13	.00
HR service provider: Assist with the implementation and administration of HR practices.	–.23*	–.05
Development of HR systems and practices: Develop new HR systems and practices	.16[t]	.08
Strategic business partner: Member of the management team; involved with strategic HR planning, organizational design, and strategic change	.27**	–.01

[a]Based on percentage of time spent on HR roles as rated by HR executives.

[b]Response scale: 1 = much below average; 2 = somewhat below average; 3 = about average; 4 = somewhat above average; 5 = much above average.

Significance level: [t]$p \le .10$, *$p \le .05$, **$p \le .01$, ***$p \le .001$.

Development of HR systems and strategic business partner are both positively related to organizational performance in 2010 but are not significantly related in 2013. The largest and most significant correlation for organizational performance in 2010 was with being a strategic business partner. This reinforces the importance of HR being involved in strategic decisions of corporations. However, in 2013, this relationship is not significant. There is no obvious reason for this change. Perhaps it reflects a change in what drives organizational performance, but more likely some outlier data caused this unexpected result.

The pattern of correlations for 2010 in table 16.1 is similar to that in table 15.1, which presents data on HR effectiveness. In both cases, the key to effectiveness is spending more time on being a strategic contributor and less time on traditional HR service activities. The major difference among them is the strength of the correlations; as expected, they are much lower for organizational performance than for HR effectiveness (table 16.1).

Business Strategy

The extent of HR's involvement in specific business strategy activities shows low relationships with organizational performance. As can be seen in table 16.2, the correlations for all business strategy activities are positive but low for both 2010 and 2013. Given the overall positive pattern, it is reasonable to suggest that having HR involved in business strategy activities is positive, but it certainly does not make a compelling case for its involvement in any specific strategy activity with the possible exception of implementation. In many respects, this is not surprising. There is a considerable distance between HR participating in a business strategy

Table 16.2. Relationship of business strategy activities to organizational performance, United States		
	Organizational Performance[b]	
Activities[a]	2010	2013
Help identify or design strategy options	.15	.02
Help decide among the best strategy options	.14	.04
Help plan the implementation of strategy	.11	.20*
Help identify new business opportunities	.12	.05
Assess the organization's readiness to implement strategies	.13	.12
Help design the organization structure to implement strategy	.12	.11
Assess possible merger, acquisition, or divestiture strategies	.18[t]	.14[t]
Work with the corporate board on business strategy	.09	.10

[a]Response scale: 1 = little or no extent; 2 = some extent; 3 = moderate extent; 4 = great extent; 5 = very great extent.
[b]Response scale: 1 = much below average; 2 = somewhat below average; 3 = about average; 4 =somewhat above average; 5 = much above average.
Significance level: [t]$p \le .10$, *$p \le .05$, **$p \le .01$, ***$p \le .001$.

activity and an organization performing more effectively than its competitors. Even at its best, the HR role in strategy development and implementation is likely to be relatively minor, and having an effective business strategy is only part of what it takes to create an effective organization.

HR Strategy

The results for the HR strategy items tend to show that there is a relatively strong, positive relationship between a number of features of the HR strategy and organizational performance. The strongest correlation in table 16.3 for 2010 is with human capital strategies that are integrated with the business strategy. This is not surprising given the potential advantage of this type of integration. For 2013, the highest correlation is with data-based human capital decisions. Four other elements of HR strategy are also significantly related to organizational performance in 2013. Data-based talent strategy, analytical support, and human capital strategy integrated with business strategy and driving change management all have statistically significant relationships with organizational performance.

Overall the results indicate that a well-designed HR-driven business strategy can have a positive impact on organizational performance. The results are not as strong as they are for HR effectiveness, but this is hardly surprising given the many factors that determine organizational performance.

HR Organization

Organizational performance is not closely related to the features of the HR organization in the corporations we studied. As can be seen in table 16.4, although all the correlations are positive, only HR talent development reached statistical significance in 2010. It reaches the .10 level in

Table 16.3. Relationship of HR strategy to organizational performance, United States

HR Strategy[a]	Organizational Performance[b]	
	2010	2013
Data-based talent strategy	.22*	.21*
A human capital strategy that is integrated with business strategy	.33***	.19*
Provides analytical support for business decision making	.24**	.16[t]
Provides HR data to support change management	.23*	.20*
Drives change management	.20*	.12
Makes rigorous data-based decisions about human capital management	.18[t]	.28***

[a]Response scale: 1 = little or no extent; 2 = some extent; 3 = moderate extent; 4 = great extent; 5 = very great extent.

[b]Response scale: 1 = much below average; 2 = somewhat below average; 3 = about average; 4 =somewhat above average; 5 = much above average.

Significance level: [t]$p \leq .10$, *$p \leq .05$, **$p \leq .01$, ***$p \leq .001$.

Table 16.4. Relationship of HR organization to organizational performance, United States

HR Organization	Organizational Performance[b]	
	2010	2013
HR service units[a]	.11	.09
Decentralization[a]	.06	.13
HR talent development[a]	.18*	.14[t]

[a]See table 6.1. for items in scale.

[b]Response scale: 1 = much below average; 2 = somewhat below average; 3 = about average; 4 =somewhat above average; 5 = much above average.

Significance level: [t]$p \leq .10$, *$p \leq .05$, **$p \leq .01$, ***$p \leq .001$.

2013. The fact that HR talent development is significantly correlated with organizational performance again points to the value of having a well-staffed and well-run HR organization. Service units are also positively, but not significantly, related to organizational performance. This provides some support for the argument that it is useful to have corporate resource teams that service the rest of the organization.

HR Activity Changes

Multiple changes in HR activity levels are significantly related to organizational performance. As can be seen in table 16.5, three activity level changes have particularly strong relationships in 2013. Employee development, recruitment and selection, and HR metrics show relatively strong statistically significant relationships with organizational performance. In 2010, all of these relationships were strong, as was the relationship with organizational design and development. This indicates that shifting more time and effort into these areas has been a high-payoff activity for these organizations. Particularly interesting are the

Table 16.5. Relationship of HR activity changes to organizational performance, United States		
	Organizational Performance[c]	
HR Activities[a,b]	**2010**	**2013**
Design and organizational development	.30***	.13
Compensation and benefits	.18*	.11
Employee development	.34***	.29***
Recruitment and selection	.35***	.19*
HR metrics and analytics	.13	.24**
HR information systems	.11	.07
Union relations	.05	.08
Social networks	—	.16[t]

[a]Response scale: 1 = greatly decreased; 2 = decreased; 3 = stayed the same; 4 = increased; 5 = greatly increased.

[b]See Table 7.1 for items in scales.

[c]Response scale: 1 = much below average; 2 = somewhat below average; 3 = about average; 4 = somewhat above average; 5 = much above average.

Empty cells indicate that the item was not asked in that year.

Significance level: [t] $p \leq .10$, * $p \leq .05$, ** $p \leq .01$, *** $p \leq .001$.

relationships with the amount of activity change having to do with talent management. They indicate that increasing the focus on talent management is potentially a high-payoff activity for many organizations.

Outsourcing

In 2010, the results for HR outsourcing showed no strong relationship with organizational performance (not asked in 2013). Training was the one significant correlation between organizational performance and thirteen different types of outsourcing, but even it was a low relationship. Some types of activities such as benefits even show a negative relationship to organizational performance. Overall the data suggest that outsourcing HR activities is not necessarily the right way to improve organizational performance, just as it is not necessarily a way to improve the performance of the HR organization

Information Technology

The results from both 2010 and 2013 for HR's use of information technology show a clear relationship between its use and organizational performance. As can be seen in table 16.6, HR functions that have completely integrated IT systems have a significantly higher performance rating than those with lesser amounts of IT use. The relationship is not as strong as is the one for HR effectiveness, but it is strong enough to establish the importance of having IT-based HR systems.

Table 16.7 shows the relationship between HRIS outcomes and organizational performance. The results generally show low positive relationships

Table 16.6. Relationship of information system use to organizational performance, United States

Information System	Organizational Performance (Means)[a]	
	2010	2013
Completely integrated HR IT system	4.3	4.2
Most processes are IT based but not fully integrated	3.8	4.0
Some HR processes are IT based	3.7	3.7
Little IT present in the HR function	3.8	3.5
No IT present	No responses	No responses

[a]Response scale: 1 = much below average; 2 = somewhat below average; 3 = about average; 4 = somewhat above average; 5 = much above average.

Table 16.7. Relationship of HRIS outcomes to organizational performance, United States

HRIS Outcomes[c]	Organizational Performance[b]	
	2010	2013
Overall effectiveness[a]	**.21***	**.13**
Employee satisfaction	**.13**	**.18***
Efficiency	**.22***	**.17***
Improve HR services	.19*	.19*
Reduce HR transaction costs	.18*	.14
Speed up HR processes	.25**	.18*
Reduce the number of employees in HR	.17[t]	.07
Business effectiveness	**.18***	**.07**
Provide new strategic information	.17[t]	.14
Integrate HR processes (e.g., training, compensation)	.16[t]	.02
Measure HR's impact on the business	**.32****	**.07**
Improve human capital decisions of managers outside HR	**.20***	**.06**
Effective	**.13**	**.12**
Create knowledge networks	**.22***	**.05**
Build social networks that help get work done	**.24****	**.10**
Offer a positive user experience	**—**	**.15[t]**
Represent a state-of-the-art solution	**—**	**.08**
Use the most advance technology	**—**	**.12**

[a]Includes items from Employee Satisfaction, Efficiency, and Business Effectiveness scales only.

[b]Response scale: 1 = much below average; 2 = somewhat below average; 3 = about average; 4 = somewhat above average; 5 = much above average.

[c]Response scale: 1 = little or no extent; 2 = some extent; 3 = moderate extent; 4 = great extent; 5 = very great extent.

Empty cells indicate that the item was not asked in that year.

Significance level: [t]$p \leq .10$, *$p \leq .05$, **$p \leq .01$, ***$p \leq .001$.

between how effective the HRIS is and the overall performance of organizations. The results are much stronger for 2010 than they are for 2013. Although the correlations are low, some of them reach statistical significance and the others are positive, further evidence that using information technology properly can have a positive impact on organizational performance. This finding is particularly interesting with respect to the network questions (knowledge, social). Both are significantly related to organizational performance in 2010, suggesting that they may be a new and potentially powerful way to improve organizational performance. It is a bit puzzling that although they are positively related, they are not significantly related to performance in 2013.

Metrics and Analytics Use

There are a number of significant relationships between the use of HR metrics and organizational performance (table 16.8). As a general rule, the greater the use of HR metrics and analytics, the more effective an organization is. The statistically significant relationships are all in the effectiveness and impact areas. None of the efficiency items are significant, but they are positive. This again makes the point that it is not how administratively efficient or effective the HR function is in doing its basic transactions

Table 16.8. Relationship of HR analytics and metrics use to organizational performance, United States		
	Organizational Performance[b]	
Measures[a]	2010	2013
Efficiency		
Measure the financial efficiency of HR operations (e.g., cost-per-hire, time-to-fill, training costs)?	.13	.14[t]
Collect metrics that measure the cost of HR programs and processes?	.14	.14[t]
Benchmark analytics and measures against data from outside organizations (e.g., Saratoga, Mercer, Hewitt)?	.09	.06
Effectiveness		
Use HR dashboards or scorecards?	.13	.20*
Measure the specific effects of HR programs (e.g., learning from training, motivation from rewards, validity of tests)?	.20*	.20*
Have the capability to conduct cost-benefit analyses (also called utility analyses) of HR programs?	.23*	.19*
Impact		
Measure the business impact of HR programs and processes?	.34***	.02
Measure the quality of the talent decisions made by non-HR leaders?	.04	.23**
Measure the business impact of high versus low performance in jobs?	.24**	.08

[a]Response scale: 1 = not currently being considered; 2 = planning for; 3 = being built; 4 = yes, have now.

[b]Response scale: 1 = much below average; 2 = somewhat below average; 3 = about average; 4 = somewhat above average; 5 = much above average.

Significance level: [t]$p \leq .10$, *$p \leq .05$, **$p \leq .01$, ***$p \leq .001$.

Table 16.9. Relationship of HR metrics and analytical effectiveness to organizational performance, United States

Effectiveness[a]	Organizational Performance[b]	
	2010	2013
Strategy contributions		
Contributing to decisions about business strategy and human capital management	.19*	.07
Identifying where talent has the greatest potential for strategic impact	.38***	.18*
Connecting human capital practices to organizational performance	.19*	.11
Supporting organizational change efforts	.10	.09
HR functional and operational contributions		
Assessing and improving the HR department operations	.16[t]	.09
Predicting the effects of HR programs before implementation	.16[t]	.09
Pinpointing HR programs that should be discontinued	.19*	.10
Logic, analysis, measurement, and process (LAMP)		
Using logical principles that clearly connect talent to organizational success	.26**	.23**
Using advanced data analysis and statistics	.23*	.28***
Providing high-quality (complete, timely, accessible) talent measurements	.32***	.05
Motivating users to take appropriate action	.30***	.07
Using big data	—	.12

[a]Response scale: 1 = very ineffective; 2 = ineffective; 3 = somewhat effective; 4 = effective; 5 = very effective.

[b]Response scale: 1 = much below average; 2 = somewhat below average; 3 = about average; 4 = somewhat above average; 5 = much above average.

Empty cells indicate that the item was not asked in that year.

Significance level: [t]$p \leq .10$, *$p \leq .05$, **$p \leq .01$, ***$p \leq .001$.

work that determines organizational performance. Rather, it is the degree to which it is able to put in place programs and make decisions that influence the way the organization develops and manages talent.

Three of the highest correlations in 2013 are being able to measure the effectiveness of HR programs and processes and organizational performance. These correlations are also relatively high in 2010. These items all have to do with the ability to make informed business decision about HR activities. In 2010 and 2013, there are significant relationships involving the impact of HR. They include measuring the business effects of HR programs and the business impact of performance in jobs. All of these have direct implications for the bottom line of corporations.

The effectiveness of an organization's HR metrics and analytics is significantly related to organizational performance (table 16.9). Three of the four strategy contributions measures, one of the functional and operational measures, and all of the logic, analysis, measurement, and process (LAMP) items are significantly related to organizational performance in 2010 or 2013, or both. There is a strong correlation between identifying where talent has the greatest potential for strategic impact and organizational effectiveness. This once again reinforces the point that informed decision making about talent is something that HR functions can do that contributes to organizational performance. These significant relationships reinforce the point that of all the things HR can do, decision making and analysis by the HR function has the largest impact on organizational performance. For example, using the logical principles that connect talent to organizational success is significantly related to organizational performance. Similarly, providing high-quality talent measurements is significantly related in 2010.

Decision Science

The decision-making results are shown in table 16.10. All of the types of decisions studied are significantly related to organizational performance in 2010 and most are in 2013. Two of the highest correlations concern business leaders' making decisions about strategy and finance. The human capital decisions (e.g., where and why human capital makes a difference) are also significant. This does not prove causation because these are correlational data and there is the possibility that because an organization is performing well, it is seen as making good decisions. Perhaps the best explanation for why this relationship exists is one based on a kind of virtuous spiral in which good decisions drive good performance, which in turn encourages managers to focus on making good talent management decisions (Lawler 2008). Overall the data strongly support having managers both within and outside the HR function who understand how and why good talent management leads to high organizational performance

Sustainability

Both the role of HR in sustainability and its sustainability activities are significantly related to organizational performance (tables 16.11 and 16.12). The overall relationship is clear: when HR is involved in sustainability, both HR functions and their organizations perform better. This raises the question of what causes this relationship. As we mentioned in chapter 15, it most likely is because well-functioning organizations choose to have their HR function involved in sustainability rather than that HR's involvement makes the organizations more effective.

HR Skills

Satisfaction with some HR skills was significantly related to organizational performance in 2010. As can be seen in table 16.13, three of the

Table 16.10. Relationship of decision science sophistication to organizational performance, United States

Decision Making[a]	Organizational Performance[b]	
	2010	2013
We excel at competing for and with talent where it matters the most to our strategic success.	.32***	.27**
Business leaders' decisions that depend on or affect human capital (e.g., layoffs, reward) are as rigorous, logical, and strategically relevant as their decisions about resources such as money, technology, and customers.	.27**	.22*
Business leaders understand and use sound principles when making decisions about:		
1. Motivation	.30***	.20*
2. Development and learning	.32***	.25**
3. Culture	.33***	.18*
4. Organizational design	.31***	.10
5. Business strategy	.40***	.25**
6. Finance	.39***	.29***
7. Marketing	.22*	.21*
HR leaders have a good understanding about where and why human capital makes the biggest difference in their business.	.33***	.26**
Business leaders have a good understanding about where and why human capital makes the biggest difference in their business.	.24*	.31***
HR systems educate business leaders about their talent decisions.	.27**	.18*
HR adds value by ensuring compliance with rules, laws, and guidelines.	.27**	.23*
HR adds value by delivering high-quality professional practices and services.	.30***	.14
HR adds value by improving talent decisions inside and outside the HR function.	.29**	.07

[a]Response scale: 1 = little or no extent; 2 = some extent; 3 = moderate extent; 4 = great extent; 5 = very great extent.

[b]Response scale: 1 = much below average; 2 = somewhat below average; 3 = about average; 4 = somewhat above average; 5 = much above average.

Significance level: $^{t}p \leq .10$, $^{*}p \leq .05$, $^{**}p \leq .01$, $^{***}p \leq .001$.

Table 16.11. Relationship of HR role in sustainability activities to organizational performance, United States

HR Role	Organizational Performance[a]
HR's role *is*	.24**
HR's role *should be*	.21*

[a]Response scale: 1 = much below average; 2 = somewhat below average; 3 = about average; 4 = somewhat above average; 5 = much above average.

Significance level: $^{t}p \leq .10$, $^{*}p \leq .05$, $^{**}p \leq .01$, $^{***}p \leq .001$.

Table 16.12. Relationship of sustainability activities to organizational performance, United States

Sustainability Activities[a]	Organizational Performance[b]
Sustainability performance and competences are explicitly built into HR processes such as selection, rewards, and development.	.15[t]
HR is involved in the design of sustainability initiatives and programs.	.26**
HR provides support and expertise in organizational design issues that affect sustainability.	.29***
HR provides change management support for building sustainability into the way my company does business.	.24**

[a]Response scale: 1 = strongly disagree; 2 = somewhat disagree; 3 = neither disagree nor agree; 4 = somewhat agree; 5 = strongly agree.

[b]Response scale: 1 = much below average; 2 = somewhat below average; 3 = about average; 4 = somewhat above average; 5 = much above average.

Significance level: $^t p \leq .10$, $^* p \leq .05$, $^{**} p \leq .01$, $^{***} p \leq .001$.

Table 16.13. Relationship of HR skill satisfaction to organizational performance, United States

HR Skills[a]	Organizational Performance[b]	
	2010	2013
HR technical skills[c]	.19*	.13
Interpersonal dynamics	.29***	.10
Business partner skills	.23*	.01
Metrics skills	.17[t]	.10
Sustainability	—	.04
Social media	—	.00
Globalization	—	−.02
Risk management	—	.07

[a]Response scale: 1 = very dissatisfied; 2 = dissatisfied; 3 = neutral; 4 = satisfied; 5 = very satisfied.

[b]Response scale: 1 = much below average; 2 = somewhat below average; 3 = about average; 4 = somewhat above average; 5 = much above average.

[c]Scale for HR technical skills recalculated for 2010 survey.

Empty cells indicate that the item was not asked in that year.

Significance level: $^t p \leq .10$, $^* p \leq .05$, $^{**} p \leq .01$, $^{***} p \leq .001$.

four skills areas that were measured in 2010 had statistically significant relationships, but none do in 2013. It is surprising that these four skills areas are not more strongly related to organizational performance.

For the 2013 survey, we added four new skill areas that are increasingly thought to be ones that HR managers should have, yet none of them are significantly related to organizational performance. The overall low relationship between HR skills and organizational performance does not argue for investing in the development of the HR staff. Nevertheless, we think it is very important to make this investment. Without it, an HR function cannot be expected to deliver the outcomes that have been shown to lead to organizational effectiveness.

Conclusion

Our results show a number of moderately strong relationships between organizational performance and the way HR is organized, managed, and staffed and its activities. As expected, the relationships are not as strong as those involving the effectiveness of HR as a function. Among the most important are the following:

- The amount of time spent on strategic issues is positively related to organizational performance.

- A number of HR strategy activities are related to organizational performance. The strongest relationship is with having a human capital strategy that is integrated with the business strategy.

- The amount of HR talent development that is done by an organization is positively related to its performance, as is the skill level in HR.

- Increasing HR's focus on talent is associated with high organizational performance.

- Having an integrated HRIS system is associated with high organizational performance.

- Employing metrics and analytics that measure the impact and quality of HR programs, processes, and talent decisions is associated with organizational performance.

- High-performance organizations have a high level of decision science sophistication with respect to talent and its impact on organizational performance.

- High-performance organizations have HR functions that are active in sustainability.

Overall the results tell an important story about how HR can contribute to organizational performance. Talent management is clearly an area where HR can have a positive impact on organizational performance by improving its data, analytics, and decision making. HR also can make important contributions to organizational performance by developing its role as a strategic contributor.

CHAPTER 17

How HR Has Changed

Our study provides unique data that answer multiple important questions about how HR is changing. Other studies have asked about the current importance of HR taking a new direction, adding new skills, adopting new HR practices, and offering new services. They have also asked HR managers to report on the amount and kind of change they think has occurred. This is the only study that has examined change by measuring the activities and effectiveness of HR functions over time.

Reports of change are almost always less valid than are comparisons among data collected at two or more points in time. The former are influenced by memory and other factors. The problem with reports of change is demonstrated in our study by the responses to our question concerning how HR time is spent. HR executives responding to each of our seven surveys from 1995 to 2013 report a significant shift in the way HR time is being spent. However, when we examine actual changes in activity levels using reports of current practice from different time periods, the percentages have not shifted. Thus, our data suggest that if we had relied on self-reported change, we would have concluded after every survey that HR had reduced the time spent on maintaining records and auditing operations by about 16 percentage points and had increased the time spent as a strategic business partner by about 13 percentage points. Yet the actual reports of time spent on strategic partnership, maintaining records, and auditing are virtually unchanged since 1995. HR has long spent about 25 percent of its time as a strategic partner. In fact, the impression of progress is the result of a bad memory that is most likely the result of wishful thinking.

There is no question that the business environment has changed dramatically in the past twenty years, but the HR function in most organizations does not look very different than it did fifteen to twenty years ago. The period since our last survey in 2010 alone saw enormous change in the business environment: a global economic recovery; the continuing economic growth of India and China; and fundamental changes in technology-driven social platforms, personalization, and device-centric applications. There is widespread agreement and much writing about the need for HR to change and how it needs to change to be more strategic and more of a business partner; offer higher-quality HR information systems (HRIS) and human capital management systems; and be more of a leader on issues such as globalization, sustainability, workplace personalization, and organizational agility (Boudreau and Ziskin 2011; Lawler and Worley 2011; Worley, Williams, and Lawler 2014).

Despite the many changes that have occurred, our data show little change from 1995 to 2013 related to how HR is organized and how it operates in large corporations. A quick perusal of the tables in this book reveals that HR has not changed very much. We can point to some areas where change has occurred, but even in those areas, the changes took place largely in the late 1990s and have leveled off or even reversed since then. In this chapter, we provide a summary of what has and has not changed and attempt to reconcile our evidence of slow or nonexistent change in HR with the widespread impression that the profession is changing.

What Has and Has Not Changed

Our analysis of the results of our 1995, 1998, 2001, 2004, 2007, 2010, and 2013 surveys establishes that some significant changes have occurred in how HR functions are organized and how they deliver services. The most significant changes are the way the HR function is organized, where HR activities and information are located, and HR's role in employee advocacy and shaping a labor market strategy. These changes may well set the stage for a greater strategic partnership, but they are largely focused on how the HR function itself is organized and managed and how it defines its relationships with its clients. The most important changes are these:

- HR is more likely to use service teams to support and serve business units.

- HR is more likely to have corporate centers of excellence.

- Companies are more likely to have similar HR practices in different business units.

- HR is paying increased attention to recruitment and selection as well as organizational design and development.

- More companies have most rather than some of their HR processes as information technology based.

- Employees are increasingly making use of HRISs on a self-service basis.

- There is greater satisfaction with the interpersonal dynamics and business understanding skills of HR professionals.

- HR decision support contributions are increasingly associated with HR's strategic role.

- HR is increasingly effective in helping to shape a viable employment relationship for the future, providing HR services, operating centers of excellence, and being an employee advocate.

Most of these changes occurred in the late 1990s. Since then, the major changes have involved information technology.

In comparing our earlier results to the 2013 results, it is clear that a number of things have not changed very much, if at all. Many of these elements reflect HR's role in shaping strategy and building effective HR skills. Among them are the following:

- The belief that HR has increased the time it spends as a strategic partner and the estimated time as a strategic partner

- The extent to which HR is shaping business strategy

- The desire of HR executives to be business and strategic partners

- The rotation of individuals into and out of HR

- The tendency of HR advice to boards to be about executive compensation and succession and not about change, governance, risk, strategy, or sustainability

- The moderate quality of the human capital decisions that business leaders make

- The relatively low levels of business leaders' use of sound principles for human capital decisions compared to their use with respect to more tangible assets

- The infrequent use of HR systems to educate business leaders about the quality of their talent decisions

- The implementation of HR metrics and analytics systems and their effectiveness

- The moderate use of efficiency and effectiveness measures and the less frequent use of measuring HR impact on decisions and strategy

- The use of fully integrated HR information technology systems

- Less than a quarter of respondents who think that more than 80 percent of HR professionals have the skills they need to be effective

- HR skill satisfaction averages below "neither satisfied nor dissatisfied" for all HR skills except those in traditional areas of HR technical skills and interpersonal dynamics

- The business partner skills of the HR professionals rated as moderate to low

- The highest effectiveness of HR in traditional areas such as providing HR services and being an employee advocate and the lowest effectiveness in areas related to business strategy

- Little improvement in the key areas that are strongly correlated with HR's role in strategy and HR functional effectiveness

Overall, when we analyze our data from 1995, 1998, 2001, 2004, 2007, 2010, and 2013, we find that more things have stayed the same than have changed. Although many of the changes we found are significant and important, the amount of change is surprisingly small. Frankly, given the tremendous amount of attention that has been given to the importance of HR being a business and strategic partner and adding value in new ways, we expected much more change. In fact, we have expected more change than we have seen in every wave of our study since it began. This "stubborn traditionalism" (Boudreau and Ramstad 2007; Boudreau and Lawler 2014a) is also apparent in the continuing flow of articles about frustration among non-HR executives with HR's unrealized potential.

Overall, much about HR has remained the same despite the enormous amount of change that is going on around it. This raises a critical question: Are there particular organizational and environmental conditions that are associated with HR being more of a business and strategic partner? The answer is yes, and looking at them can help us understand what it takes to change how HR operates in organizations.

Strategic Focuses

Our 2013 study found a strong relationship between what is happening in the HR function and an organization's strategic focuses. In particular, three of the five focuses—information, knowledge, and innovation—were positively related to most of the strategic and advanced features of HR functions. This is a bit different from the survey in 2010, which also showed a positive association with the sustainability focus. In the 2013 results, sustainability sometimes emerged as positively associated with strategic and advanced HR elements, though less so than in 2010. Generally it appears that an emphasis on information, knowledge, and innovation creates a much more favorable situation for the HR function because it places a premium on acquiring, developing, deploying, and retaining talent.

Overall, our results clearly show that strategy focuses influence the way the HR function operates and its success as a business partner. When there are strong focuses on information knowledge and innovation, HR performs more high-valued-added activities and is more strategic, and the HR function is more positively regarded.

Our strategy results raise the issue of the direction of causality. One possibility is that an organization's strategy causes HR to take on a particular role. The alternative is that a more strategic HR role causes organizations to attempt or adopt strategies that rely more on knowledge and talent quality. Our guess is that the most common causal direction is from strategy to the nature of HR, not the reverse. One implication is that how an HR organization operates in a company may be largely determined by the company's business strategy. Perhaps HR is more the victim than the guilty party in cases where it is not a business or strategic partner. Certainly every senior HR leader we have worked with has said that it is easier to find an organization that understands and supports strategic HR than to try to change an organization that does not.

Management Approaches

Of the five management approaches we asked about, two of them had a strong and consistent positive relationship with the nature of the HR function in organizations. The high-involvement and sustainable approaches were associated with HR being more involved in business strategy activities, employee development, working with the board, and with advanced levels of decision science, decision support, and HR metrics and analytics. This is not surprising. These approaches, more than the others, require a clear focus on human capital and an organization that understands how talent and organizational design decisions affect strategic success.

The bureaucratic and the low-cost-operator approaches had negative relationships to most of the HR items. This is not surprising. These management approaches do not look to talent as a source of competitive advantage, so it is not surprising that they do not invest in building effective HR organizations.

The results for the global competitor approach tend to fall in the middle. It does have a positive relationship to the importance of HR, but the relationship is not as strong as it is for the high-involvement and sustainable approaches. This may reflect the fact that global competitors focus on many approaches to strategic success, including low cost. They may also use elements of the bureaucratic management approach in order to coordinate their global operations and operate their international units. In contrast, the high-involvement approach explicitly focuses on talent involvement as a key to performance, and the sustainable approach specifically emphasizes the quality of the employment relationship as a key performance indicator, in addition to its contribution to organization success.

As with the results for strategic focuses, there is the question of what comes first: the management approach or an HR function that is a strong business and strategic participant. As with the strategic focuses, our best guess is that it is more often the high-involvement and the sustainable approaches that lead to the strong HR role, but there are probably organizations where HR has had a major influence when an organization adopts the high-involvement approach and the sustainable approach.

Boudreau and Lawler (2014a) note that some approaches do not appear to be friendly to the advancement HR, which may explain why the profession has been so slow to change. They add that HR leaders who want to advance their profession need to consider whether it is better to battle the headwind of working in low-cost or bureaucratic organizations or to move to organizations that have or are willing to adopt sustainable and innovation-focused approaches.

International Differences

There are some interesting differences among the seven countries studied, and not surprisingly most of the differences involved China. It is one of two least developed of the countries studied (the other is India) and the only communist country studied. The key country differences include the following:

- China's HR organizations are lower than other countries on time spent as a strategic business partner.

- China's HR organizations are less involved in helping with succession and compensation issues.

- China's HR organizations are much less involved in business strategy activities, including implementation, assessing readiness, and identifying options.

- Chinese HR organizations do not have HR strategies that drive change management and are integrated with the business strategy.

- Chinese HR organizations are low on adding value by improving talent decisions and knowing where human capital makes a difference.

- HR organizations in the United States are the most frequent users of outsourcing and HR service units; Chinese are the least frequent.

- Chinese HR organizations are lowest on using HR metrics and analytics and on doing talent assessments.

- Employee assistance is outsourced most in the United States, Canada, and Australia and least in China.

- Chinese organizations make the least use of information technology; the United States makes the most.

- Chinese organizations rate the effectiveness of their metrics and analytics higher than any other country rates theirs.

- Chinese HR executives are the least satisfied with the skills of their HR staffs.

- Chinese HR executives rate the performance of their functions the lowest and the importance of HR performance the lowest.

Overall the picture is clear: HR organizations are very similar in India and in the Western countries studied and report higher levels of strategic partnership and HR functional effectiveness than China does. The similarity among these countries is not surprising since most of the organizations studied are large global operators. Still, there are cultural and legal differences among the countries that might lead to some major differences, but our data indicate they have not. The lower strategic activity in China suggests that the level of national economic and political development is a determinant of HR's role in organizations.

The development difference may also explain the management approach taken in the other countries versus China. Boudreau and Lawler (2014b) reported an analysis using the 2010 wave of data from this study, comparing the US sample to the China sample. In the 2010 survey, the China sample characterized its management approach significantly more as "low-cost operator" and significantly less as "global competitor," "high involvement," and "sustainable." In the 2013 survey, a similar pattern emerged, though the China sample reported similar levels of the high-involvement approach. As we noted earlier, the low-cost-operator approach is associated with lower levels of HR strategic partnership and HR functional effectiveness. Boudreau and Lawler (2014b) suggest that because in comparison to Western organizations, Chinese organizations show a stronger correlation between organizational size and the use of the low-cost operator approach, the performance it supports may make it more prevalent in China and in turn hinder the development of more advanced and strategic HR practices in China.

HR as a Strategic Contributor

The data concerning what determines the strategic role of the HR function are clearly consistent with the argument that HR can and should be more of a strategic contributor. Yet the data also show that HR is not a strategic contributor in most organizations. It appears to have some influence when it comes to how staffing relates to strategy and in influencing organizational structure and its relationship to implementing strategy. But our results suggest that HR plays a less prominent role when it comes to the development of strategy, consideration of strategic options, and other strategy areas, including acquisitions and mergers.

A number of HR capabilities and practices are significantly associated with a stronger strategic role for HR, including these:

- Having an HR strategy that is integrated with the business strategy

- The use of information technology by HR

- Focusing on HR talent development

- Using HR service teams that provide expertise and support the business

- Having HR activities that focus on organizational design, organizational development, change management, employee development, and metrics

- Using computer systems for training and development

- Having an effective HRIS system

- Having effective HR metrics and analytics

- Having business leaders who make rigorous, logical human capital decisions

- Having an HR staff with technical, organizational dynamics, business partner, and metrics skills

- Having effective decision support

- Having an HR function that effectively provides services

- Strong HR involvement and support of sustainability initiatives

Overall, HR being a strategic contributor demands that high levels of business knowledge and skill be present in HR. It also requires HRISs that have the right metrics and analytics, and organizational designs and practices that link HR managers to business units. Last, but not to be overlooked, is the need for effective and efficient delivery of HR services.

HR Effectiveness

The factors leading to HR effectiveness are a combination of approaches that promote efficiency in routine transactional processing and allow HR professionals to focus on expanding their knowledge base, providing expertise, and partnering with others. In chapter 14, we reported the results of whether organizational needs are being met across our twelve elements of HR effectiveness, which provide an actionable agenda for HR functions. It is also marked by another characteristic: most of the practices are rated between 6 and 7 on a ten-point scale of met needs. Only the traditional elements of "providing HR services" and "being an employee advocate" are rated higher than 7. That these measures have shown little change since 1995 strongly suggests that one of the reasons that HR is not increasing its effectiveness is that it has not done the things that it needs to do in order to be and to be perceived as more effective.

The results in chapter 15 showed that in virtually every major area we studied, there is a positive association between key advanced HR activities and functional characteristics and the strength of HR's role as a strategic partner. Despite the clear path this shows, the time spent on strategic partnership has not changed, and the nature of HR's role in strategy remains largely the traditional support role rather than a shaping or major partner role.

Organizational Effectiveness

In a similar vein, our results in chapter 16 show that many HR practices are significantly related to organizational performance. The results confirm our prior findings that organizational performance is higher when HR professionals focus on talent, use metrics and analytics to address HR effectiveness and impact, and develop their skills and knowledge. In our 2013 survey, new questions revealed that HR's role in sustainability is also positively related to organization performance.

What HR needs to do to improve its effectiveness is clear and not surprising. What is surprising is that it continues to do business as usual in a rapidly changing world. This has been a consistent finding since the mid-1990s and remains one of the most striking results of all our surveys.

Obstacles to Change

There are a number of possible explanations for why HR has not changed more. One is that HR executives simply do not believe that HR needs to change. But based on the results of our surveys and many others, this does not seem to be true. In all of our surveys, HR executives have said they have changed and plan to change and have said that it is important that they act as more of a business partner. Of course, they may just be saying what is professionally and politically correct and giving lip-service to the idea of being a business partner.

A second possible reason for the failure of HR to change is that in most organizations, there is no great demand for this change. HR's existing role and activities are well institutionalized and have created a kind of codependency relationship. The individuals in the HR function are satisfied with their current role and are comfortable delivering traditional HR services in a traditional mode; at the same time, the recipients of these services are satisfied with HR primarily being an administrative function that does what they consider onerous HR work for them. This situation leads to an institutionalized devaluation of the HR function because of its low level of contribution to the business and to an unwillingness to let it change because it serves many organization members well enough as it is (Boudreau and Lawler 2014a). However, our results showing an increase in the use of centralized HR services, HRIS, and the movement of HR activities into the hands of employees and their managers may signal the end of highly attentive and personal HR services.

The managers outside HR whom we surveyed in 2010 acknowledged the importance of HR being a strategic partner, but they also focused on the importance of HR's contributing to talent management (Lawler and Boudreau 2012). Ironically, it is possible that their focus on talent may be operating against upgrading the strategic role of HR. It may focus a disproportionate amount of professional HR time on delivering services related to recruiting, orienting, developing, and retaining employees, leaving HR little time and few resources to spend on upgrading the competencies and systems needed in order for it to be a contributor to strategy development.

Recruiting, developing, and retaining a highly mobile and competitive workforce can often impose high demands on HR time and energy and can lock HR professionals into activity patterns that are difficult to change. Certainly a common refrain we hear from HR leaders is that they rarely have time to think about big picture issues or to develop in areas beyond their specific functional responsibilities. We have found that the attention being paid to almost all HR activities has increased since we began our surveys, suggesting that although there is agreement that some HR activities add greater value than others, HR functions are still required to spend an increasing amount of time on activities that may have low strategic value.

The skills of the professionals in the HR function offer an additional reason for the limited change in the HR function. Just how difficult it is to change the HR function becomes apparent when we look at the kinds of skills that members of the HR function must have in order to be rated highly and to perform the roles of strategic contributor and business partner. HR professionals need skills ranging from relatively routine administrative processing skills to organizational dynamics and business skills. Although business and organizational dynamics skills are the most highly related to HR's effectiveness, our results suggest that the HR function cannot be ineffective in its core administrative functions if it wants to be respected. Interestingly, in our surveys, HR does not score very high in administrative skills, especially with respect to managing contractors and managing HRISs. The latter is particularly concerning since it is the future of HR operations and strategy.

Business and strategic contributor effectiveness requires knowledge and skills in areas such as change management, strategic planning, and organizational design. It also requires a knowledge of decision science for human capital that provides logical and unique strategic insights by using human capital principles. HR professionals have traditionally had little experience with these areas, which involve complex judgments. Such expertise is both hard to acquire and in short supply. Becoming expert in business partnering demands the acquisition of not only explicit knowledge but also tacit knowledge that comes from experience. Applying this expertise demands the ability to influence line management and to be part of effective teaming relationships with others who have deep business knowledge.

The results of our surveys show that HR professionals are seen as having increased some of their interpersonal dynamics skills and their business understanding skills since 1995. However, they are still perceived to fall short in most business skills and in metrics and analytical skills as well. HR leaders also often lack cross-functional business experience. Understanding HR strategy is at best a ticket to a seat at the table. Expertise in business strategy is required to set the table and add value once there. Thus, HR is in a bit of a catch-22: it must get to the table and gain experience in order to gain the knowledge and skills it needs to get there!

In a related study at the Center for Effective Organizations, John Boudreau and Ian Ziskin surveyed several hundred HR professionals in eleven leading organizations on the current and ideal role of HR leaders in the talent applications of emerging trends such as gamification, big data, segmentation, and sustainability. Across the board, that research showed that the ideal role was akin to being a leader or key contributor, but the current role was much less involved, often rated only as "occasional input." Participants commented that while leaders inside and outside HR recognized the importance of getting ahead of such trends, the day-to-day demands of traditional HR made it virtually impossible to systematically evolve to leadership roles.

Conclusion

HR wants to be a strategic partner and the door is open because of the growing recognition that talent is a key determinant of an organization's effectiveness. But HR cannot get through the door in many organizations, much less take a seat at the table. The good news is that our results consistently identify a pattern of HR activities, skills, and relationships that are associated with HR effectiveness and a stronger strategic role. Difficult as it may be to make them happen, the changes that are required emerge consistently and are easy to identify.

CHAPTER 18

What the Future of HR Should Be

What should the future be for the HR function? What does HR need to do to become a strategic contributor? When we reported on our 1998 results (Lawler and Mohrman 2000, p. 71), we wrote, "Change has just begun. The next decade will probably see dramatic change in the human resource function in most companies. The opportunity exists for human resource management to become a true strategic partner, and to help decide how organizations will be managed, what human resource systems will look like, and how human resource services will be created and delivered."

Our 2013 results suggest that many of the changes we predicted have not yet taken place. Yes, there has been some change, but it is not the kind of game-changing change that we thought would happen. Nevertheless, we have not altered our view that transformational change in HR is needed. If anything, it is needed much more now than it was in 1998. The world of work has undergone tremendous change since 1998. Today organizations in the United States and the rest of the developed world have an ever higher percentage of their employees doing knowledge work. Information technology has changed how work is done and what work is done. The economy has become more global. Environmental sustainability has become an increasingly important global issue. Human capital has become increasingly important as a source of competitive advantage, as has intellectual capital (Lawler and Worley 2011). Furthermore, the rate of change is likely to increase (Worley, Williams, and Lawler 2014).

Our results show that when organizations focus on developing their competencies, capabilities, and knowledge assets, especially in combination with a strong focus on the strategy of the firm, HR is a strong strategic and business contributor and the HR function is markedly different from the way it has traditionally operated. Thus, there is good reason to believe that if organizations increasingly pursue strategic focuses and management approaches that draw on deep and widespread human capital excellence, HR will change.

HR as a High-Value Contributor

We pointed out in chapter 1 that as a business, HR potentially can have three product lines. The first is to execute the processes and activities required to provide services such as compensation, administration, staffing, development and deployment.

The second role is to respond to business plans developed by others, helping business units and general managers realize their plans. In this role, HR provides advice and services concerning how to develop, design, and install HR practices in areas such as employee relations, talent management, organizational development, change management, and connecting HR practices with business operations.

The third role is helping to develop and implement the strategic direction of an organization. It requires acquiring, developing, and accessing an organization's human capital and creating the organizational capabilities required to support its strategic direction. It also requires shaping strategy by providing a unique perspective through the lens of the talent market and human behavior. This requires HR to have leaders who understand business strategy and how it relates to organizational capabilities and core competencies and how those connect to pivotal talent and organizational design decisions. In this role, HR leaders need to use their knowledge to help the organization set its strategic direction and develop its design and business plans in ways that are consistent with a talent decision science.

HR Administration

The HR administrative services of an organization are increasingly becoming a commodity. Historically, they were delivered by an in-house HR function, often in a labor-intensive and costly manner. Three alternative approaches are emerging as ways to acquire and operate the technology and skills needed to deliver HR services.

The first is to use web-based custom systems that are designed and operated by the organization. This model is currently being used by IT companies such as Google, IBM, Cisco, Hewlett-Packard, and Microsoft. Some of these systems are impressive and allow individuals, on a self-service basis, to perform a number of important HR tasks and access a great deal of information. More powerful personal devices such as phones and tablets promise a future of HR apps that may make such activities easier and more user friendly. Video authoring tools promise a future in which individuals may be able to easily record and post their knowledge to a library in the cloud, enabling virtual social learning. However, it is highly unlikely that most companies will ever develop the kind of custom systems that large technology companies have developed because it is too expensive and time-consuming.

A second model is to acquire software and systems from vendors using one of two approaches. The first is to buy an integrated web-based system from a major enterprise resource planning (ERP) vendor (e.g., Oracle, SAP, Workday). The second is to acquire individual HR applications for specific tasks like compensation administration, staffing, and training from different software vendors. While using separate best-in-class applications for each function may improve performance within each function, our results suggest there is great value in integration. The best use of HR data often is integration across multiple HR processes, but this can be costly and time-consuming. Integrated total HR systems may provide the remedy because they are already integrated.

We may see the evolution of a core set of data standards (Cascio and Boudreau 2012) against which multiple software vendors can develop their applications. A new item in our 2013 survey asked about software as a service hosted in the cloud and found that it achieved a higher-rated effectiveness level than all levels of outsourcing, suggesting that a more modular and cloud-based model may be the most effective.

The third model is to use business process outsourcing. A number of major corporations have signed contracts to outsource all or most of the administrative aspects of their HR management processes. Case studies of four early adopters showed significant cost savings, as well as enabling some movement toward HR becoming more of a strategic partner (Lawler, Ulrich, Fitz-enz, and Madden 2004). Other large firms (e.g., Unilever) have adopted this approach. However, the results of our 2013 survey suggest that outsourcing may not be growing quickly and may even be declining. Our results suggest that it is seen as most effective when it is done on a "very limited" or "moderate" level, not at a "substantial" level.

Our findings in 2013 present some interesting results concerning the future of HR technologies. They show a continuing trend for more HR administration to be done by employees on a self-service basis and that more employee self-service is associated with a stronger HR role in strategy, perhaps because it frees up time for HR to get involved in strategic activities. In the 2013 survey, we added new items on the use of social networks, mobile technology, and software as service. Each was rated as being used less than a "moderate extent," but greater use of each of them was associated with HR's increase in strategic role. Thus, there is some evidence that employee self-service, social networks, mobile technology, and software as service may be enablers of other actions that HR can take to become more of a strategic contributor.

Overall, we believe that information technology can be a key delivery vehicle for HR services and can contribute to an enhanced strategic role for HR. It has the potential to free up HR to do more strategic work and to collect important talent and organizational effectiveness data. In addition, the value of information systems in conveying HR knowledge and decision frameworks to managers and employees represents an untapped opportunity for improving an organization's talent management.

Business Partner

But what about HR activities that involve responding to the business plans others have formed and implementing and preparing the organization to execute those plans? Can this role be outsourced? Can or should these activities be put on the web?

HRISs can collect, aggregate, and analyze ever-increasing amounts of data about the human resources of an organization, at ever-lower costs and higher speeds. HR data can contribute to change management, business plan development and implementation, and business operations by making human capital information readily available and obtaining feedback and suggestions about HR process improvement and effectiveness. These enablers can enhance human judgment in problem solving and decision making but can never replace it.

As for outsourcing the business partner role, consultants can provide insight into the HR implications of business plans and organizational change. However, our view is that tailoring HR programs and practices to specific strategies and business plans and implementing them will always need the contributions of internal skilled HR professionals to provide the services, information, and knowledge that are necessary for HR to be an effective business partner.

Performing the business partner role entails solving problems and making decisions that are value laden, highly uncertain, and context specific; they require understanding the business, its strategy, the nature of the workforce, and the required competencies. It entails the application of tacit, experience-based knowledge of employee relations, as well as knowledge of the HR discipline and the ability to combine HR knowledge with the perspectives of other disciplines, such as business management, marketing, information technology, and technology.

The key question for us is not whether HR professionals should perform the business partner role, but whether current HR professionals are the ones to do it. The results of our study suggest that the comfort level and effectiveness of today's HR professionals remain highest in the traditional HR areas, such as HR technical and interpersonal skills, compliance, implementing (not shaping) strategy, and giving corporate boards advice on HR issues such as executive compensation and succession. To become better at helping the organizations to implement business plans, HR professionals need to develop their capabilities in areas such as organizational design, change management, vendor and contract management, decision support, finance, and strategy analysis.

Strategic Contributor

Perhaps the most intriguing results of our study are those that have implications for the strategic contributor role. As organizations face a more complex and rapidly changing sustainability-conscious environment, there is an increasing need for HR leaders to not only respond to business strategies, but to shape them based on talent and organizational competencies and capabilities. In addition, the rapid rate of change, the need to develop new strategies and quickly translate them into talent strategies, and the likelihood that the availability of talent will be a key strategic differentiator have greatly combined to increase the importance of HR being an effective strategic contributor.

The role of strategic contributor requires individuals who understand how business strategies and plans connect to talent and organizational design and management. They also need to know how to shape business strategies to fit emerging human capital opportunities and threats. Some of this work can be outsourced to HR strategy consultants, but we believe that in most organizations, there needs to be an internal group with good HR knowledge who can manage consultants and can shape organizational strategies. Ideally, HR's strategic role ultimately needs to be led by a senior executive in the organization, not a consultant.

The importance of the HR strategic role and the need to fill it with somebody who understands business may be one reason that our research finds that almost a quarter of all chief HR executives come from the business rather than from the HR function. In essence, some companies seem to have decided that the HR strategic partner role is too important to be entrusted to someone with solely an HR background. This is not completely surprising; our results show a long-term tendency for satisfaction with HR's skills to be higher when it comes to HR technical and interpersonal skills than for business partner, metrics, and decision support skills.

As tempting as it is to staff the top HR role with a business executive, there is a danger if the chief HR officer has little HR functional knowledge. Just as with other functions such as IT, operations, legal, supply chain, and finance, this role requires a strong knowledge of not only business and strategy but also knowledge of the function. In the case of HR, it requires the capacity to understand the principles and practices that underlie labor markets and human behavior at work just as knowledge about portfolio theory or customer behavior is a prerequisite to be the chief financial officer or chief marketing officer (Boudreau and Ramstad 2007). Indeed, effective strategic partnership may require that HR leaders retool their current logic frameworks to better apply the principles of disciplines such as marketing, finance, and operations directly to such HR functions as staffing, rewards and talent management (Boudreau 2010).

The arrival of big data on the HR scene provides data-supported enablers that can strengthen HR's position as a strategic contributor. Big data can potentially help HR professionals make significant contributions to strategy formulation by providing both cost and organizational effectiveness data with respect to HR practices. They can provide information about how to develop certain key competencies and about the existing levels of organizational effectiveness and organizational capabilities. These are all critical to the strategy planning process. They can codify and teach decision frameworks and principles that enhance strategic decisions (Boudreau and Ramstad 2007). They also can enable HR executives to translate what they know about an organization and its capabilities into change programs, thus allowing the organization to develop the capabilities to implement new strategic plans and new directions (Lawler and Worley 2006).

Our survey results suggest that for decades, the skills, resources, and time to deliver on a powerful new role remain stubbornly lacking in the HR function of most organizations. There is a real possibility that organizations will grow impatient with the HR profession's failure to develop strategic HR leaders and decide to take their chances by populating HR leadership positions with individuals who possess the business, analytical, and change skills necessary to formulate human capital strategy—even if those individuals are not well versed in HR.

Talent Management for the HR Profession

Quite possibly the biggest change that needs to occur in HR has to do with how talent is managed in the HR function, not elsewhere in the organization. In many respects, talent management in HR is a case of the shoemakers' children lacking shoes. Our results suggest that HR often does not have the right talent, and too often it has talent that is inferior to that in other key parts of the organization even though HR professionals need to have a comparable set of skills and knowledge.

HR professionals need the following abilities:

- To understand and be able to formulate a business model for the HR function and to contribute to the firm's business mode
- To understand business operations and be able to craft HR management approaches that reflect their organization's competitive situation

- To understand organizational and work design and change management principles and approaches and be able to play a leadership role when these issues are considered

- To understand different models of staffing, compensation, and other HR management practices so that they can effectively implement HR systems that support the business plans of the organization

- To educate and develop business leaders who make human capital decisions that are as logical, rigorous, and strategic as are their decisions about money, technology, and customers

- To identify the pivot points in the business that drive strategic and organizational effectiveness, and then connect human capital decisions to those pivot points

There are some reasons to think that at least at the senior levels, the talent level in HR has been improving. More CEOs now recognize the importance of having a talented HR executive and have acted on this recognition. Organizations have been particularly willing to promote women to senior HR management positions. Many highly talented female business leaders have become HR executives because it is their best career opportunity. This has created a gender diversity in HR that offers significant opportunities for the HR profession to provide a unique perspective at the executive and board levels of organizations. Because organizations must consider more diverse employee populations and customers, this is an important change.

The skills and knowledge that HR professionals need are not easily acquired. They are likely to exist only in organizations that take HR talent management seriously and have an integrated approach to talent management. This has important implications for HR's performance management and staffing practices at all levels of the HR function. At the entry level, for example, HR needs to significantly increase the quality of those it hires. Today few of the best students in the leading business schools pursue HR careers because of low starting salaries and a perception that HR is not a good place to start a career. As a result, there often is a scarcity of highly talented business school students with an academic concentration in HR. Thus, organizations should consider hiring non-HR majors who are very talented and interested in HR. Indeed, the ground may be shifting; some business school students have been very articulate about the wisdom of their decision to pursue an HR career (Breitfelder and Dowling 2008). However, at least until it does shift, HR needs to hire more non-HR majors.

Once HR professionals are hired, it is important that they spend time working outside HR. Our data suggest that this does not happen very often and that most organizations have no plans to increase it. This is a problem because without experience in non-HR jobs, HR professionals miss important opportunities to understand the business; they also miss the chance to build personal credibility by doing a non-HR job well.

It may be even more important to have non-HR managers and professionals rotate into HR than it is for HR professionals to rotate out. At this point, very few US corporations have CEOs or senior executives other than the head of HR who have worked in HR. Increasing the number of senior managers who have HR experience has important benefits. One is that it can improve their performance when they make human capital decisions and they work with HR. Another is that it makes top organizational talent available to the HR function and brings to HR the perspective of non-HR executives regarding HR's value proposition.

Our results show that business leaders are held to higher standards regarding their capability to use sound principles in areas such as finance and marketing as compared to human capital and talent management. Considering the acknowledged importance of talent to competitiveness, it would seem prudent to give senior leaders deep experience in HR so they can build their understanding of this important area.

The value of shared and valid principles about human capital and talent management has important implications for future HR executives. HR professionals should be trained and should develop and use research-based knowledge about labor markets, human behavior, and organizational effectiveness. They need to move beyond just being good to work with and knowledgeable about people and employee relations. They need to know and act on the large amount of research that has been done on talent management, organizational design, and a host of other organizational effectiveness issues. Making decisions on instinct or "knowing people" is not enough. Evidence-based decision making is needed along with a savvy understanding about how to transform organizations through evidence-based change.

HR Organizational Design

How should the HR function be managed and structured? Should it be a large function, employing approximately one out of every one hundred employees, and organized primarily using a service delivery paradigm focused on activities such as compensation, training, and staffing? There is good reason to believe that it should not. HR needs to use a deeper and more strategic perspective on how it adds value to justify its cost. Strategic influence, business decision support, organizational agility, and sustainability need to define the HR value proposition; providing low-cost, high-quality services is not sufficient (Worley et al. 2014).

One possible approach to the design of the HR function is to centralize operations and infrastructure within a chief operating officer function for HR. Such a function would span both the business partner and the administrative components of the HR function, providing specialized support in areas such as compensation, development, and performance management. This structure would free the chief HR officer (CHRO) of many of the ongoing tasks associated with running the HR department and allow him or her to focus on the strategic role of human capital in the organization, as well as on being a member of the executive team.

An increasingly common feature of HR function design, particularly in companies with multiple business units, is to place an HR executive in each business unit. Their role involves contributing to business unit plans and tailoring HR practices to the workforce needs of the unit. They are also expected to be liaisons to the corporate HR staff and services on behalf of their business units. This liaison role is likely to be increasingly important in the future. Instead of locating many of the HR services in the business unit, many multidivision corporations are creating shared service units and corporate centers of excellence for the business units to draw on. They also are outsourcing HR transactional services and require business units to use them. In both approaches, the role of the business unit HR executive is to both translate business strategies into necessary HR responses and coordinate the centralized HR services for the business unit. In this design, there is an increasing use of "double-hatting" HR executives to ensure connections between HR functional expertise and business unit goals. For example, the head of learning and development may double-hat as the business partner for a major organizational division or product line where learning and development are particularly pivotal.

In some organizations, the HR organization appears to be becoming a type of front-back organization where the business unit HR leaders are the front, customer-focused part (Galbraith 2014). The back is the vendors, shared services units, and centers of excellence that are available to the business units. Our results show that the front-back approach to HR function design has increased in popularity since 1994 and there is reason to believe that some versions of it will be the most popular approaches in the future. Nevertheless, it is worth considering an alternative organization for the HR function since it does not directly position HR to make it a maximum contribution to organizational effectiveness.

Potentially, HR can be in three businesses (administration, business partner, and strategic contributor) that are related but require different competencies and capabilities. One comparison here is sales and marketing; another is accounting and finance. They are related but require different competencies and capabilities; therefore, they are split and operate at different levels of an organization's hierarchy. Applying this logic to HR would mean creating an HR function that does administration and business partnering with respect to strategy implementation and HR service delivery to the organization. Another function would be created that has overall responsibility for organizational effectiveness.

The organizational effectiveness corporate function would combine business strategy and planning, human capital management, organizational development, and organizational design. It would be headed by a chief organization effectiveness officer (COEO) and would have responsibility for strategy formulation, implementation, and talent management. In this approach, the COEO would report to the CEO, and the CHRO would report to the COEO.

Having an organizational effectiveness function is a good fit for many of today's knowledge work organizations because it integrates expertise in business strategy and talent management. It is unlike the typical organizational design of most large organizations because it recognizes and creates a function charged with managing the fit between talent and strategy. All too often, this fit is not considered because no one, except perhaps the CEO, is responsible for the fit. It is a particularly good fit for organizations that need to be agile because they face a rapidly changing environment.

Looking Ahead

The opportunity for the HR function to add value is great, but at this time, it is more promise than reality. For promise to become reality, HR executives need to develop new skills and knowledge, and HR needs to be able to execute HR management and administrative activities effectively. Doing the basics well is the platform on which the HR organization needs to build its role as a business partner. Doing so is critical, because it demonstrates the capacity of the HR function to operate effectively as a business, and it potentially can provide the information that enables HR to be an effective business partner and strategic contributor. But it is not enough; HR must also make strategic contributions to the organization.

Indeed, the context for HR management increasingly requires boundaries that span the HR function, the organization, and the dynamic environment within which the organization operates. As organizations adopt definitions of sustainable effectiveness that include the social and environmental impacts of organizations and face the need to embrace constant and dynamic change, it will change even today's aspirations for HR as a business partner that contributes to a human capital–based competitive advantage (Lawler and Worley 2011). Consider the following six trends that have been identified as pivotal to the future of HR (Boudreau and Ziskin 2011):

1. Hero leadership to collective leadership

2. Intellectual property to agile cocreativity

3. Employment value proposition to personal value proposition

4. Sameness to segmentation

5. Fatigue to sustainability

6. Persuasion to education

These trends illustrate the complexity of issues that organizations will face in the future. Where will expertise arise to help organizations craft a point of view and framework for sustainability, agility, cocreation with multiple constituents, mass-customized value proposition and talent segmentation, and the evolution of leadership as vested in a top team to something that pervades the entire organization? These are not "HR issues"; they are strategy and organizational design issues that will be central to the success of most organizations and vital topics for all businesses. And they draw on the unique disciplines that traditionally underlie HR, including psychology, political science, anthropology, values, culture, and engagement.

Should CEOs expect their CHROs to take the lead on these issues? Are HR leaders and their organizations prepared for such leadership? In many cases today, such issues fall outside the HR function or in the "white spaces" between today's HR job descriptions (Boudreau and Ziskin 2011).

The need for a new business model for HR has been accepted and acknowledged by most HR executives, but the HR function still appears to be at the very beginning of the changes that are needed in order for it to become a reality. Our study reveals that the change process is slower than it should be. It identifies a clear action agenda that can yield an HR function capable of adding more value to the business. We believe there will be enormous change in the design and operation of HR functions, but we are not sure when it will occur. We have said it before, and we say it again: the HR function needs to look seriously at reinventing itself. The old approaches and models are not good enough. If they are not changed, the HR function will become a minor player in tomorrow's organizations.

REFERENCES

Boudreau, J. W. 2010. *Retooling HR*. Boston: Harvard Business School Press.

Boudreau, J. W., and R. Jesuthasan. 2011. *Transformative HR*. New York: Wiley.

Boudreau, J. W., and E. E. Lawler. 2014a. Stubborn traditionalism in HRM: Causes and consequences. *Human Resource Management Review* 24 (3): 232–44.

Boudreau, J. W., and E. E. Lawler III. 2014b. The strategic role of HR in the U.S. and China: Relationships with HR outcomes and effects of management approaches. In *Strategic talent management: Contemporary issues in international context*, ed. P. Sparrow, H. Scullion, and I. Tarique. Cambridge: Cambridge University Press.

Boudreau, J. W., and P. M. Ramstad. 1997. Measuring intellectual capital: Learning from financial history. *Human Resource Management* 36 (3): 34–56.

Boudreau, J. W., and P. M. Ramstad. 2003. Strategic HRM measurement in the 21st century: From justifying HR to strategic talent leadership. In *HRM in the 21st century*, ed. M. Goldsmith, R. P. Gandossy, and M. S. Efron, 79–90. Hoboken, NJ: Wiley.

Boudreau, J. W., and P. M. Ramstad. 2005a. Talentship and the evolution of human resource management: From "professional practices" to "strategic talent decision science." *Human Resource Planning Journal* 28 (2): 17–26.

Boudreau, J. W., and P. M. Ramstad. 2005b. Talentship, talent segmentation, and sustainability: A new HR decision science paradigm for a new strategy definition. In *The future of human resources management*, ed. M. Losey, S. Meisinger, and D. Ulrich. Washington, DC: Society for Human Resource Management.

Boudreau, J. W., and P. M. Ramstad. 2005c. Where is your pivotal talent? *Harvard Business Review* 83 (4): 23–24.

Boudreau, J. W., and P. M. Ramstad. 2006. Talentship and human resource management and analysis: From ROI to strategic organizational change. *Human Resource Planning Journal* 29 (1): 25–33.

Boudreau, J. W., and P. M. Ramstad. 2007. *Beyond HR: The new science of human capital*. Boston: Harvard Business School Press.

Boudreau, J. W., and I. Ziskin. 2011. The future of HR and effective organizations. *Organizational Dynamics* 40 (4): 255–67.

Breitfelder, M. D., and D. W. Dowling. 2008. Why did we ever go into HR? *Harvard Business Review* 86 (7–8): 39–43.

Brockbank, W. 1999. If HR were really strategically proactive: Present and future directions in HR's contribution to competitive advantage. *Human Resource Management* 38 (4): 337–52.

Brundtland, G. H. 1987. *Report of the World Commission on Environment and Development: Our Common Future.* New York: United Nations.

Cascio, W. F. 2000. *Costing human resources,* 4th ed. Cincinnati, OH: South-Western.

Cascio, W. F., and J. W. Boudreau. 2011. *Investing in people: Financial impact of human resource initiatives,* 2nd ed. Upper Saddle River, NJ: FT Press.

Cascio, W. F., and J. W. Boudreau. 2012. Short introduction to strategic human resources. Cambridge: Cambridge University Press.

Csoka, L. S., and B. Hackett. 1998. *Transforming the HR function for global business success.* New York: Conference Board.

Galbraith, J. R. 2014. *Designing organizations: Strategy, structure, and process at the business unit and enterprise levels.* San Francisco: Jossey-Bass.

Gates, S. 2004. *Measuring more than efficiency.* Research Report R-1356-04-RR. New York: Conference Board.

Gubman, E. 2004. HR strategy and planning: From birth to business results. *Human Resource Planning* 27 (1): 13–23.

Huselid, M. A., B. E. Becker, and R. W. Beatty. 2005. *The workforce scorecard.* Boston: Harvard Business School Press.

Lawler, E. E. 1995. Strategic human resources management: An idea whose time has come. In *Managing human resources in the 1990s and beyond: Is the workplace being transformed?* ed. B. Downie and M. L. Coates, 46–70. Kingston, Canada: IRC Press.

Lawler, E. E. 2008. *Talent: Making people your competitive advantage.* San Francisco: Jossey-Bass.

Lawler, E. E., and J. W. Boudreau. 2009. *Achieving excellence in human resource management.* Stanford, CA: Stanford University Press.

Lawler, E. E., and J. W. Boudreau. 2012. *Effective human resource management: A global analysis.* Stanford, CA: Stanford University Press.

Lawler, E. E., J. W. Boudreau, and S. A. Mohrman. 2006. *Achieving strategic excellence: An assessment of human resource organizations.* Stanford, CA: Stanford University Press.

Lawler, E. E., A. Levenson, and J. W. Boudreau. 2004. HR metrics and analytics: Uses and impacts. *Human Resource Planning Journal* 27 (4): 27–35.

Lawler, E. E., and S. A. Mohrman. 2000. *Creating a strategic human resources organization.* Los Angeles: Center for Effective Organizations.

Lawler, E. E., and S. A. Mohrman. 2003. *Creating a strategic human resources organization: An assessment of trends and new directions.* Stanford, CA: Stanford University Press.

Lawler, E. E., S. A. Mohrman, and G. S. Benson. 2001. *Organizing for high performance: The CEO report on employee involvement, TQM, reengineering, and knowledge management in Fortune 1000 companies.* San Francisco: Jossey-Bass.

Lawler, E. E., D. Ulrich, J. Fitz-enz, and J. Madden. 2004. *Human resources business process outsourcing.* San Francisco: Jossey-Bass.

Lawler, E. E., and C. G. Worley. 2006. *Built to change: How to achieve sustained organizational effectiveness.* San Francisco: Jossey-Bass.

Lawler, E. E., and C. G. Worley. 2011. *Management reset: Organizing for sustainable effectiveness.* San Francisco: Jossey-Bass.

Lev, B. 2001. *Intangibles: Management, measurement, and reporting.* Washington, DC: Brookings.

Mohrman, A. M., J. R. Galbraith, E. E. Lawler, and Associates. 1998. *Tomorrow's organization: Crafting winning capabilities in a dynamic world.* San Francisco: Jossey-Bass.

Mohrman, S. A., and E. E. Lawler. 2014. Designing organizations for sustainable effectiveness: A new paradigm for organizations and academic researchers. *Journal of Organizational Effectiveness: People and Performance* 1 (1): 14–34.

Mohrman, S. A., E. E. Lawler, and G. McMahan. 1996. *New directions for the human resources organization: An organization design approach.* Los Angeles: Center for Effective Organizations. Mohrman, S. A., J. O'Toole, and E. E. Lawler. 2015. *Corporate stewardship: Achieving sustainable effectiveness.* Sheffield, UK: Greenleaf.

O'Toole, J., and E. E. Lawler. 2006. *The new American workplace*. New York: Palgrave Macmillan.

Ulrich, D. 1997. *Human resources champions*. Boston: Harvard Business School Press.

Ulrich, D., and W. Brockbank. 2005. *The HR value proposition*. Boston: Harvard Business School Press.

Ulrich, D., W. Brockbank, D. Johnson, K. Sandholtz, and J. Younger. 2008. *HR competencies: Mastery at the intersection of people and business*. Alexandria, VA: SHRM.

Ulrich, D., J. Younger, W. Brockbank, and M. Ulrich. 2012. *HR from the outside in: Six competencies for the future of human resources*. New York: McGraw-Hill.

Worley, C. G., T. Williams, and E. E. Lawler III. 2014. *The agility factor: Building adaptable organizations for superior performance*. San Francisco: Jossey-Bass.

APPENDIX A
Research Partners

United States

Conference Board–USA
Rebecca L. Ray, Senior Vice President—Human Capital
Yolanda Lannquist, Research Analyst

Executive Network
Mike Dulworth, President and CEO
Kiley Merrill (HR Roundtable Group), Network Director
Ari Neubauer, Membership Services

Human Resources Planning Society
Christopher Mundschenk, HR People and Strategy

Institute for Corporate Productivity
Jay Jamrog, Senior Vice President of Research
Kevin Oakes, Chief Executive Officer
Kevin Martin, Chief Research and Marketing Officer
Erik Samdahl, Director of Marketing

Australia

Australian Human Resources Institute
Anne-Marie Dolan, Manager—Development and Research/HR Manager

Canada

The Conference Board of Canada
Ruth Wright, Associate Director—Leadership and Human Resources Research
Erica Bernstein, Research Associate and Network Officer
Alicia Cameron, Research Associate and Analyst
Heidi Martin, Research Associate and Network Manager

China

Institute of Organization and Human Resources, School of Public Administration, Renmin University of China

Chaoping Li, Associate Professor

Bwise Management Training & Consulting

Paul Wang, Consultant

Europe

Corporate Research Foundation

Mike Haffendon, Cofounder

Lynn Little

World Trade Group

Ben Quarless, Content and Community Manager

Kate Marston, Head of Online Marketing and Operations

University of Chieti-Pescara (The G. d'Annunzio University)

Lorenzo Lucianetti, Aggregate Professor

India

National HRD Network

Archana Arcot

Aparajita Pant

APPENDIX B
Research Design

Our study examines the extent to which the design and activities of the HR function are actually changing by analyzing survey data from 1995, 1998, 2001, 2004, 2007, 2010, and 2013. We examine the use of practices that are expected to represent the new directions that human resource organizations must take in order to fit with the changes that are occurring in the organizations they serve. We also examine how these changes are related to the strategic role of HR, its effectiveness, and the effectiveness of organizations. Finally, we examine the impact of how the HR function is designed and operates on its effectiveness. It focuses in depth on twelve areas:

1. *HR activities.* In order to assess how HR has changed, questions were asked about how the activities of HR have changed. Of particular interest is whether HR is doing less administration and more strategic work.

2. *HR role and activities.* Because of changes in the business environment, it is reasonable to expect that the HR function may have changed. A major focus of the study is to learn to what extent the HR function is changing, particularly with respect to becoming a strategic partner. It also looks at which organizational designs and HR practices are associated with HR being a strategic partner. Of particular concern is whether attention to strategic services, such as organizational design and development, is related to the effectiveness of the HR function and organizational effectiveness. We also focus on finding out how much increase or decrease there has been in the emphasis on traditional HR functions such as HR planning, compensation, recruitment, selection, and HR information systems. Of particular interest is whether HR is doing less administrative and more strategic work.

3. *Decision science for talent resources.* Numerous books and articles that discuss talent have highlighted the fact that organizations are increasingly competing for human capital and that their ability to successfully compete can be a source of competitive advantage. They also, of course, need to effectively manage the talent. Our study therefore focuses on whether organizations have developed a decision science for their important talent decisions and whether this is related to how effectively they manage it and to organizational effectiveness.

4. *Design of the HR function.* We examine whether changes have occurred in the way the HR function is organized in order to increase the value that it delivers. Because of their role in determining the balance between efficiency and customer-focused support, we look at the adoption of shared services and centers of excellence. We also look at the use of self-service and HR generalists.

5. *Outsourcing.* Outsourcing is becoming an increasingly popular way to deliver HR services and gain HR expertise. Potentially it is a way to deal with changes in the demand for HR services as well as a way to control costs. Thus, we focus both on how common different approaches to outsourcing are and how effective they are.

6. *Information technology.* HRIS systems can potentially radically change the way HR services are delivered and managed. Thus, the study examines how companies are using information technology in their HR

functions. It also focuses on how effective organizations consider their HR information systems to be in influencing employee satisfaction and providing strategic information.

7. *Metrics and analytics.* It is important to know both what measures HR organizations collect and how they analyze them. Thus, our study looks at what metrics are being collected and used. It also looks at how effectively metrics and analytics are being used.

8. *Sustainable performance.* Organizations are increasingly being asked to perform well not just financially but socially and environmentally as well. This raises the question of what HR can and should do to ensure that organizations perform well in all three areas.

9. *HR skills.* Critical to the effectiveness of any HR function are the skills of the HR professionals and staff. Thus, the study examines how satisfied organizations are with their HR professionals' skills in a variety of areas. It also looks at the importance of the skills HR professionals need in order to serve as true business and strategic partners.

10. *HR effectiveness.* The effectiveness of the HR function is a critical issue. Particular emphasis in our study is placed on the effectiveness of the HR function in doing many of the new activities that are required in order for it to be a business and strategic partner. These include managing change, contributing to strategy, managing the outsourcing of HR, and operating shared service units. Perhaps the crucial issue with respect to effectiveness concerns what practices lead to an effective HR organization. Thus, the study focuses on what HR structures, approaches, and practices are associated with the effectiveness of an HR organization.

11. *Organizational performance.* The effectiveness and structure of the HR function is just one of many influences on an organization's overall performance, but it can be a significant influence. Human capital is an important driver of organizational performance in most organizations. Thus, the relationship between organizational performance and how the HR function is designed and operates is an important focus of the study.

12. *International.* In our first five surveys, we gathered data only from US corporations. The economy has become increasingly global since we began this research in 1995, and thus it is particularly important to consider how HR functions in different countries. For the first time in our 2010 survey, we collected data from corporations in five countries in addition to US corporations. In 2013, we collected data from the United States as well as from the same five countries, and from India.

Method

This is the seventh in an every-three-year study examining whether change has occurred in the HR organizations of large and medium-sized corporations and what makes HR function effectively. In the first study in 1995, surveys were mailed to HR executives at the director level or above in 417 large and medium-sized service and industrial firms (Mohrman, Lawler, and McMahan 1996). The executives chosen in the HR function had broad visibility across the corporation. We received responses from 130 companies (response rate 19.6 percent). In the second study, done in 1998, we mailed surveys to similar executives at 663 similar firms; 199 usable surveys were returned (response rate 17.9 percent) (Lawler and Mohrman 2000). In the third survey, done in 2001, 966 surveys were mailed and 150 usable surveys were received (15.5 percent response rate) (Lawler and Mohrman 2003). For the 2004 study, surveys were again mailed to HR executives with corporate visibility of the HR function in large and medium-sized companies (Lawler, Boudreau, and Mohrman 2006).

For the 2007 survey, questionnaires were once again mailed to HR executives in medium and large companies. For the first time, data were also gathered by using the Internet. The Institute for Corporate Productivity (i4cp) created a web-based version of our survey and used it to collect data from 43 companies, giving us a total sample of 106 companies. All of the 2010 and 2013 survey data were collected using the Internet. HR executives were given a link and asked to respond.

For the first time in 2004, data were collected from non-HR senior managers. In 2007, 2010, and 2013, data were again collected from non-HR senior managers in US corporations. A cover letter to the HR executives in the United States asked that the survey be distributed to individuals who were not in HR but were in a position to evaluate the function. In 2010, the manager's questionnaire was made available by a link and the questions were answered online. A complete copy of the 2010 manager survey with frequencies, means, and variances for the United States is in Lawler and Boudreau (2012). As part of this study for 2013, limited data were collected from US managers, but we do not report them in this book.

For the first time in 2010, data were collected from more than one country. In addition to the United States, data were collected from HR executives in Australia, Canada, Europe, the United Kingdom, and China. For the 2013 study, we added India to the list of countries. All data were collected via the Internet.

In all countries except China, the survey was in English. In China, it was in Mandarin. Access was provided by the organizations listed in appendix A, which also lists the individuals who worked with us in each country.

Sample

As in our past surveys, data were collected from HR executives in companies with one thousand or more employees. Responses were received from Australia (*n* = 23), Canada (*n* = 45), China (*n* = 78), Europe (*n* = 43), India (*n* = 53), the United Kingdom (*n* = 31), and the United States *(n* = 143).

The median company in the US example had fourteen thousand employees, while the median company in the international survey had forty-two hundred employees. The revenue of the US firms was also greater: $5.0 billion (median) versus $2.0 billion (median) for the international sample.

The companies in our sample are in a wide variety of industries. Among the least common are mining and art/entertainment. The international and US samples have relatively similar profiles with respect to industries. The largest difference is health care. The US sample has many more health care companies, most likely because the United States has more of these companies because of its private enterprise approach to delivering health care.

Staffing of the HR Function

In the US firms studied, the average number of employees in the HR function was 351. The ratio of total employees to HR employees was 100 to 0.91. This ratio is lower than that found in 2001 (1.11), 2004 (1.00), and 2007 (0.94) and slightly higher than in 2010 (0.88).

Despite the introduction of information technology and the downsizing of corporate staff groups, there has been no dramatic decrease in the size of the HR function relative to the rest of the organization. In fact, if there is a trend, it is toward having more HR staff per employee. Why this is true is unclear at this point. It may reflect the increased importance of the function and an increase in its workload or simply that it is a well-institutionalized part of most organizations that is difficult to reduce in size.

The respondents were asked to state the background of their current heads of human resources. In 76.1 percent of US companies, the top HR executive came up through the HR function. In the other 23.9 percent of cases, these executives came from other functions, including operations, sales and marketing, and legal. This result is similar to the findings of the 2001, 2004, 2007, and 2010 surveys. The percentage of chief HR officers who come from HR varies significantly on a country-to-country basis. The low is 65.2 percent in Australia, and the high is 84.9 percent in India.

Why do some firms continue to place executives in charge of the HR function who are not traditional HR executives? There are three likely reasons. First, senior executives without an HR background are being put in charge of HR in order to develop them because they are candidates for the CEO job. Second, they are being put in charge of HR in order to make it run more like a business and be more of a business partner. Third, failed line managers are being put into HR because it is a "safe" preretirement job. The survey did not ask why this is being done, so we can only speculate that in the majority of cases, it is done in order to change the HR function or develop an executive. In today's business world, it is too important a position to use as a dumping ground.

Measures

The 2013 HR survey is a slightly altered version of the previous surveys. It covers fourteen general areas:

1. General descriptive information about the demographics of the firm and the HR function

2. The organizational context that the HR function serves, including its broad organizational form, management approach, and the amount and kinds of strategic change and organizational initiatives being carried out by the company (expanded in 2007 and some items changed in 2010)

3. The changing focus of the HR function measured in terms of how much time it is spending in different kinds of roles compared with five to seven years ago

4. The degree of emphasis that a number of HR activities are receiving and the involvement of HR in business strategy

5. The HR function's use of various organizational practices to increase efficiency and business responsiveness and the extent to which it is investing in a number of initiatives to support change

6. The use of outsourcing and its effectiveness (altered in 2007 and 2010, not asked in 2013)

7. The use of information technology and its effectiveness (new in 1998, expanded in 2001, reduced in 2007)

8. The use of HR metrics and analytics as well as their effectiveness (new in 2004, expanded in 2007)

9. HR's role in sustainability programs—what it is and what it should be (new in 2013)

10. How the effectiveness of HR programs and activities is measured (new in 2004, expanded in 2007)

11. How HR leaders and business leaders make decisions that involve human capital (new in 2004)

12. The skill requirements for employees in the HR function and satisfaction with current skills

13. The perceived effectiveness of the HR function and the importance of a variety of HR activities

14. Overall organizational performance in comparisons to competitors

A complete copy of the 2013 survey with frequencies and means for each item in the US sample is in appendix C.

Method Limitations

Survey research of the type used in this study has a number of limitations. The following are among the most important:

1. The data for each company are provided by only one individual. They are asked to respond to a number of questions that require broad knowledge of the company in order to answer effectively. Clearly not all individuals answering the survey could reasonably be expected to have the breadth of knowledge that is required to give an accurate answer to each question. In some cases, individuals skipped questions when they presumably did not know the answers. In any case, their responses are best looked at as guestimates by individuals rather than as fully informed data-based information. Because there is only one respondent per firm, in most cases, it is impossible to check the interrelatedness of the responses.

2. It is impossible to accurately calculate the response rate to the survey. Because of the method we used to distribute the survey, we are unable to determine how many people were actually asked to respond. In any case, it is safe to assume that the response rate is very low. The survey is long, and it is not something that everyone who got a chance to respond would be able to respond to accurately and be interested in spending the time required. Although this is a limitation of our study, it does not mean that the data are misleading. In the case of most countries, we have a reasonable number of responses so that we have at least some idea as to what things are like in those countries.

3. It is hard to determine whether the samples from the different countries are comparable. Clearly there are differences in organization size and most likely the kinds of industries that were sampled. This reflects the reality that the countries typically have different size organizations and concentrations in different industries. Thus, to some degree, the comparisons between countries reflect differences in the size of company and industry, as well as nationality. Given this, it is important to be cautious in interpreting the country comparison data. The best conclusion about the methodology is to regard the data as providing good starting points for thinking about how HR functions over time in different countries. Thus the information is not definitive, but these are the only data of their kind that exist, and as a result, they warrant serious consideration. They certainly provide a much better guide to what is happening with respect to HR than many of the articles that are written based on interviews with a few heads of HR about what they are doing in their companies.

4. The same words can mean different things to different people, particularly if they are from different countries and have different native languages. Since we used English in virtually all our surveys, the data may be compromised to some degree by the different meanings being attached to the same words by people in different countries, or for that matter by people in the same country. There are large cultural differences between and within countries, which may make people think differently or interpret words like *quality, frequency, often,* and so on differently. Words can also change their meaning over time, so someone responding to the same question in 1995 may not make the same response in 2013 because the terms used in the question have gradually evolved or been redefined. This may be particularly true in the case of management terms, which seem to constantly be redefined by the ongoing, highly active literature in the field of management. Overall, this means that we must be careful in interpreting changes or lack of changes in longitudinal data.

APPENDIX C

2013 Effective HR Management Survey:
Global Study USA Feedback Report (N = 143)

THIS SECTION ASKS QUESTIONS ABOUT YOUR COMPANY AND HR IN YOUR ORGANIZATION.

	Mean	S.D.*
1. What is the annual revenue of your company (in $billions)?	$14.0	$22.9
2. Approximately how many employees are in your company?	38,438.4	66,757.3
3. Approximately, how many full-time equivalent employees (FTEs, exempt and nonexempt) are part of the HR function? (This number should include both centralized and decentralized staff).	351.1	531.7

4. What is the background of the current head of HR? (please check one response)	
76.1%	Human Resource Management
23.9%	Other Function(s), which one(s):

5. How would you gauge your company's performance, relative to its competitors …	Much Below Average	Somewhat Below Average	About Average	Somewhat Above Average	Much Above Average	Mean	S.D.
a. Societal and environmental sustainability performance.	1.4	6.3	31.5	41.3	19.6	**3.71**	**.90**
b. HR function performance.	2.1	13.3	30.8	46.2	7.7	**3.44**	**.89**
c. Overall company performance.	2.1	6.3	23.1	39.2	29.4	**3.87**	**.98**

6. To what extent do these describe how your organization operates?	Little or No Extent	Some Extent	Moderate Extent	Great Extent	Very Great Extent	Mean	S.D.
a. Bureaucratic (hierarchical structure, tight job descriptions, top-down decision making).	10.5	34.3	27.3	23.8	4.2	**2.77**	**1.06**
b. Low-cost operator (low wages, minimum benefits, focus on cost reduction and controls).	32.6	27.7	27.7	9.2	2.8	**2.22**	**1.09**
c. High involvement (flat structure, participative decisions, commitment to employee development and careers).	7.0	30.3	31.0	26.8	4.9	**2.92**	**1.03**
d. Global competitor (complex interesting work, hire best talent, low commitment to employee development and careers).	11.3	23.2	33.8	23.9	7.7	**2.94**	**1.11**
e. Sustainable (agile design, focus on financial performance and sustainability).	7.1	12.8	39.7	29.8	10.6	**3.24**	**1.04**

*S.D. = Standard Deviation

7. To what extent is each of the following strategic initiatives present in your organization?	Little or No Extent	Some Extent	Moderate Extent	Great Extent	Very Great Extent	Mean	S.D.
f. Building a global presence.	24.5	9.8	11.2	31.5	23.1	**3.19**	**1.51**
g. Acquisitions.	13.5	12.8	24.8	32.6	16.3	**3.26**	**1.26**
h. Customer focus.	2.1	4.9	14.7	35.0	43.4	**4.13**	**.98**
i. Technology leadership.	6.3	21.0	30.8	21.0	21.0	**3.29**	**1.20**
j. Talent management.	3.5	14.7	34.3	34.3	13.3	**3.39**	**1.01**
k. Knowledge@ / intellectual capital management.	4.9	25.9	41.3	23.1	4.9	**2.97**	**.94**
l. Sustainability.	2.1	22.4	38.5	26.6	10.5	**3.21**	**.98**
m. Innovation.	4.9	19.6	29.4	33.6	12.6	**3.29**	**1.07**

THIS SECTION ASKS QUESTIONS ABOUT THE HUMAN RESOURCE FUNCTION IN YOUR COMPANY.

---

8. For each of the following HR roles, please estimate the percentage of time your HR function spends performing these roles. Percentages should add to 100% for each column.

PERCENTAGES SHOULD ADD TO 100% FOR EACH COLUMN:	CURRENTLY	5-7 YEARS AGO
a. **Maintaining Records** (Collect, track and maintain data on employees)	15.2%	26.8%
b. **Auditing/Controlling** (Ensure compliance with internal operations, regulations, and legal and union requirements)	13.0%	17.2%
c. **Providing Human Resource Services** (Assist with implementation and administration of HR practices)	25.7%	28.6%
d. **Developing Human Resource Systems and Practices** (Develop new HR systems and practices)	19.0%	13.2%
e. **Strategic Business Partnering** (Member of the management team; involved with strategic HR planning, organization design, and strategic change)	27.1%	14.2%
TOTAL	100%	100%

---

9. Which of the following best describes the relationship between the human resource function and the business strategy of your corporation? (Please check one response.)

Mean = 2.92; S.D. = .75	
3.5%	Human Resource plays no role in business strategy (**if checked, go to QUESTION 11**).
21.7%	Human Resource is involved in implementing the business strategy.
53.8%	Human Resource provides input to the business strategy and helps implement it once it has been developed.
21.0%	Human Resource is a full partner in developing and implementing the business strategy.

10. With respect to strategy, to what extent does the HR function...?	Little or No Extent	Some Extent	Moderate Extent	Great Extent	Very Great Extent	Mean	S.D.
a. Help identify or design strategy options.	9.4	31.2	37.0	21.0	1.4	2.74	.95
b. Help decide among the best strategy options.	11.7	26.3	32.1	27.0	2.9	2.83	1.05
c. Help plan the implementation of strategy.	2.2	10.1	31.9	46.4	9.4	3.51	.88
d. Help identify new business opportunities.	34.1	40.6	21.7	3.6	0.0	1.95	.84
e. Assess the organization's readiness to implement strategies.	6.5	18.8	28.3	32.6	13.8	3.28	1.12
f. Help design the organization structure to implement strategy.	5.1	8.7	23.9	38.4	23.9	3.67	1.09
g. Assess possible merger, acquisition or divestiture strategies.	13.1	25.5	29.9	25.5	5.8	2.85	1.12
h. Work with the corporate board on business strategy.	24.1	32.1	28.5	13.1	2.2	2.37	1.06

Your company's HR organization:

11. To what extent does each of the following describe the way your HR organization currently operates?	Little or No Extent	Some Extent	Moderate Extent	Great Extent	Very Great Extent	Mean	S.D.
a. Administrative processing is centralized in shared services units.	6.3	18.9	20.3	39.2	15.4	3.38	1.14
b. Transactional HR work is outsourced.	30.1	34.3	21.0	11.9	2.8	2.23	1.09
c. Centers of excellence provide specialized expertise.	7.7	14.0	21.7	35.7	21.0	3.48	1.19
d. Decentralized HR generalists support business units.	8.5	12.7	13.4	38.7	26.8	3.63	1.24
e. People rotate *within* HR.	20.4	26.8	26.1	16.9	9.9	2.69	1.25
f. People rotate *into* HR.	47.6	35.7	15.4	1.4	0.0	1.71	.78
g. People rotate *out of* HR to other functions.	55.9	32.9	10.5	0.7	0.0	1.56	.71
h. HR practices vary across business units.	23.1	39.9	18.9	11.9	6.3	2.38	1.15
i. Some transactional activities that used to be done by HR are done by employees on a self-service basis.	5.6	23.1	32.2	30.1	9.1	3.14	1.05
j. HR "advice" is available on-line for managers and employees.	28.7	28.0	18.2	16.8	8.4	2.48	1.29
k. There is a low HR/employee ratio.	16.1	21.7	34.3	21.7	6.3	2.80	1.14
l. There is a data-based talent strategy.	21.1	31.0	28.2	16.9	2.8	2.49	1.09
m. There is a human capital strategy that is integrated with the business strategy.	14.7	21.7	32.9	24.5	6.3	2.86	1.14
n. Provides analytic support for business decision-making.	14.7	28.7	39.9	14.0	2.8	2.62	.99
o. Provides HR data to support change management.	9.2	31.0	34.5	19.7	5.6	2.82	1.04
p. Drives change management.	7.7	25.2	24.5	35.7	7.0	3.09	1.09
q. Makes rigorous data-based decisions about human capital management.	21.0	31.5	35.0	10.5	2.1	2.41	1.00
r. Uses social networks for HR activities such as recruiting, performance management, and work assignments.	15.4	26.6	32.2	20.3	5.6	2.74	1.12
s. Uses mobile technology to support HR activities such as recruiting, self-service, communication, etc.	32.2	28.0	23.1	11.9	4.9	2.29	1.18
t. Uses Software as a Service (SaaS) model (subscription based, hosted in the cloud).	26.6	26.6	19.6	21.0	6.3	2.54	1.26

12. How has the amount of focus or attention to the following HR activities changed over the past 5–7 years as a proportion of the overall Human Resource activity and emphasis?	Greatly Decreased	Decreased	Stayed the Same	Increased	Greatly Increased	Mean	S.D.
a. Human capital forecasting and planning.	1.4	2.1	24.6	56.3	15.5	**3.82**	.77
b. Compensation.	0.0	3.5	35.2	45.1	16.2	**3.74**	.77
c. Benefits.	1.4	7.0	38.7	41.5	11.3	**3.54**	.84
d. Organization development.	0.7	6.3	21.8	52.8	18.3	**3.82**	.83
e. Organization design.	0.7	4.9	33.1	45.8	15.5	**3.70**	.81
f. Training and education.	2.1	11.3	35.9	36.6	14.1	**3.49**	.94
g. Management development.	1.4	6.4	21.3	47.5	23.4	**3.85**	.90
h. Union relations.	11.4	17.9	56.4	9.3	5.0	**2.79**	.94
i. HR information systems.	1.4	7.0	16.9	57.0	17.6	**3.82**	.85
j. Performance appraisal.	1.4	6.3	35.9	43.0	13.4	**3.61**	.85
k. Recruitment.	0.0	3.5	21.3	53.2	22.0	**3.94**	.76
l. Selection.	0.0	2.8	29.6	54.2	13.4	**3.78**	.71
m. Career planning.	0.7	7.8	43.3	39.7	8.5	**3.48**	.79
n. Legal affairs.	0.7	9.9	62.7	20.4	6.3	**3.22**	.74
o. Employee assistance.	1.4	10.6	74.6	12.7	0.7	**3.01**	.56
p. Competency / Talent assessment.	0.0	2.8	28.2	53.5	15.5	**3.82**	.72
q. HR metrics and analysis.	0.0	2.8	25.5	53.9	17.7	**3.87**	.73
r. Executive compensation.	0.7	2.1	30.5	42.6	24.1	**3.87**	.83
s. Developing social networks.	0.7	3.5	31.9	59.6	4.3	**3.63**	.66

13. In general, how effective do you think the following approaches to HR outsourcing are?	Very Ineffective	Ineffective	Neither	Effective	Very Effective	Mean	S.D.
a. No outsourcing	29.5	36.7	25.2	7.9	0.7	**2.14**	.96
b. Very limited: only a few transactional services (e.g. payroll)	3.7	29.4	27.2	36.8	2.9	**3.06**	.96
c. Moderate outsourcing	1.4	10.8	25.9	56.1	5.8	**3.54**	.82
d. Substantial outsourcing	11.6	31.2	33.3	21.0	2.9	**2.72**	1.02
e. Software as a service (hosted in cloud)	1.4	4.3	31.9	42.8	19.6	**3.75**	.87

14. Please check the one statement that best describes the current state of your HR Information technology:	
Mean = 2.37, S.D.= .73	
7.4%	Completely integrated HR information technology system.
55.9%	Most processes are information technology based but not fully integrated.
29.4%	Some HR processes are information technology based.
7.4%	There is little information technology present in the HR function.
0.0%	There is no information technology present. **(If checked, skip to Question 17.)**

15. How likely are you to replace or upgrade your core HRIS platform in the next three years?						
Will not Happen	Slightly Likely	Moderately Likely	Very Likely	Certain to Happen	Mean	S.D.
27.1	18.6	11.4	17.1	25.7	2.96	1.58

16. To what extent do you consider your information technology system to …	Little or No Extent	Some Extent	Moderate Extent	Great Extent	Very Great Extent	Mean	S.D.
a. Be effective.	6.5	31.7	33.8	27.3	0.7	2.84	.93
b. Satisfy your employees.	15.2	35.5	37.7	10.1	1.4	2.47	.92
c. Improve HR services.	11.6	23.9	34.8	26.8	2.9	2.86	1.04
d. Reduce HR transaction costs.	12.2	27.3	33.1	20.1	7.2	2.83	1.11
e. Provide new strategic information.	21.7	29.0	29.0	16.7	3.6	2.51	1.12
f. Speed up HR processes.	13.7	22.3	30.2	28.8	5.0	2.89	1.12
g. Reduce the number of employees in HR.	25.2	31.7	26.6	12.2	4.3	2.39	1.12
h. Integrate HR processes (e.g. training, compensation).	20.9	28.8	29.5	16.5	4.3	2.55	1.12
i. Measure HR's impact on the business.	31.7	27.3	26.6	13.7	0.7	2.24	1.07
j. Improve the human capital decisions of managers outside HR.	26.1	31.9	26.8	12.3	2.9	2.34	1.08
k. Create knowledge networks.	47.5	22.3	20.9	8.6	0.7	1.93	1.05
l. Build social networks that help work get done.	56.1	18.7	13.7	10.8	0.7	1.81	1.08
m. Offer a positive user experience.	19.6	31.2	32.6	15.2	1.4	2.48	1.02
n. Represent a state-of-the-art solution.	35.5	25.4	26.8	8.7	3.6	2.20	1.13
o. Use the most advanced technology	36.7	29.5	20.9	10.1	2.9	2.13	1.11

17. Does your organization currently …	Yes, Have Now	Being Built	Planning For	Not Currently Being Considered	Mean	S.D.
a. Measure the business impact of HR programs and processes?	21.9	26.3	36.5	15.3	2.45	1.00
b. Collect metrics that measure the cost of HR programs and processes?	41.6	20.4	24.8	13.1	2.09	1.09
c. Have the capability to conduct cost-benefit analyses (also called utility analyses) of HR programs?	25.0	11.0	31.6	32.4	2.71	1.17
d. Use HR dashboards or scorecards?	46.7	26.3	17.5	9.5	1.90	1.01
e. Measure the financial efficiency of HR operations (e.g. cost-per-hire, time-to-fill, training costs?)	48.9	21.9	23.4	5.8	1.86	.97
f. Measure the specific effects of HR programs (such as, learning from training, motivation from rewards, validity of tests, etc.)?	17.5	19.7	35.0	27.7	2.73	1.05
g. Benchmark analytics and measures against data from outside organizations (e.g. Saratoga, Mercer, Hewitt, etc.)?	48.5	15.4	21.3	14.7	2.02	1.14
h. Measure the quality of the talent decisions made by non-HR leaders?	10.9	14.6	31.4	43.1	3.07	1.01
i. Measure the business impact of high versus low performance in jobs?	10.9	14.6	27.7	46.7	3.10	1.02

18. How effective are the information, measurement, and analysis systems of your organization when it comes to the following?	Very Ineffective	Ineffective	Neither	Effective	Very Effective	Mean	S.D.
a. Connecting human capital practices to organizational performance.	8.6	39.8	29.7	21.1	0.8	2.66	.93
b. Identifying where talent has the greatest potential for strategic impact.	7.0	28.1	27.3	35.9	1.6	2.97	1.00
c. Predicting the effects of HR programs before implementation.	10.1	37.2	32.6	20.2	0.0	2.63	.92
d. Pinpointing HR programs that should be discontinued.	11.8	34.6	28.3	24.4	0.8	2.68	1.00
e. Supporting organizational change efforts.	5.5	19.5	25.8	42.2	7.0	3.26	1.03
f. Assessing and improving the HR department operations.	7.0	17.1	24.0	47.3	4.7	3.26	1.03
g. Contributing to decisions about business strategy and human capital management.	7.0	21.9	26.6	41.4	3.1	3.12	1.02
h. Using logical principles that clearly connect talent to organizational success.	6.2	30.2	25.6	34.9	3.1	2.98	1.02
i. Using advanced data analysis and statistics.	14.1	38.3	30.5	15.6	1.6	2.52	.97
j. Providing high-quality (complete, timely, accessible) talent measurements.	7.8	32.6	31.8	26.4	1.6	2.81	.97
k. Motivating users to take appropriate action.	9.3	30.2	32.6	27.1	0.8	2.80	.97
l. Utilizing "Big Data"	21.1	38.3	25.0	14.1	1.6	2.37	1.02

19. To what extent are these statements true about your organization?	Little or No Extent	Some Extent	Moderate Extent	Great Extent	Very Great Extent	Mean	S.D.
a. We excel at competing for and with talent where it matters most to our strategic success.	3.1	19.7	40.9	29.9	6.3	3.17	.92
b. Business leaders' decisions that depend upon or affect human capital (e.g. layoffs, rewards, etc.) are as rigorous, logical and strategically relevant as their decisions about resources such as money, technology, and customers.	10.2	30.7	30.7	24.4	3.9	2.81	1.04
c. HR leaders have a good understanding about where and why human capital makes the biggest difference in their business.	3.9	18.0	32.0	41.4	4.7	3.25	.94
d. Business leaders have a good understanding about where and why human capital makes the biggest difference in their business.	3.9	23.4	37.5	30.5	4.7	3.09	.94
e. HR systems educate business leaders about their talent decisions.	27.3	39.8	24.2	6.3	2.3	2.16	.98
f. HR adds value by ensuring compliance with rules, laws, and guidelines.	4.7	21.3	28.3	36.2	9.4	3.24	1.04
g. HR adds value by delivering high-quality professional practices and services.	3.9	13.3	29.7	46.1	7.0	3.39	.94
h. HR adds value by improving talent decisions inside and outside the HR function.	2.3	16.4	28.1	39.1	14.1	3.46	1.00
i. Business leaders understand and use sound principles when making decisions about:	Little or No Extent	Some Extent	Moderate Extent	Great Extent	Very Great Extent	Mean	S.D.
1. Motivation.	7.0	32.0	40.6	19.5	0.8	2.75	.88
2. Development and learning.	3.1	30.7	48.8	14.2	3.1	2.83	.82
3. Culture.	7.8	25.8	32.0	26.6	7.8	3.01	1.08
4. Organizational design.	10.2	36.7	28.9	22.7	1.6	2.69	.99
5. Business strategy.	0.0	10.9	23.4	54.7	10.9	3.66	.82
6. Finance.	0.8	3.9	18.0	56.3	21.1	3.93	.79
7. Marketing.	3.9	12.5	39.8	34.4	9.4	3.33	.95

20. How much does your Corporation's Board call on HR for help with the following?	Little or No Extent	Some Extent	Moderate Extent	Great Extent	Very Great Extent	Mean	S.D.
a. Executive compensation.	4.0	5.6	5.6	31.0	54.0	4.25	1.06
b. Addressing strategic readiness.	12.9	25.8	32.3	24.2	4.8	2.82	1.09
c. Executive succession.	4.8	9.5	8.7	37.3	39.7	3.98	1.14
d. Change consulting.	18.5	26.6	29.0	20.2	5.6	2.68	1.16
e. Developing board effectiveness / corporate governance.	30.9	22.8	26.0	18.7	1.6	2.37	1.16
f. Risk assessment.	19.2	24.8	34.4	18.4	3.2	2.62	1.09
g. Information about the condition or capability of the work force.	10.7	20.5	33.6	26.2	9.0	3.02	1.12
h. Board compensation.	17.6	13.4	18.5	27.7	22.7	3.24	1.41
i. Sustainability.	26.2	25.4	30.3	15.6	2.5	2.43	1.11

Regarding the skills and knowledge of your organization's current HR professional/managerial staff:

21. How satisfied are you with current HR professional/managerial staff in each of these areas?	Very Dissatisfied	Dissatisfied	Neutral	Satisfied	Very Satisfied	Mean	S.D.
a. Team skills.	0.0	12.0	23.2	52.0	12.8	3.66	.85
b. HR technical skills.	1.6	9.5	23.0	50.0	15.9	3.69	.91
c. Business understanding.	1.6	22.4	28.0	40.0	8.0	3.30	.96
d. Interpersonal skills.	0.0	5.6	19.0	54.0	21.4	3.91	.79
e. Cross-functional experience.	4.8	37.3	38.9	15.9	3.2	2.75	.89
f. Consultation skills.	4.0	25.8	31.5	31.5	7.3	3.12	1.01
g. Leadership/management.	4.0	15.9	25.4	42.1	12.7	3.44	1.03
h. Global understanding.	4.8	31.2	38.4	20.8	4.8	2.90	.95
i. Organization design.	5.6	33.3	31.7	27.0	2.4	2.87	.95
j. Strategic planning.	8.0	35.2	36.8	17.6	2.4	2.71	.93
k. Information technology.	5.6	26.2	34.9	33.3	0.0	2.96	.91
l. Change management.	4.0	26.2	29.4	38.1	2.4	3.09	.95
m. Metrics development.	8.7	39.7	34.1	15.9	1.6	2.62	.91
n. Data analysis and mining.	15.2	36.0	28.0	19.2	1.6	2.56	1.02
o. Sustainability.	6.4	26.4	48.8	17.6	0.8	2.80	.83
p. Social media.	6.4	32.8	39.2	20.8	0.8	2.77	.88
q. Globalization.	7.3	27.6	43.1	17.9	4.1	2.84	.94
r. Risk management.	4.0	26.4	37.6	27.2	4.8	3.02	.95

22. What percentage of your company-wide HR professional / HR managerial staff possesses the necessary skill set for success in today's business environment? (Circle one response.)

None 0%	Almost None 1-20%	Some 21-40%	About Half 41-60%	Most 61-80%	Almost All 81-99%	All 100%	Mean	S.D.
0.9	1.8	17.7	37.2	36.3	6.2	0.0	4.25	.94

23. Please rate the following activities on a scale of 1 to 10 or not applicable.
In view of what is needed by your company:

How well is the HR organization meeting needs in each of the areas below?	Not Meeting Needs	2	3	4	5	6-	7	8	9	All Needs Met	Not Applicable	Mean	S.D.
a. Providing HR services.	0.0	0.8	0.8	2.4	4.8	12.1	21.8	42.7	10.5	4.0	0.0	7.40	1.39
b. Providing change consulting services.	2.4	3.2	10.4	14.4	10.4	15.2	21.6	17.6	4.8	0.0	0.0	5.76	2.01
c. Being a business partner.	1.6	2.4	3.2	7.2	7.2	17.6	20.0	20.0	16.0	4.8	0.0	6.78	2.01
d. Improving decisions about human capital.	1.6	1.6	5.6	11.2	10.4	21.6	14.4	21.6	10.4	1.6	0.0	6.31	1.96
e. Managing outsourcing.	3.8	2.9	6.7	7.6	17.1	15.2	16.2	20.0	5.7	4.8	13.3	6.10	2.18
f. Operating HR centers of excellence.	3.4	4.2	7.6	4.2	8.4	10.1	22.7	26.9	10.9	1.7	4.2	6.43	2.20
g. Operating HR shared service units.	1.8	4.4	4.4	9.6	11.4	14.9	14.9	21.9	12.3	4.4	7.7	6.43	2.17
h. Helping to develop business strategies.	5.7	4.9	6.5	11.4	12.2	22.0	18.7	14.6	3.3	0.8	0.7	5.59	2.10
i. Being an employee advocate.	0.8	1.6	1.6	5.6	2.4	11.2	22.4	25.6	22.4	6.4	0.0	7.38	1.81
j. Analyzing HR and business metrics.	1.6	8.8	8.0	16.0	13.6	22.4	16.0	10.4	3.2	0.0	0.0	5.34	1.94
k. Working with the corporate board.	2.5	6.7	3.3	7.5	10.8	6.7	17.5	15.8	22.5	6.7	3.5	6.68	2.43
l. Preparing talent for the future.	0.8	0.0	6.5	10.5	8.9	21.0	21.8	21.8	7.3	1.6	0.7	6.40	1.78

24. Please rate the following activities on a scale of 1 to 10 or not applicable.
In view of what is needed by your company:

How *important* is it that HR does these well?	Not Important	2	3	4	5	6	7	8	9	Very Important	Not Applicable	Mean	S.D.
a. Providing HR services.	0.0	0.8	0.0	0.0	1.6	8.9	11.3	27.4	15.3	34.7	0.0	**8.46**	**1.50**
b. Providing change consulting services.	0.0	0.0	0.8	0.0	5.6	8.1	20.2	28.2	15.3	21.8	0.0	**8.02**	**1.51**
c. Being a business partner.	0.0	0.0	1.6	0.0	0.0	3.2	4.0	21.8	18.5	50.8	0.0	**9.02**	**1.33**
d. Improving decisions about human capital.	0.0	0.0	0.8	0.0	1.6	5.6	6.5	17.7	29.0	38.7	0.0	**8.80**	**1.36**
e. Managing outsourcing.	0.9	3.6	8.1	7.2	18.0	11.7	21.6	14.4	8.1	6.3	9.1	**6.24**	**2.12**
f. Operating HR centers of excellence.	0.0	0.8	1.7	1.7	5.8	5.8	19.2	24.2	23.3	17.5	2.8	**7.90**	**1.70**
g. Operating HR shared service units.	0.9	2.6	0.9	2.6	7.7	6.0	16.2	21.4	21.4	20.5	4.9	**7.75**	**2.02**
h. Helping to develop business strategies.	0.0	0.8	3.3	1.6	10.6	4.9	19.5	19.5	22.0	17.9	0.0	**7.69**	**1.89**
i. Being an employee advocate.	0.0	0.0	0.8	1.6	10.5	8.9	14.5	25.8	22.6	15.3	0.0	**7.79**	**1.65**
j. Analyzing HR and business metrics.	0.0	0.0	0.8	0.0	4.1	9.0	11.5	23.0	27.9	23.8	0.0	**8.30**	**1.49**
k. Working with the corporate board.	0.0	0.8	4.2	2.5	4.2	12.5	10.0	27.5	16.7	21.7	2.8	**7.77**	**1.93**
l. Preparing talent for the future.	0.0	0.0	0.8	0.0	1.6	0.8	4.1	14.6	20.3	57.7	0.7	**9.21**	**1.22**

25. Please indicate your agreement or disagreement with the following statements about your company's environmental and social sustainability activities:	Strongly Disagree	Somewhat Disagree	Neither Disagree or Agree	Somewhat Agree	Strongly Agree	Mean	S.D.
a. Sustainability performance and competences *are* explicitly built into HR processes such as selection, rewards, and development.	16.7	29.2	20.8	27.5	5.8	**2.77**	**1.19**
b. Sustainability performance and competences *should be* explicitly built into HR processes such as selection, rewards, and development.	0.0	11.7	22.5	40.8	25.0	**3.79**	**.95**
c. HR *is involved* in the design of sustainability initiatives and programs.	13.3	20.8	22.5	31.7	11.7	**3.08**	**1.24**
d. HR *should be involved* in the design of sustainability initiatives and programs.	0.8	12.5	18.3	40.8	27.5	**3.82**	**1.00**
e. HR *provides* support and expertise in organization design issues that impact sustainability.	10.0	14.2	21.7	40.0	14.2	**3.34**	**1.18**
f. HR *should* provide support and expertise in organization design issues that impact sustainability.	0.8	3.3	12.5	44.2	39.2	**4.18**	**.84**
g. HR *provides* change management support for building sustainability into the way my company does business.	10.8	14.2	24.2	39.2	11.7	**3.27**	**1.17**
h. HR *should* provide change management support for building sustainability into the way my company does business.	0.8	3.3	13.3	40.8	41.7	**4.19**	**.85**

26. Please indicate what HR's role is and should be in your company's sustainability activities.

	a. HR's role is:	b. HR's role should be:
No role	17.6%	0.8%
Minor role	36.1%	13.4%
Active support	33.6%	37.8%
Major support	7.6%	34.5%
Leader	5.0%	13.4%
Mean	**2.46**	**3.46**
S.D.	1.03	.92

This table is based on the entire data set for 2013 (both US and global Responses)

In which country is your company based? (Percent of total)

0.0	Argentina	12.2	India	1.8	Switzerland
5.1	Australia	0.5	Ireland	0.0	Thailand
0.0	Austria	0.5	Israel	0.0	Turkey
0.7	Belgium	1.8	Italy	0.2	United Arab Emirates
0.2	Brazil	0.0	Japan	7.2	United Kingdom
10.4	Canada	0.0	Mexico	33.0	United States of America
0.0	Chile	1.6	Netherlands	1.6	Other
18.0	China	0.2	New Zealand		
0.0	Czech Republic	0.0	Norway		
0.5	Denmark	0.0	Poland		
0.5	Egypt	0.0	Portugal		
0.2	Finland	0.0	Russia		
0.2	France	0.0	Saudi Arabia		
0.7	Germany	0.5	Singapore		
0.0	Greece	0.7	South Africa		
0.0	Hong Kong	0.2	South Korea		
0.0	Hungary	0.5	Spain		
0.0	Iceland	0.9	Sweden		

Please select the industries below that match your firm's primary businesses.

2.1%	Agriculture/Forestry	12.6%	Manufacturing (consumer)
6.3%	Business and professional services	21.0%	Manufacturing (industrial)
3.5%	Communications/broadcasting/publishing	0.7%	Mining
13.3%	Computers/technology/software	1.4%	Services/Hospitality/Arts
2.1%	Construction	2.1%	Transportation and warehousing
1.4%	Energy	1.4%	Utilities
11.2%	Financial services	7.0%	Wholesale and retail trade
16.8%	Health care	5.6%	Other
0.7%	Government / public administration / nonprofit		